T. W. JEFFRIES

SECRETS OF THE SPIES WHO CHANGED HISTORY

The True Story Behind

The plans they stole

The men they killed

The information they sold

The cunning methods they used

The perils they faced

AND THE DESTINIES THEY CHANGED!

Over three thousand years of espionage brought together in one volume of suspense, intrigue and heart-stopping excitement! Edited by one of the world's greatest authorities on espionage—Kurt Singer.

SPIES WHO
CHANGED HISTORY

Edited and with an Introduction

by

KURT SINGER

E 70

ACE BOOKS, INC.

23 West 47th Street, New York 36, N.Y.

For GORHAM MUNSON
the editor and critic whose "touches"
are artistry and who has taught me so much.

One spy in the right place is worth twenty
thousand men in the field—Napoleon

See now where the bold man did and dared
in the Wooden Horse, where we all were
hidden, the best men of the army, to bring
death and ruin upon Troy.—Homer, *The
Odyssey*

ACKNOWLEDGMENTS

Grateful appreciation is expressed herewith to all authors, publishers, newspapers, magazines, government agencies and agents who courteously granted permission to include copyrighted material.

W. H. Allen & Co. of London for excerpts from the following books by Kurt Singer: SPIES AND TRAITORS; WORLD'S GREATEST WOMEN SPIES; MORE SPY STORIES; SPIES OVER ASIA; GENTLEMEN SPIES.

B. P. Singer Features of Buena Park, California for the following article: MOKUSATSU.

T. S. Dennison & Co. of Minneapolis, Minn, for excerpts from the following books by Kurt Singer: SPY OMNIBUS; SPIES FOR DEMOCRACY.

The Oxford University Press for excerpts from Homer's THE ODYSSEY.

Prentice Hall, Inc. of New York for excerpts from the following book by Kurt Singer: THREE THOUSAND YEARS OF ESPIONAGE.

Carl Van Doren's BENEDICT ARNOLD: TRAITOR IN SUSPENSE from SECRET HISTORY OF THE AMERICAN REVOLUTION, by Carl Van Doren, copyright 1941 by The Viking Press, New York City, N. Y., and from THREE THOUSAND YEARS OF ESPIONAGE, Prentice Hall, Inc., New York City, N.Y.

Richard Wilmer Rowan's SCHULMEISTER: NAPOLEON'S DARING SPY and WILHELM STEIBER: KING OF THE SLEUTH HOUNDS, copyright 1928 by the Viking Press, New York City, N.Y. and THREE THOUSAND YEARS OF ESPIONAGE, Prentice Hall, Inc., New York City, N.Y.

Al Newman's BRITAIN'S PET SPY from *Newsweek Magazine*, May 28th, 1945, and THREE THOUSAND YEARS OF ESPIONAGE, Prentice Hall, Inc., New York, N.Y.

Edwin Muller's THE MAN WHO DID BUSINESS WITH HIMMLER from the *Reader's Digest*, Jan. 1946 and WORLD'S BEST SPY STORIES edited by Kurt Singer, Wilfred Funk, New York City, N.Y.

TABLE OF CONTENTS

AN INTRODUCTION

ODYSSEY INTO SPYLAND

"See now what the bold man did and dared in the
Wooden Horse, where we all were hidden, the best
men of the army, to bring death and ruin upon
Troy."

--Homer, THE ODYSSEY

TREASON is my business. I have dealt with it for twenty-five
years—long years, dangerous years. I have been wanted for
"high treason" by both the Communists and the Nazis. I have
seen revolutions, perfidious deceptions and sedition. I know
the grim game of subversion where vicious and naive people
sold out their own native countries and thus changed history. And all for the vainglorious dream of power.

Napoleon, who a century and a half ago employed some
of the best spies and double-spies of all times, stated: "One
spy in the right place is worth 20,000 men in the field."

Stalin must have felt the same way when Richard Sorge,
the greatest spy of World War II, short-waved his prize
message out of the Nazi Embassy in Tokyo, laconically
stating: "Japan will remain neutral toward the USSR and
will not attack Siberia."

With this message, the Russians changed their own destiny
and world history. They withdrew their military forces from
the Japanese border and converted their strength to the
battle of Stalingrad, thus creating the tidal wave of victory.
Major history was written, too, when the Soviet atomic spy
ring, including Dr. Alan May, Klaus Fuchs and the two
Rosenbergs, extracted from the United States and transmitted
to Moscow the secrets of the Hiroshima atom bomb.

When Judge Irving Kauffman sentenced Ethel and Julius
Rosenberg to die in the prison at Sing Sing, he solemnly said:
Only the Lord can find mercy for what you have done. I
believe your conduct, in putting into the hands of the Russians the A-bomb before our best scientists predicted Russia
could perfect the bomb, already has caused the Communist

9

aggression in Korea, with resultant casualties exceeding 50,000 Americans. Millions of innocent people may pay for your treason. Indeed, by your betrayal, you undoubtedly have altered the course of history to the disadvantage of your country."

Had the atom bomb not been in the hands of the Soviet nation, the Korean war might well have been avoided. All important spies have stepped into the path of history, leaving their prints and changing the courses of those paths.

From the ancient days when the Egyptians spies were sewn into flour sacks to the present-day aerial photographers spies have been masters and not pawns of history.

The spy in the last half of the Twentieth Century is not a man with secret ink and a tiny camera in his little finger-ring an agent who snoops through desk drawers. The spy of today is an emissary from one "world" on earth to destroy another "world." He does not come from Mars, yet he comes from a world that is ideologically as strange. The modern Communist spy is a revolutionist, a man or woman determined to eliminate the world of individuality, the world of free enterprise, the world of Democracy. For these fanatics, the objective is the Soviet dictatorship of the world.

The United States of America is relatively new in the global spy game, but she has learned rapidly.

Mr. Allen Welsh Dulles, Director of Central Intelligence himself came near to changing history.

During World War II, when Dulles was stationed in Berne Switzerland, he organized, with the help of Hans Gisevius a plan to assassinate Adolf Hitler. The bomb was detonated the Führer was injured but not killed. World War II whipped itself into increasing fury and more millions of innocent people went to their deaths.

Vidkun Quisling turned the destiny of his native Norway when he and a handful of men handed his country over to the Nazis. For years he had conspired with Hitler, and during the naval and air invasion on April 9, 1940, landing places had been prepared and the defensive Norwegian troops given leaves. With the Nazi troops in Norway, Quisling became the fascist ruler, inheriting the power from King Haakon.

The masses are not needed. To change history, a handful of people will suffice. Hitler began his meteoric ascent into the political firmament with seven people in Munich. Lenin was supported by two dozen men and women when the

SPIES WHO CHANGED HISTORY

Soviet Revolution was organized in 1917. Today only five per cent of the population of the Soviet Union belong to the Communist Party, but they are the total masters of the Red Empire. One per cent of the world's population are Communists, but this small minority group controls one-third of the world's territory.

This book attempts to demonstrate the ways by which individual spies and modern spy rings constantly swerve the flow of history from its natural course.

William C. Corcoran will never be forgotten as a man who changed history for the British. A devoted patriot and diplomat, Corcoran served as U.S. Consul in Gothenburg, Sweden. During the Second World War, he kept his ears to the ground and his vision toward the sea. His friends among the ship captains and seamen made it possible for him to report that Nazi ships often went to a secret harbor near Stettin, a Baltic seaport. With this as a lead, reconnaissance planes discovered the strategic spot and found the V-2 rocket and robot bomb center of Peenemünde, from which the blitz of London was being launched. Corcoran, with the help of his agents, saved millions of lives in London. Peenemünde was leveled and bomb-torn London saved from further devastation.

It was the same Billy Corcoran who found friends at a Swedish ball bearing factory. The officials of the manufacturing company denied that they had or would ever sell their equipment for use in Nazi aircraft. After lengthy and careful work, Consul Corcoran was able to produce copies of the invoices of ball bearing shipments to Hitler's Germany, thus forcing a closedown on further trade with the Nazi Air Force. This piece of alert intelligence work helped to shorten the war by cutting down strategic material needed by the swastika-marked planes.

All successful spies change history, spies on both sides of a conflict. Dr. Richard Sorge saved Stalin's empire during the battle of Stalingrad just as Ernst Friedrich Wollweber saved the Soviets in Berlin and Eastern Germany. Wollweber's name appears often in this book. He and his spy master, Laurenti Beria, who was later executed, took Berlin; it was only with the cunning of this trained spy chief that East Berlin was conquered for the communist world.

Without such successful spies as Wollweber, the history of Berlin would not read as it does. Wollweber was only a part, important part, of the "beefsteak movement": outside Nazi brown, inside commie red. For years the pudgy little Soviet

11

agent led the Communist Internationale spy service and organized ship sabotage that erased the natural chapter in the story of both Spain and Sweden. "The Red Orchestra" gives the details of this story. Today Wollweber can be considered one of the most dangerous spies alive, a man who is in charge of the entire Soviet Satellite Secret Service.

The motives for being a spy? They vary from the lust for power to political fanaticism, from a craving for adventure to a subconscious desire to die. Money seems to be the least important goal in the game.

Rebecca West, in her *Meaning of Treason*, claims that many agents and spies convicted during the last fifteen years, such as John Amery, Norman Baillie Stuart, William Joyce, were pathological cases. She says about them: "The psychotic will very readily take sides against his own country. He is as if commanded by Heaven to be a prop for any neighboring power which desires to swallow his fatherland. He hates the people around him, he hates his fellow countrymen, because he hates the real world."

There is a certain amount of evidence that the traitor or quisling is often a disturbed personality. Norwegian doctors insist that the executed Major Vidkun Quisling had suffered from a grave case of syphilis of many years standing. When the disease reached the third stage, he was attacked by paralysis, accompanied by mental symptoms, and for some years had been a dangerous megalomaniac.

My own experience in dealing with and "hunting" for foreign agents has convinced me that many abnormal people join the brigades of spies. There are also some physically handicapped people who have developed complex feelings of inferiority, and are active in communist and fascist movements.

Psychiatrists all over the world claim that some traitors belong to a group which technically is called "psychopathic." This term means that the individual is not in the customary sense insane, but suffers from an open instability of thought, feeling, and behavior. The fact that so many spies are working for both sides, friend and enemy, underlines this theory to a great extent.

Dr. Edward Glover, an eminent British psychiatrist, who attended the trial of Dr. Klaus Fuchs, analyzes the character and the mind of a traitor as follows: "His character is perverted, often incalculable and frequently antisocial. Above all he tends to be devoid of guilt, indeed, may take a certain pride in his more bizarre achievements. In earlier days the psychopath was actually described as a 'moral imbecile'."

Dr. Glover continues his analysis of spies and traitors: "The wartime quisling was, in fact, more than half gosling: a weak, immature, and childish character. The quisling and the traitor have much in common with the schoolboy who sneaks to the teacher whom he secretly hates, but whose attention he nevertheless covets."

The professional spy service will recruit all types of spies, from the homosexual or other abnormal personalities to the dollar-a-year man.

There is the spy who will team up with the secret services because "people are apt to overlook me. I must show that I'm somebody."

Then comes the neurotic who fits Dr. Afred Adler's description of a man who wants "to be superior to difficulties. Every step he takes will lead forth to self-deception."

Many have to struggle with a feeling of inadequacy. Secret service gives a spy the chance to feel adequate and superior. Professor John Dewey called it "striving for security in his fashion."

Most interesting are the pathological views of some of the spies when caught. Either they say, "I was found out because I was not clever enough; I'll do better next time," or they volunteer to confess in order to get new protection from a new master. I saw the court proceedings of Dr. Leopold Kuehn, the spy who gave light signals to the Japanese pilots during the attack against Pearl Harbor. He offered his services to America. He betrayed most of his subagents and saved his own neck.

When I once asked an agent why he had become a Nazi spy and discussed it with him during his imprisonment, he said, like many criminals, "They treated me mean. I hate them. I don't need them any more. I'll pay back. Can't I work now for you? I'll do anything you want me to do."

The desire for success and a total lack of moral concepts can be found in many cases. These individuals also often lack what Dr. Wilhelm Menninger calls "the death instinct," and he adds that they overevaluate "heroic exhibitionism."

Though no spy can wear a uniform, he is often classified as an officer in the intelligence service. The psychotics like it.

Nobel prize winner Bertrand Russell in his *Why Men Fight* perhaps comes close to the real truth and motive: "When men find themselves not fully contented and not able to procure what will cause contentment, imagination brings before their minds the thought of things they believe would make them happy."

Spies have believed there is both money and glamour in espionage. There is not. Communist and Nazi spies have often worked without fee, under party orders. Still the Nazis once paid $250,000 to the Albanian agent Cicero, who copied secret documents of the Yalta and Teheran conferences.

This book tells the story of counterfeit money which was used to change history through espionage. But all action produces counter action: while "Cicero" was photographing documents in the British Embassy in Turkey in order to give away Allied landing places to the Axis, the Allies changed history again with their "Man Who Never Was," a dead man carrying faked and erroneous papers to inform Hitler that British and American troops would land in Southern France. The ruse worked. German troops massed against the "invasion" in France while the Allies swarmed into Southern Italy.

Counterfeit money was used for espionage during World War II, but individual spies generally received a pittance. I knew agents who never received more than fifty dollars a week, plus expenses.

Gerhart Eisler, who was called Soviet spy No. 1 in America, lived in the greatest poverty in New York. Magda Fontanges, who was Mussolini's mistress and later a Gestapo spy, worked for only $42.50 a month during the war.

Dr. C. G. Jung may have the perfect reason for the motive of many agents: "the senseless emptiness of their lives." The outstanding spies and saboteurs, traitors and fifth columnists were not interested in money. Trebitch Lincoln, who served as a spy for many nations, was an adventurer. He did not care if he had millions in Europe, or lived as a poor Buddhist priest in Tibet. Dr. Allan Nunn May and Dr. Klaus Fuchs did not do their work for money. Neither did the officer, whose name I cannot reveal, who betrayed British secrets to the Israeli underground during the British-Israeli disturbances. Von Rintelen, Germany's master spy of World War I, was a patriot who organized the wildest espionage acts—from blowing up factories to fomenting strikes. He never returned to Germany. He died in England. He did his duty and hated the Prussians at the same time. He did not even want their money.

In this book, I'll try not only to give portraits of the spies but also discuss the motivations of traitors—the fanatics, like

14

Eisler; the quislings; the pseudo-intellectuals, like the Rosenbergs; the government spies and the master minds; the great spy organizers of the world who changed the path of history.

The Eichmann case is not the story of a spy who changed the hands on the timeclock of history, but the story of the capture of the man responsible for the extermination of six million Jews is a lesson about the aberrations of modern history never to be forgotten. There is a price each nation and each individual must pay for murder.

The West is not guiltless, but since 1945 the West has not conquered or controlled other nations as the Soviet Empire has done. The U-2 incident exploded as a famous spy case. Francis G. Powers, the lone pilot, has influenced world history, and his exploit will be much talked about as one of the major events in post-war American-Soviet relationships.

While it is impossible in these pages to give a total and complete account of all in the long parade of spies who have changed history, I believe this book presents the greatest spy cases, those which turned tides and those which reveal personal tragedies in a brutal war of secret brigades.

Kurt Singer
California
Late Summer 1960

THE TWELVE SPIES OF MOSES

. . . And the Lord spoke unto Moses saying,

"Send thou men, that they may search the land of Canaan . . ."

And Moses sent them to spy out the land of Canaan, and said unto them, . . . "go up into the mountain:

And see the land, what it is; and the people that dwelleth therein, whether they be strong or weak, few or many;

And what the land is that they dwell in, whether it be good or bad; and what cities they be that they dwell in, whether in tents or in strongholds;

And what the land is, whether it be fat or lean, whether there be wood therein, or not. And be ye of good courage, and bring of the fruit of the land." Now the time was the time of the first ripe grapes.

So they went up, and searched the land from the wilderness of Zin unto Rehob, as men come to Hamath.

And they ascended by the south and came unto Hebron . . .

And they came unto the brook of Eshcol, and cut down from thence a branch with one cluster of grapes, and they bore it between two upon a staff; and they brought of the pomegranates, and of the figs. . . .

And they returned from searching of the land after forty days.

And they went and came to Moses, and to Aaron, and to all the congregation of the children of Israel, unto the wilderness of Paran to Kadesh; and brought back word unto them, and unto all the congregation, and showed them the fruit of the land.

And they told him, and said, "We came unto the land whither thou sentest us, and surely it floweth with milk and honey; and this is the fruit of it.

Nevertheless the people be strong that dwell in the land; and the cities are walled, and very great: and moreover we saw the children of Anak there . . .

And there we saw the giants, the sons of Anak, which come of the giants: and we were in our own sight as grasshoppers, and so we were in their sight."

When Fieldmarshal Viscount Montgomery of El Alamein was asked whom he called the greatest general of all times, he answered without hesitance: "Moses. He trained his soldiers for forty years in the desert. He trained his people, he trained his spies."

The twelve spies of Moses mentioned in the Old Testament, Numbers XIII, were sent to the promised land of Canaan around 1480 B.C. Moses selected one man from every tribe of the Children of Israel, which made a band of twelve who were ordered to do reconnaissance work in Canaan. They were led by Osee ben Nun, who is also known by the name of Joshua. Their mission took forty days. When they returned, they reported what they had seen in the "land where milk and honey flows."

These spies came out of the wilderness of the desert; they had survived the Exodus from Pharaoh's Egypt and they recommended Canaan as the land which God had alloted to Abraham and his seed. Had these spies reported differently, modern Israel would be located today at another area, and Middle Eastern history would be different from what it is to a great degree.

RAHAB THE HARLOT, BETRAYER OF JERICHO

The beauteous Rahab has been canonized by the Catholic Church and September 1 appointed as her Saint's Day. She is considered the ancestress of no less than eight prophets. The Bible states that she was the wife of Joshua, and that they founded the extraordinary line starting with Boaz. Other historians disagree and say that Rahab became the wife of Salmon, one of the original spies, and that these two were the parents of Boaz and thus the ancestors of King David and Jesus of Nazareth.

In any case, Rahab of Jericho, may be considered the first of female fifth columnists, active in the year 1451 B.C.

And Joshua the son of Nun sent out of Shittim two men to spy secretly, saying, "Go view the land, even Jericho." And they went, and came into a harlot's house, named Rahab, and lodged there.

And it was told of the king of Jericho, saying, "Behold, there came men in hither tonight of the Children of Israel to search out the country."

And the King of Jericho sent unto Rahab, saying, "Bring forth the men that are come to thee, which are entered into thine house, for they be come to search out all the country."

And the woman took the two men and hid them, and said thus, "There came men unto me, but I wist not whence they were.

"And it came to pass about the time of shutting of the gate, when it was dark, that the men went out; whither the men went, I wot not. Pursue after them quickly; for ye shall overtake them."

But she had brought them up to the roof of the house, and hid them with the stalks of flax, which she had laid in order upon the roof.

And the men pursued after them the way to Jordan unto the fords, and as soon as they which pursued after them were gone out, they shut the gate.

And before they were laid down, she came up unto them upon the roof; and she said unto the men, "I know that the Lord hath given you the land, . . . now therefore I pray you, swear unto me by the Lord, since I have shewed you kindness, that ye will also shew kindness unto my father's house, and give me a true token:

"And that ye will save alive my father and my mother, and my brethren, and my sisters, and all that they have, and deliver our lives from death."

And the men answered her, "Our life for yours, if ye utter not this our business. And it shall be, when the Lord hath given us the land, that we will deal kindly and truly with thee."

Then she let them down by a cord through the window; for her house was upon the town wall, and she dwelt upon the wall. And she said unto them, "Get you to the mountain, lest the pursuers meet you, and hide yourself there three days, until the pursuers be returned. And afterward may you go your way."

And the men said unto her, "We shall be blameless of this thine oath, which thou has made us swear.

Behold, when we come into the land, thou shalt bind this line of scarlet thread in the window which thou didst let us down by: and thou shalt bring thy father, and thy mother, and thy brethren, and all thy father's household, home unto thee.

"And it shall be, that whosoever shall go out of the doors of thy house into the street, his blood shall be upon his head, and we will be guiltless; and whosoever shall be with thee in the house, his blood shall be on our head, if any hand be upon him.

"And if thou utter this our business, then we will be quit of thine oath which thou hast made us to swear."

And she said, "According unto your word, so be it."

And she sent them away, and they departed; and she bound the scarlet line in the window.

And they went, and came unto the mountain, and abode there three days, until the pursuers were returned; and the pursuers sought them throughout all the way, but found them not.

So the two men returned, and descended from the mountain, and passed over, and came to Joshua the son of Nun, and told him all things that befell them.

And they said unto Joshua, "Truly the Lord hath delivered into our hands all the land; for even all the inhabitants of the country do faint because of us. . . ."

And it came to pass at the seventh time, when the priests blew with the trumpets, Joshua said unto the people, "Shout, for the Lord hath given you the city.

"And the city shall be accursed, even it and all that are therein, to the Lord: only Rahab, the harlot, shall live, she and all that are with her in the house, because she hid the messengers that we sent . . ." and they took the city.

And they utterly destroyed all that was in the city, both man and woman, young and old, and ox, and sheep, and ass, with the edge of the sword.

But Joshua had said unto the two men that had spied out the country, "Go into the harlot's house, and bring out thence the woman and all that she hath, as ye swore unto her."

And the young men that were spies went in and brought out Rahab, and her father, and her mother, and her brethren, and all that she had; and they brought out all her kindred, and they left them without the camp of Israel.

And they burnt the city with fire and all that was therein. (From: *Joshua*, II and VI.)

THE TATTOOED SPY

by

Herodotus

Herodotus, who has been called the Walter Lippmann of his time, describes in Book V of his "Persian Wars" one of the oldest and most cleverly executed spy tricks of human history.

About 500 B.C. Histiaeus decided to rebel against his king, and wanted to send the news of the revolt to his brother-in-law and cousin Aristagoras who acted as a regent while Histiaeus was at King Darius' court. The following is Herodotus' own story of the amazing ruse which he used to send his message through the enemy lines.

Histiaeus, when he was anxious to give Aristagoras orders to revolt, could find only one safe way, for the rooms were guarded, of making his wishes known. He took the trustiest of his slaves, shaved all the hair from his head, and then pricked letters upon the skin, and waited till the hair grew again. As soon as the hair was grown, he sent the man to Miletus, giving him no message except, "When you come to Miletus, ask Aristagoras to shave your head, and look at it."

Now the marks on the head, as I have already mentioned, were a command to revolt.

ALEXANDER THE GREAT, INVENTOR OF POSTAL ESPIONAGE

THE SUN was setting after a scorching day and the shadows spread out over the market place. The broadest shadow was cast by the Parthenon, where the shield of Pallas Athena still proclaimed the glory of the once-proud city.

They were still proud, even in defeat, those Athenians. And they still did not understand how they could have permitted themselves to be ruled by that Macedonian boy, that ruthless, ambitious twenty-five-year-old named Alexander.

Among the great columns a number of men walked at leisure, discussing their philosophies, their tragedies, and the latest political disasters. Slaves and satirists, philosophers and bankrupt businessmen, a shadow hung over the souls of all these men like the shadow that hung over the city.

"How Socrates must have suffered in his humiliation," one remarked.

"But he was never really humiliated," replied Phidias, who had once proudly borne arms for Athens.

These men knew that the end had come upon them. They knew, too, that it was better to fight the dictator and tyrant, Alexander of Macedon, than to join him as his allies and his slaves.

In all the streets could be heard the voices and clinking

coins of his recruiting officers. Reveling drunks proclaimed through the city that from now on they would fight for the great Alexander who was going to conquer the world.

Phidias, a bold, young, strapping fellow, looked with a contemptuous smile at these countrymen of his who were selling themselves to Alexander for a few pieces of silver. He himself was Alexander's own age, and he too intended to join the tyrant's army. But he would do so in order to learn the new conqueror's weaknesses and strong points so that the day might come when the democratic republic of Athens would be free and strong again.

It was a strange spring, that year 334 B.C. Few Athenians could endure the shame of being ruled again by a dictator and a man probably of low origin. For it was rumored in the promenades of the Acropolis that Alexander's mother was a woman of half-barbarian blood. From her Alexander had inherited his fervent and visionary mind, it was said.

By now fifty thousand men had been assembled for the march into Asia. Alexander, with his Macedonians, Illyrians, Thracians, and other groups from the various Greek states, was preparing to conquer Asia Minor. Phidias bade his friends farewell, for he was now an officer in the army of Alexander. The invincible boy king's new army was concentrated at Arisbe on the Hellespont. Alexander, after piously visiting the site of Troy and bringing offerings to the Homeric heroes, opened his campaign. His first goal was Sardis, the ancient capital of Lydia. The Persian fleet tried unsuccessfully to stop him.

Seeing the skill and vigor with which the great general directed his forces, Phidias could not help feeling a certain admiration for him. But Phidias had his own political ambitions. While Alexander was winning battles, Phidias hoped to spread disunity among his allies and discontent among his officers and his men.

Alexander got wind of this work. So long as he was winning battle after battle, it did not much matter to him what a few agitators were saying. But when he encountered stubborn resistance from the Persians at Halicarnassus, he decided that it was time to nip any rebellion in the bud. In the winter of 334 B.C. the Persians were stubbornly defying Alexander's siege. The war was at a standstill temporarily, and the king had time to look around in his own camp. He intended, after conquering the Persians, to have himself proclaimed king of Persia. These men of his own army would form his army of occupation. Therefore he had to know in advance who was and who was not trustworthy.

The plan Alexander devised for discovering the sentiments of his men was simple but ingenious. One morning he called his highranking officers together and, so the historians report, declared: "I, Alexander, am as lonely and homesick as all of you must be. It may be years before I shall again see my dear ones at home. Therefore I have decided to send couriers, mounted upon the fastest horses, to Macedon, Thrace, and Athens. Any of you who wish to send a message home may do so by these same couriers."

The officers cheered their king loudly for this unprecedented favor. And two days later the couriers left Helicarnassus laden with messages for the heroes' wives and children, fathers, and mothers, messages describing their own heroic lives and the great war they were fighting for the glory of Alexander.

The couriers did not travel far. They turned aside, as they had been ordered, and delivered their letters to Alexander, who had set up a secret private headquarters for his purpose. There the king read and evaluated each letter. It was in this way that the great strategist originated the art of postal censorship, a common practice of war that has outlived the Macedonian phalanx by two thousand years.

Among the letters Alexander found several from Phidias, all filled with invective against the king. Phidias died for his treason without ever learning how Alexander the Great had discovered his contemplated conspiracy. When the unfortunate agitator protested his innocence, the king listened with cold indifference. His reply was simply to repeat the order for Phidias' execution.

Without Alexander the Great's unique and shrewd postal espionage system, it is entirely possible he might have met defeat. From such humble beginning modern postal methods without opening the envelopes; ultra-violet ray devices; have been developed: X-ray processes for reading letters secret inks; scientific "unbreakable" codes and the diplomatic pouch.

Postal Espionage can be defined as "communicated information." Alexander stopped it at its source.

SPIES OF SCIPIO AND HANNIBAL

Scipio Africanus (237-183 B.C.), the great opponent of
Hannibal, annihilator of Carthaginian and Numidian forces,
who routed Carthage from her outposts on the Ebro in Spain
and drove her deep into the African valleys, has been called
by modern military strategists, such as Captain Liddell Hart,
a greater general than Napoleon. In the course of his career
he perpetrated some ingenious military tricks which deserve
mention in the history of espionage. His surprise tactics have
been a model for military scientists.

Old Sextus Julius Frontinus, author of one of the earliest
books on military strategy, *The Stratagems*, makes the following analysis of Scipio's campaign against Syphax, King of
the Numidians.

> Scipio Africanus, seizing the opportunity of send-
> ing an embassy to Syphax, commanded specially
> chosen tribunes and centurions to go with Laelius,
> disguised as slaves and entrusted with the task of
> spying out the strength of the king. These men, in
> order to examine more freely the situation of the
> camp, purposely let loose a horse and chased it
> around the greatest part of the fortifications, pre-
> tending it was running away. After they had re-
> ported the results of their observations, the destruc-
> tion of the camp by fire brought the war to a close.

Polybius, another historian whose information evidently de-
rives from Laelius, treats the destruction of the camp in this
wise.

> The whole place was filled with wailing and
> confused cries, panic, fear, strange noises, and
> above all raging fires and flames that overbore all
> resistance, things any one of which would be suf-
> ficient to strike terror into a human heart, and how
> much more this extraordinary combination of them
> all. It is not possible to find any other disaster which,
> however magnified, could be compared with this,
> so much did it exceed in horror all previous events.
> Therefore of all brilliant exploits performed by
> Scipio this seems to me the most brilliant and most
> adventurous.

Before the incident of the great fire, a small slip almost betrayed Scipio's spies completely. One of King Syphax's officers thought he recognized a certain man among the slaves of Laelius, Scipio's emissary. He challenged the man with the words, "You are not a slave but a general." Laelius trembled inwardly, fearing complete unmasking. He resorted to a bold gesture. Turning sharply he slapped the face of the disguised slave and, as Frontinus reports it, spat at the man and between blows abused him thus: "You dog, you dirty slave, low creature, how dare you presume even to resemble a Roman general!"

King Syphax's men were convinced that no genuine Roman general could submit to such treatment and that the man must therefore be a slave and nothing else. The ruse was successful.

Polybius records another anecdote about Scipio Africanus which illustrates his way of dealing with captured spies. Hannibal repeatedly smuggled scouts into the Roman camp, and it once happened that three of these spies were captured and brought before Scipio. The great general spared their lives, but administered a lesson which they would never forget. This is the anecdote, taken from Polybius.

> Scipio was so far from punishing them, as is the usual practice, that on the contrary he ordered a tribune to attend them and point out clearly to them the exact arrangement of the camp. After this had been done he asked them if the officer had explained everything to their satisfaction. When they answered that he had done so, Scipio furnished them with provisions and an escort, and told them to report carefully to Hannibal what had happened to them.

This attitude of self-confidence bordering on arrogance on the part of the Romans made a deep impression, of course, on Hannibal. The latter must have learned of the treatment of his spies with the deepest chagrin.

Livy, in a celebrated passage, pictures Hannibal's feelings:

> On their return, Hannibal was so much struck with admiration of Scipio's magnanimity and daring that he conceived . . . a strong desire to meet him and converse with him. Having decided on this

he sent a herald saying that he desired to discuss the whole situation with him, and Scipio, on receiving the message, accepted and said he would send to Hannibal, fixing a place and hour for the meeting.

Upon one occasion the two generals, Scipio and Hannibal, encountered each other "within a javelin's throw." Livy is our authority for this, and he marvels that these generals, fighting more bitterly against one another than any in previous history, would have had an encounter because they both happened to be going for water at the same time and place. We must assume that both were busy finding out what they could about each other's forces.

Polybius writes more of Hannibal's intrigues and master strokes of espionage:

> For years before he undertook his campaign against Rome, he had his agents in Italy and they were observing everyone and everything. He charged them with transmitting to him exact and positive information regarding the fertility of the trans-Alpine plains and the valleys of the Po, their populations, their military spirit and preparations and, above all, their disposition to the government at Rome. There was nothing too large in promises that the Carthaginian was not ready to make in return for their support against the hated city.

Hannibal brilliantly exploited the use of fire in warfare. At one time his battalions were stationed in Sicily, where they laid siege to one of the harbor cities whose buildings perched on high hills, overlooking the Carthaginian troops. The siege went on for many months. The besiegers were making no headway and the counterattacks of the city were becoming fiercer and more dangerous. Hannibal decided that cunning must bring him victory where force had failed. But the city's defenders permitted no vessel to enter the harbor, and no person to enter the gates. Couriers that Hannibal had sent out had been caught.

Finally Hannibal dispatched his most trusted spy. This spy was to try to enter the city disguised as a veteran of past Sicilian wars. He was to remain in the city and make no attempt to return. His instructions were of the simplest: stay in the city and let fire be your weapon.

The first part of the spy's task was successful. He took a house on one of the hills and lived a retired life. There he cooked his own meals over an outdoor fire, kept odd hours and often found it necessary to roast a bite to eat while other folk were sleeping.

The smoke and fires had, of course, purposes beyond the preparation of meals. They were cyphered messages dealing with the city's defenses. Hannibal was able to see them quite clearly. Long after the city had fallen its inhabitants learned how the smoke and fire from one man's house had defeated them for all their impregnable fortifications.

SAMUEL PEPYS ON ESPIONAGE

Pepys' diaries have amused us all with their frankness, honesty, and informality. Though Samuel Pepys (1633-1703) reached the position of Secretary of the British Admiralty under Charles II, he admitted that his mother had been no more than a "washmaid of my Lady Veere," that her brother had been a butcher at Whitechapel. Not much is known about his youth, though school records show us that on one occasion he was publicly admonished for having been "scandalously overseen in drink." It is also known that he wrote a sophomoric romance called Love is a Cheat, *a manuscript which he later destroyed.*

In 1660 he secured an appointment to a clerkship in the Naval Office. Utterly incompetent at the beginning, he applied himself to his duties with such zeal that he eventually rose to be Secretary of the Admiralty and retained the office even under James II. His journals were written in a shorthand of his own. They comprise six volumes and form a candid account of court manners, secret diplomacy and everyday life.

Pepys merrily confesses to espionage, telling of the theft of a key from the pocket of a sleeping Dutch diplomat. With the key the Dutchman's desk was rifled of much important information.

Elsewhere, he deplores the changed times: whereas Cromwell spent 70,000 pounds a year on espionage, the present king allotted only 700 pounds annually to it. Yet Pepys

*wonders much that, for all the pinched budget, much useful
information could be obtained.)*

From Samuel Pepys' Diary:

February 14, 1668,

Secretary Morrice did this day in the House, when they
talked of intelligence, say that he was allowed but £700 a
year for intelligence, whereas, in Cromwell's time, he did
allow £70,000 a year for it; and was confirmed there in by
Colonel Birch, who said that thereby Cromwell carried the
secrets of all the princes of Europe at his girdle.

February 17, 1668,

They did here in the House talk boldly of the King's bad
counselors, and how they must be all turned out, and many
of them, and better, brought in: and the proceedings of the
Long Parliament in the beginning of the war were called to
memory: and the King's bad intelligence was mentioned,
wherein they were bitter against my Lord Arlington, saying,
among other things, that what ever Morrice's was, who desired he had but £750 a year allowed him for intelligence,
the King paid too dear for my Lord Arlington's in giving him
£10,000 and a barony for it.

Dec. 27, 1668,

Saw the King at chapel but staid not to hear anything, but
went to walk in the party with W. Hewer, and there among
others met with Sir G. Downing, and walked with him an
hour, talking of business, and how the late war was managed,
there being nobody to take care of it: and he telling, when
he was in Holland, what he offered the King to do, if he
might have power, and then, upon the least word, perhaps
of a woman, to the King, he was contradicted again. And
particularly of the loss of all that we lost in Guiniy. *He told
me that he had so good spies, that he hath had the keys
taken out of De Witt's* pockets when he was a-bed, and his*

---

* John de Witt, Grand Pensionary of Holland, was later
killed by a Dutch mob enraged at the elevation of William of
Orange after the French Army overran Holland and the
British fleet successfully destroyed the Dutch fleet. K.S.

*closet opened, and papers brought to him, and left in his
hands for an hour, and carried back and laid in the
place again.* He says that he hath always had their most
private debates, that have been but between two or three
of them brought to him in an hour after, and an hour after
that, hath sent word thereof to the King . . .

BENEDICT ARNOLD, TRAITOR IN SUSPENSE

by Carl Van Doren

When in 1741 a son was born to the famous Arnold family
of Connecticut, the father expressed the wish that the young
Benedict Arnold should become the greatest soldier the
Colonies had yet produced. The family was old and honored;
one of Benedict Arnold's great-grandfathers had been governor of Rhode Island for three successive terms. Therefore
there was nothing extravagant about the father's ambition
for his son.

The young Benedict Arnold did not have the patience to
complete his education. At fifteen he ran away from home
to seek adventure. He enlisted in an expedition against the
French, but did not stick out the campaign and straggled
back home. Then he settled in New Haven; though only
twenty-one, he carried on trade with the West Indies and
made quite a success of it.

During the rapid turns of fortune of the Revolutionary War
Benedict Arnold participated first as a captain, then as
colonel and finally as a brigadier general. His military exploits in New England and Canada made him famous overnight. He was made a major general, and fought with George
Washington in New Jersey. In 1778 he received the command of Philadelphia.

There his private conduct was much criticized. He offended
against the society of the Philadelphia Quakers with his
gambling, drinking, flirting, and extravagance.

In 1778 four charges were brought against him and, which
he insisted on a quick court-martial and was virtually cleared;
two trivial cases were brought to George Washington's attention. Possibly it was at that time that he felt himself injured
and that he first thought of co-operating with the British. It
was equally possible that he felt the war was going on too
long and was becoming tedious; it was beginning to pall,

28

had the classroom of his boyhood and the adventurous life of his adolescence. In any event, although Washington praised his military achievements, Arnold played his Commander-in-Chief false. He employed a liaison man, Joseph Stansbury, to conspire with Sir Henry Clinton, the British Commander-in-Chief. He met with Major John André, the British officer chosen by Sir Henry as intermediary, and together they worked out plans for the betrayal of the American troops at West Point.

Arnold was the sole commander of West Point. Therefore it was a simple matter for him to weaken the garrison. The price he set on this was 20,000 pounds, which he knew was high. For many weeks he waited in suspense to learn whether the British would meet his proposal.

Carl Van Doren, the eminent historian, makes this point in his Secret History *of the American Revolution that waiting was punishment indeed for Arnold's treachery.* K.S.

Though Arnold was at Headquarters at Kakiat by July 30 (1780) and hurried off a note to tell the British that the Americans would cross the Hudson the next day, he did not then see Washington. But on the 31st, "while the army was crossing at King's Ferry," Washington remembered, "I was going to see the last detachment over, and met Arnold, who asked me if I had thought of anything for him. I told him that he was to have the command of the light troops, which was a post of honour, and which his rank entitled him to. Upon this information his countenance changed and he appeared to be quite fallen; and instead of thanking me, or expressing any pleasure at the appointment, never opened his mouth."

The general orders for the next day had perhaps already been drafted, for on the 1st they announced that Arnold would command the left wing. But on the 3rd, after he had once more pleaded his three-year-old wound as his excuse, the assignment was changed and he was instructed to "proceed to West Point and take the command of that post and its dependencies." These included the forts at Stony Point and Verplanck's below West Point, on each side of the Hudson, and the posts east of the river from Fishkill to King's Ferry as well as the corps of infantry and cavalry "advanced towards the enemy's lines" as far south as North Castle (near Armonk). Since the main army was preparing to return to New Jersey, this would leave Arnold in charge not only of the river forts but also of the disputed district north of New York through which Clinton would have to send any land troops marching to assist an expedition by water.

In the maneuvers of Washington and Clinton during the last days of July and the first of August, Arnold had a secret share. When Clinton on the 26th took his transports through Hell Gate on their way, he hoped, to attack the French at Newport, he already believed that Arnold might soon command West Point and conspire to surrender it. Believing this Clinton could risk a movement against the French with part of his forces, leaving the rest to hold New York till his return. But he had such grudging and delaying support from Arbuthnot and the fleet, Clinton claimed, that he brought the transports to at Huntington, decided he could not afford to be held up so long as it seemed he would be, and was back at threatened New York on the 31st. Washington, who that day got his army across the Hudson, crossed expecting to move south and attack New York in Clinton's absence. On hearing of Clinton's return, Washington changed his plans, left Arnold in the Highlands, and moved the main army to Tappan in New Jersey. An attack on New York might still be possible. In the meantime the army at Tappan would be between West Point and Clinton if he attacked first, as Washington thought not too unlikely. Clinton put off his attack. The prospects of success would be much brighter once Arnold had established himself and completed his plans for treachery.

On the 3rd, the day Arnold received his instructions for West Point, he wrote from Fishkill to Mercy Scollay in Boston about the Warren children in whom he had for more than two years kept up his interest. Congress had in July voted to allow, through the Massachusetts authorities, a major general's half pay for the maintenance of Warren's second son and two daughters (the elder son being already provided for), to commence with Warren's death and to continue till the youngest of them should be of age. Arnold claiming more credit for Congress's action than he probably deserved, regretted that he had not himself been able to do what he would have liked, while the children were being cared for by Mercy Scollay and her father. "The public are indebted to me for a considerable sum which I advanced for them in Canada, and for four years pay which I cannot obtain. I must request you will present the account of expenses incurred to the president and council of Massachusetts Bay without any mention of my name, and request payment, which I make not the least doubt they will not only comply with but reimburse the sum advanced . . . If the state refuses to pay the account I shall esteem myself obliged to . . . Your observations on the charitable disposition of people of opulence is very just. Charity, urbanity, and the social virtues seem swallowed up in the tumult and confusion of the times, and self wholly engrosses the nabobs of the present day."

Characteristically, Arnold was offering to be generous again and also hinting that he, "without any mention of my name," might be reimbursed for what he had already given. As on his trip to Connecticut in June, he was busy with schemes for realizing his American assets before he went over to the British.

Possibly on the 4th, certainly by the 5th, Arnold was at Robinson's House opposite West Point. "I have not been on the Point since I came here," he wrote on the 5th to Robert Howe. "I shall carefully inspect both sides of the river and take quarters where I think myself free from danger and in a condition to render the greatest service. At present I apprehend no danger in these quarters, which are the most convenient for an invalid." He stayed on at this manor house of Beverley Robinson, used by the Americans as headquarters, and occupied immediately before Arnold by Howe. One of the surgeons who had been there in 1778 thought that Robinson in the choice of his country seat must have been "guided altogether by a taste for romantic singularity and novelty. It is surrounded on two sides by hideous mountains and dreary forests, not a house in view, and but one within a mile." Arnold seems to have been neither repelled nor attracted by the wild scenery or the isolation of the house. It was safer than a house on the Point might be—for him and for his wife and youngest child who were soon, Arnold planned, to join him. They would be out of range of British guns attacking the fortress. And the Highlands command might still be exercised from the east side of the Hudson, as it had been for the past three years.

Major Franks, who had been aide to Arnold in Philadelphia, was now with him again; and on the 5th Arnold wrote to Lieutenant Colonel Richard Varick at Hackensack. "I am in want of a secretary, having within a few days been appointed to this command. General Schuyler"—then at Washington's Headquarters—"informed me yesterday that he believed it would be agreeable to you, as the duty would engross only a part of your time and leave a considerable time for you to prosecute your studies, if you choose. . . As this has the appearance of a quiet post, I expect Mrs. Arnold will soon be with me." Varick had been military secretary to Schuyler in the northern army, and a friend to Arnold during the Saratoga campaign. Out of active service since the past January, Varick had resumed his interrupted legal studies at his father's house, but had found himself so often called on for militia duty that he was glad to return to the army as Arnold's writing aide. In accepting the offer on the 7th Varick spoke of his pleasure at the chance to serve "under an officer than whom none in the army claims greater respect from, and will be more agreeable to, me than yourself . . . The presence of Mrs. Arnold will certainly make our situation in the barren Highlands vastly more agreeable, and I am persuaded will more than compensate for every deficiency of nature." But Varick needed a week to get proper clothes for his new appointment, and could not reach Robinson's House till the 13th.

In the selection of his aides Arnold did not look for disaffected men whom he might take into his confidence. Any confidant would add to the peril of the undertaking. Franks had broken with his loyalist father in Montreal while the Americans were there in 1776 and had been with Arnold most of the time since. Arnold was used to Franks as aid and could feel sure that Varick, as Schuyler said, would a capable secretary. Nor can there be much doubt that Arnold chose aides—both in their twenties—who would be congenial not only to him but also to his wife, transported from elegant Philadelphia to what she might think a lonely wilderness.

Arnold's solicitude for Peggy appears in many of his letters: references to her coming, efforts to get beds, dishes, and other household equipment suitable for her. And there is a revealing passage in a letter to Howe on September 12. Howe, a bachelor of nearly fifty with a reputation for gallantry, had congratulated Arnold on his good fortune in being so happily married. "I thank you, my dear Sir," Arnold replied "for your friendly wishes to me and Mrs. Arnold . . . and for the favourable opinion you are pleased to entertain of the state of our connubial connexion. Be assured, Sir, no sensations can have a comparison with those arising from the reciprocity of concern and mutual felicity existing between lady of sensibility and a fond husband. I myself had enjoyed a tolerable share of the dissipated joys of life, as well as the scenes of sensual gratification incident to a man of nervous constitution; but, when set in competition with those I have since felt and still enjoy, I consider the time of celibacy in some measure misspent." In these stiff sentences, with these heavy words, Arnold was unmistakably implying that he found in Peggy a wife that any husband, a mistress that any lover, might covet. The Shippens all thought of her as demure and shy. Arnold knew better.

II

It will be remembered that Arnold, at Robinson's House by the 5th, did not know till the 24th that his price of £20,000 for the surrender of West Point to the British had been agreed to; and it is conceivable that he might never have consented to the bargain on less satisfactory terms. But whether or not he was fully bent on treason during August (1780), he was bound to act with at least the appearance of his customary vigor, so as not to be suspected. Washington furnished definite instructions for the West Point command, and he was attentive to all that went on in Arnold's department. Arnold could treacherously weaken the post only by stealth, in spite of Washington's supervision and in the face of objections sure to come from Colonel John Lamb, commandant of artillery at West Point; Lieutenant Colonel Udny Hay, in command of the troops at Fishkill; Colonel James Livingston, commanding the works at Verplanck's and Stony Point; and Colonel Elisha Sheldon, in charge of the forces watching the enemy lines. Whatever Arnold might do for the sake of the British had to seem to be for the sake of the Americans.

For instance, there was his asking Lafayette at Headquarters for the names of his spies in New York. Though Arnold may have meant to put an end to that information, he could claim that he wished to facilitate it, now he was in the Highlands command. Lafayette refused to tell the names, because he had promised not to, but he did not then think of Arnold as more than zealous in the matter. Nor did Howe (the former commander), turning West Point over to Arnold, consider it strange when Arnold said in his letter of August 5: "As the safety of this post and garrison in a great measure depends on having good intelligence of the movements and designs of the enemy, and as you have been fortunate in the agents you have employed for that purpose, I must request (with their permission) to be informed who they are, as I wish to employ them for the same purpose. I will engage upon honour to make no discovery of them to any person breathing."

Howe naturally did not know that Arnold, after his visit to West Point in June, had written Clinton (the British Commander) that some of his spies on Howe were in Howe's pay also. On the 14th Howe replied much as Lafayette had done. The agents were not willing to have their names divulged to anybody. The two most intelligent of them "are persons of character and property who cannot without utter ruin get out of the enemy's power and yet, devoted to America, have agreed to serve in a way they do not like but which is the only way they can at present serve her in." Another agent, on Long Island, would continue to report under the name of John Williams, if Arnold would make no attempt to find out his real name. Arnold on the 16th hoped the secret agents would in time give him their confidence. "You have my honour," he assured Howe, "that I will not be solicitous about the real name of Mr. Williams, and you may pledge my faith to him that if accident should disclose to me his real name I will not discover it. I will take proper precautions that no gentlemen of my family open any letters addressed to me as Private." But Howe's spies seem never to have served Arnold. Perhaps they were wary because they did not know him as they knew Howe. Perhaps they distrusted Arnold. One of them insisted that "a general officer high up was in compact with the enemy." Though no suspicion yet pointed particularly at Arnold, spies must be careful.

Arnold, being a double-dealer, had a double use for secret agents. He might get information from them which he honestly needed as commander, or which as treacherous informer he might forward to New York. Most of all, he desired a channel of communication with Clinton by way of the Hudson instead of the long way round through Philadelphia. He may have wished that he could get hold of some spy who had served both Clinton and Howe and who would become Arnold's messenger.

In the hunt for secret agents Arnold formed what was to be his fateful connection with Joshua Hett Smith. Smith lived near Haverstraw on the west bank of the Hudson, not far below King's Ferry, in a country house belonging to his refugee brother William Smith, the royal chief justice of New York. Joshua Smith had been an active Whig in the early years of the Revolution, member of the New York provincial congress, and energetic in the patriot militia of his neighborhood. Married to a South Carolina woman, he had in 1778 made the acquaintance in Charleston of Robert Howe, and after his return to Haverstraw and Howe's appointment to West Point had zealously concerned himself with obtaining and transmitting the reports of Howe's secret agents. Howe seems to have recommended Smith to Arnold, who had met him in Philadelphia two years before. Arnold may have stopped at Smith's House on the ride to King's Ferry at the end of July, and he then or soon afterwards asked Smith about the sources of Howe's information. Smith, in a letter to Arnold of August 13, preferred not to be too explicit on paper but promised to come to Robinson's House and furnish the secret details. He hospitably offered to entertain Peggy Arnold if she should pay her husband a visit. She might "make my house a stage until your barge can meet her at the ferry." Smith wished Arnold might grant passes to two loyalist women and their children, so they could go to New York and join their husbands. This, Smith said, would be humane to the women and children, and burdensome to the British who would have to feed and house them.

Nothing in the letter indicated any disaffection on Smith's part, nor in Arnold's answer of the 16th, thanking Smith for his "civilities tendered to Mrs. Arnold," and saying the passes were enclosed. They were actually not sent. Varick, who had arrived at Robinson's and taken up his duties, was suspicious of Smith, chiefly on account of his brother. There was always danger that women sent into New York with a flag might carry messages—and Arnold did later smuggle his first message from West Point to André by such means. On Varick's insistence, Arnold held up the passes and wrote on the 17th to Governor George Clinton of New York asking for instructions in regard to flags of truce. Clinton on the 22nd replied that passes of the kind were to be granted to inhabitants of the state only with the permission of the civil government. Arnold accepted the ruling, but defended Smith's character till Varick was irritated.

Then there was the affair of the woodcutters. On August 12 Arnold wrote to Washington: "Colonel Hay (commander at Fishkill) requested 200 men to cut wood and make brick for the use of the garrison next winter. He informs me that the wood must be transported a considerable distance by water; that the vessels employed are so badly found with cables, anchors, and sails that they cannot ply after the middle of October. I find on inquiry that the wood is destroyed in the vicinity of the garrison, and unless a stock is laid in this fall they will be put to the greatest difficulty for fuel next winter. Colonel Hay is of opinion that with 200 men he can furnish a sufficient quantity for the garrison. I wish your Excellency's directions in this matter." Washington the next day thought providing wood in season so essential that Arnold should allow Hay the men he required.

Here again Arnold appeared to be merely prompt and forehanded. But a letter from Hay to Arnold on the 15th, three days after the letter to Washington, proposed the wood-cutting scheme as if Hay had not yet heard of it. "I beg leave to mention the necessity of adopting some certain plan by which a quantity of wood may immediately be cut for, and be conveyed to, the garrison at West Point. When you view the distance from which that article must be brought by land if not laid in before the river shuts, you will be fully convinced of the necessity of procuring an immediate and, as far as possible, a full supply. I would likewise observe that there are but few vessels in this river that have either sails or cables fit for the fall; of consequence the conveyance of wood as well as forage and provisions must become very precarious."

It is of course possible that Hay had already spoken to Arnold, and wrote his letter only for the headquarters record. But Arnold wrote the next day: "I have ordered 200 good axemen to be drafted tomorrow morning and put under your direction to procure wood, etc., for the garrison." This was the number Arnold had told Washington that Hay required, though Hay in his letter had not specified it or any other. It looks as if Arnold had originated the idea and set the figure himself, while letting both Washington and Hay think that Hay was responsible. Was Arnold acting as a commander genuinely interested in the winter's fuel, or was he acting as a traitor set on weakening the post he intended to surrender? Colonel Lamb at West Point sharply protested on the 18th. He had already sent 200 militiamen to Hay at Fishkill for a guard. "What occasion there is for such a guard at that place I cannot possibly conceive. Half the number will be sufficient." And now he must send an equal number to cut wood. "If such drafts as are called for are made from the garrison we shall neither be able to finish the works that are incomplete nor in a situation to defend those that are finished." But the woodcutters soon went off up the river to Staatsburg. As Arnold must have calculated, they would provide fuel for West Point if it was still to be an American fort that winter; and they could not be on hand to help defend it if it was to be taken by the British that summer.

Arnold had been accused of taking up, or partially dismantling, the chain which had been laid across the Hudson at West Point to prevent the passage of enemy ships. There is no evidence that he did. Major Villefranche, the French engineer sent by Washington to superintend the reconstruction of the works, reported on the 19th that he had examined the chain and thought new logs should be installed as soon as possible under the chain. Arnold on the 22nd applied to Governor Clinton for teams to be used in drawing the chain out for repairs (teams which Clinton could not provide), and complained the next day to Timothy Pickering, quartermaster general of the Continental army: "I am informed . . . that the middle part of the chain . . . is sinking and in dangerous situation, on account of the logs, which it has hitherto floated on, being water-soaken; that unless this be speedily remedied it will be out of our power to raise it but with great expense of time and trouble; that new timber cannot be hauled for want of teams, of which we have not half sufficient for the daily necessities of the garrison." Instead of taking up the chain, Arnold did nothing. He had in June reported to Clinton that it could be broken by a single heavily loaded ship. There was enough treachery in neglecting the chain altogether.

III

In the midst of the heavy routine duties of his command, Arnold found time to carry on a persistent if disappointing correspondence about his private affairs. Titus Hosmer, on whom Arnold had depended to represent him in Hartford, died suddenly August 4, and Caleb Bull took his place. Arnold on the 15th asked whether Bull had yet received the notes on the Connecticut treasury, for Arnold's back pay, and what they were worth. If they could be sold, he wished "to convert them into specie or sterling bills that I may have an opportunity of improving the money in a purchase." Three days later Arnold sent Bull an order on the state treasury for the notes, and requested him to put the *Active* claim in charge of some other lawyer or lawyers, "with a suitable fee and a promise, in case their exertions shall prove successful in obtaining speedy justice to the captors of the *Active*, of $1,000 specie which I will pay to him or them who will undertake and prosecute the affair to issue . . . Of this offer you will please to make no mention to any other person." Bull on the 26th replied that he had found a lawyer who thought he could manage the claim, but that the treasury notes could not be obtained "till three of the committee are together to adjust your accounts, which I shall get done as soon as possible." This was two days after Arnold had learned that he might have his price for the surrender of West Point. He seems to have given up his expectation of money from Connecitut, and to have dropped the futile correspondence with Bull.

Nor was Arnold more successful in his efforts to raise money in New London or New Haven. On the 10th he wrote to Nathaniel Shaw, Continental prize agent for Connecticut, who was then in New London. Joseph Packwood, according to Arnold, had returned from a profitable voyage to the West Indies in the sloop *John* more than a year ago and had never accounted to the owners, of whom Arnold was one. Shaw might settle the business. Apparently no answer ever came from Shaw to Arnold. On the 22nd Jacob Thompson of New Haven reported that Arnold's accounts were not yet settle   His china had been sold, but the enemy had taken the money from Mr. Shipman,* Mr. Shipman said. The house had not been sold, but Captain Sloan (Arnold's lieutenant) had come back from a prosperous voyage, moved in, and repaired the roof. "He will take every meathard (method) to secure the house from further damegg he intends to purchase it if he goes safe the next voyg." On the 28th Arnold wrote to Thompson in detail, and again on the 31st; and on the 31st he dispatched Jesse Penfield with several letters to Thomapson and others in New Haven. In particular, he wanted a feather bed belonging to his sister Hannah, which was to be brought from Cheshire to Fishkill with every care to keep it from getting dirty or wet on the road. The bed may have reached Arnold just before he fled West Point, but not, it appears, any of the money he thought due him in New Haven.

Like most Continental officers without sound private incomes Arnold was in serious need. On August 3 the general officers had presented a memorial to Congress, asking for

* This money was due to Benedict Arnold.

increase of pay. Congress, itself desperate, in its resolution of the 12th observed: "that patience and self-denial, fortitude and perseverance, and the cheerful sacrifice of time, health, and fortune are necessary virtues which both the citizen and soldier are called to exercise while struggling for the liberties of their country; and that moderation, frugality, and temperance must be among the chief supports, as well as the brightest ornaments, of that kind of civil government which is wisely instituted by the several states in this union." Nor were the various adjustments of compensation in the resolutions of the 12th and the 24th much more satisfying to the officers than these moral remarks.

Arnold was infuriated. The promise that he, as major general, would after the war get seven years' half pay and 1100 acres of land meant nothing to him now. Writing on the 27th to Parsons (commanding some of Benedict Arnold's troops), in command of the Connecticut forces, Arnold sent a copy of the resolutions which he bitterly said were "founded on principles of genuine Congressional virtue, magnanimity, benevolence, patriotism, and justice. I hope they meet with a proper reception by all who are interested in them. The insult added to injury is too pointed to pass unnoticed." Both to Nathaniel Greene* on the 23rd and to Parsons on September 8 Arnold proposed that a committee of 1,000 or 1,500 men from all ranks of the army be sent to Congress "to present a spirited but decent memorial setting forth their claims and requesting immediate justice as far as the public are able. This measure I think would be attended with happy consequences to the country; for if justice is not done to the army their necessities will occasion them to disband, and the country will of course be left to the ravages of the enemy." Arnold was, when he made this proposal to Parsons, already in communication with André on the subject of a meeting to arrange for the surrender of West Point; in the meantime, it might be worth while to encourage a sense of grievances in Parsons, who had just been ordered to take command of all Arnold's troops advanced towards the British lines.

Possibly with a sense of his own grievances, Arnold at headquarters had no scruple about trading in public stores for his own benefit. Catherine Martin, wife of a sergeant major in the 3rd Pennsylvania and housekeeper for Arnold, noticed that he secretively kept his stores "in his own private

* Quartermaster General.

room, and afterwards in a room appointed for the purpose, to which no person had access except himself," his servant, and the housekeeper. Arnold seems to have drawn the salt meat and rum allowed him and his household from the commissary in bulk, stored them, and then as he chose exchanged them for fresh meat or vegetables from farmers—as he allowed other officers who found they could not buy country produce for money. Besides this, Arnold's aides found that he sold wine, pork, and salt for cash, which he pocketed. As the memorandum book in which he noted down such sales is missing, there is no certainty how much he disposed of. Varick managed to prevent one sale of rum—to a Tory skipper—and thought he had prevented another of three barrels of pork. But Arnold, giving his orders about the pork "in so singularly low a tone of voice as not to be audible where Colonel Varick sat writing in the same room," got the barrels taken out of the cellar and moved down to the landing without the knowledge of his punctilious aide. Arnold's defence of his conduct was simple: he claimed he had back rations coming to him as part of his unsettled accounts and would hereafter draw all his rations and sell what he did not need.

Faithful as Franks (his aide in Philadelphia) had long been to Arnold, and much as Varick admired his chief, Arnold's official family was not harmonious. When Varick arrived on the 13th he found Franks dissatisfied. Arnold for some months had been short and fault-finding. The money Franks had brought from Canada had depreciated in value, and he felt he must soon discover a way of earning more for the support of his sister. He thought of going to Spain, where his friend Brockholst Livingston was now private secretary to John Jay, minister at that court. Three years with Arnold was enough. But Franks was in no great hurry, and he willingly set off for Philadelphia on the 23rd to escort Peggy Arnold and her child back to West Point.

Varick had come to his post in the belief that his work as secretary would not occupy all his time but would give him leisure for his studies. In this he was disappointed. Because of his "constant confinement to the writing table," he refused to have anything to do with Arnold's household or stores or in any way to act "as caterer or steward." Arnold had brought so many stores to Robinson's House, Franks said a day or two after Varick's arrival, that if the enemy should make a surprise attack "either our baggage or our stores must be lost. I (Varick) replied that the stores should go to the devil before I should lose my baggage, and that with Arnold's conduct in that respect I had no concern." But Varick was too honest not to object to Arnold's peculations, as he was too patriotic not to object to Arnold's friendship with Joshua Hett Smith (the spy). Yet while Varick thought Arnold was sly and avaricious, he did not at all suspect him of treachery.

IV

A man as arrogant as Arnold must have hated the indignity of being watched and checked by his aides, though he may have been too much absorbed in his conspiracy to fret over minor inconveniences. A month after he left Philadelphia he had still not heard from Clinton. Arnold waited in anxious tension. His terms might be rejected. Even if they were accepted, the answer had to come by a dangerous road, with many chances of detection which would mean ruin and probably death. How the answer came is not certain. A guess is that it was brought by an innocent messenger, Jonathan Copp, who on the 21st wrote from Fishkill that he had last Thursday seen Mrs. Arnold "perfectly well" and that he had with him a parcel and letters from her which would be forwarded. If these included the letters from British Headquarters, they did not reach Arnold for three days more; and it was six days after that before he found an opportunity and a messenger for his reply.

Just why William Heron of Redding, Connecticut, decided to go on a treacherous errand to New York at the end of August remains a mystery. He had hitherto been publicly an active patriot, member of the assembly, and trusted friend of General Parsons. Parsons, understanding that Heron's errand was to collect a debt, sent him to Arnold for the necessary pass. "Mr. Heron is a neighbour of mine, for whose integrity and firm attachment to the cause of the country I will hold myself answerable . . . I am certain he will conduct with strict honor any matter he undertakes."

As Heron later told his story to the Americans, he applied to Arnold for the pass on the 29th and was told to come back the next morning at eight. "I waited on him according to his directions. He intimated (by Colonel Varick) that I must wait two hours before he could dismiss me. I stayed (I believe) a longer time than that. I sat in the room with Colonel Varick, when the general came in and desired the colonel to write a permit (or a flag) for me, which he did, and the general signed it. The general then retired to his room and immediately sent word to me that he wanted to speak to me. I waited on him, and as soon as I entered the room (he being alone) he asked me if I thought the person with whom I expected to transact my business at the enemy's lines would transmit that letter (meaning a letter he held out to me) to the person to whom it was directed. I answered in the affirmative. He said if I could rely on him he should be obliged to me if I could give him (meaning the person I was to meet) a particular charge with regard to the delivery of the letter. As soon as I received the letter and viewed the superscription, which was written in a feigned hand, I must confess that I felt a jealousy or a suspicion that I never before experienced concerning any person of his rank."

Arnold said that the letter, originally sealed with a wafer had been opened for examination and sealed again with wax. But when Heron scrutinized it he found the wafer "entirely whole." This must, he reflected, be a letter which Arnold himself was sending secretly to New York, taking special pains that Varick should not know about it. Might not Arnold have written it while Heron waited, seizing this occasion to get some forbidden message safely carried? "Considering the impression the foregoing circumstances made on my mind, will not be thought strange if I deemed it my duty to deliver the letter in question to General Parsons, instead of carrying it where it was directed, which I accordingly did on my return from the lines."

What is to be thought stranger is that Heron did not transmit the letter addressed to "Mr. John Anderson, merchant, to the care of James Osborne to be left at the Rev. Mr. Odell, New York." For Heron in New York made terms with the British and became their spy for the duration of the war. On September 4 he talked for three hours with Chief Justice William Smith, brother of Arnold's friend at Haverstraw, said he had dined with Arnold at Robinson's House, and reported a general discontent among the Highlands officers, as well as widespread despair among the people everywhere. "Undoubtedly the majority of the Continentals have long been for a reunion with Great Britain." Smith, hearing the kind of talk loyalists liked and almost always heard, took down a long record of Heron's conversation and noted in his own manuscript memoirs: "It is very material. I gave him some informtion of which he will make good use." But Heron with un-explained caution took Arnold's letter back to Redding and gave it to Parsons on the 10th. Parsons, reading it, did what Arnold hoped any chance reader would do: supposed it "to refer merely to commerce" and did not turn it over to Washington till after Arnold's treason had come to light.

The intercepted letter played no part in the conspiracy, but it is a part of Arnold's story. It was written as from Gustavus about Moore (Arnold).

"On the 24th instant," he wrote, "I received a note from you without date, in answer to mine of the 7th July; also a letter from your house (British Head-quarters) of 24th July in answer to mine of the 15th with a note from Beckwith of the 30th July; with an extract of a letter from Mr. James Osborne of the 24th." Peggy or Stansbury had presumably thought only part of Odell's letter worth forward-ing. "I had paid particular attention to the contents of several letters. Had they arrived earlier, you should have had my answer sooner. A variety of circumstances has prevented my writing you before. I expect to do it very fully in a few days, and to procure you an interview with Mr. Moore, when you will be able to settle your commercial plan, I hope, agreeable to all parties. Mr. Moore assures me that he is still of opinion that his first proposal"—for £10,000 indemnification win or lose—"is by no means unreasonable, and makes no doubt, when he has a conference with you, that you will close with it." Arnold seemed incapable of realizing that he could not, somehow or other, have the price he had set his mind on. "He expects when you meet that you will be fully authorized from your house; that the risks and profits of the co-partnership may be fully and clearly understood.

A speculation might at this time be easily made to some advantage with ready money (British forces), but there is not the quantity of goods (men and stores) at market (West Point) which your partner seems to suppose, and the number of speculators (American forces) below I think will be against your making an immediate purchase (attack).

Clinton had spoken of 3000 men to be surrendered at West Point for £20,000, and Arnold had nothing like that number in the garrison. From then on he was less concerned with scattering his men than with concentrating them at West Point. He wanted his full price for the surrender, though the capture might be harder and bloodier. He may even have counselled delay with a thought to his own surer profit.

> I apprehend goods will be in greater plenty and much cheaper in the course of the season; both dry and wet (provisions and rum?) are much wanted and in demand at this juncture. Some quantities are expected in this part of the country soon.
>
> Mr. Moore flatters himself that in the course of ten days he will have the pleasure of seeing you. He requests me to advise you that he has ordered a draft on you in favour of our mutual friend Stansbury (liaison officer and paymaster for Sir Henry Clinton) for £300, which you will charge on account of the tobacco (the balance kept for Arnold in New York).

As Heron guessed, he had probably been kept waiting while Arnold wrote this letter. For it was only an acknowledgment of the offers received, and an acceptance of them. Arnold had not yet had time, and could not that Wednesday morning take time, to arrange in clear detail the indispensable interview with André.

West Point, key to the Hudson Valley, sometimes called the American Gibraltar, was not surrendered to the British after all. Sir Henry Clinton's adjutant, General John André the intermediary, had met Benedict Arnold near Stony Point New York, on the night of September 21, 1780. Their preparations for the mock attack were completed, but two days later, while returning by land, André was captured by the Americans with incriminating papers and maps on him. The officer in charge of the captured British officer failed to divine the underlying plot and simply sent warning of the proposed attack to Arnold as Commander of West Point. Thus warned, Arnold had ample time to escape aboard the British battleship, Vulture.

Arnold's career of duplicity seems to have been guided by plain self-interest, rather than any glamorous idealism of heroism. If causes interested Arnold at all, they were of secondary importance to his immense pride. He had not the slightest difficulty in swinging over to the British cause when it seemed to further his personal advancement. Although the West Point plot was muffed and he forfeited his £20,000, he was commissioned a brigadier general in the British Army and was awarded 6,315 pounds for his property losses in the American "zone." As a British officer he led an expedition to Virginia, where he ordered the burning of Richmond. In 1781 he led an attack against American troops in New London.

Finally he returned to London with the rest of the defeated British. There he was consulted by the King and the Government on American affairs. Though treason may seem profitable, traitors are despised and mistrusted everywhere and Arnold could not settle down in his adopted country. He spent the next ten years of his life, until 1791, in St. John, N.B., where he again carried on trade with the West Indies. He returned to London in 1791 after the outbreak of war between Britain and France and made a large fortune outfitting privateers.

He nursed a hope of returning to the America he had betrayed. This, of course, could never be realized. On June 14, 1801, he died in London, quite alone and without obituaries.

If Benedict Arnold had not been discovered to be a British spy, he might have changed the history of the United States in a very similar fashion as did Major Vidkun Quisling during World War II. Both names have gone down in history as being synonymous with the word "traitor."

SCHULMEISTER, NAPOLEON'S DARING SPY

by Richard Wilmer Rowan

IN A century and a quarter of almost continuous warfare, and of incessant intrigue and international secret service there has not appeared a more daring spy than Karl Schulmeister, the Alsatian who served Napoleon I. Stieber of Prussia, a half-century later, was at least as unscrupulous, and probably a more gifted organizer of wholesale espionage. The American, Lafayette Baker, was possibly as bold as Schulmeister. Montgaillard was a more devious plotter. But none of these three, and no other engaged in secret service, combined all the qualities and resources which made the Alsatian the most dangerous man of his day.

Schulmeister, as reckless an adventurer as Bonaparte himself, possessed not only the cruel audacity common to all great espionage agents but also he had talent as an actor, astounding wit, and extraordinary physical courage and endurance. Born on August 5, 1770, in New-Freistedt, he was the son of a ... ...-hed Lutheran minister; but he grew up to have the pleasa... conviction that he was of noble Hungarian lineage, and the time came when he helped to forge the documents which "proved" it. An eagerness for elegances suitable to exalted rank led him, when at length he could afford it, to employ the most noted dancing masters of the Continent. He aspired to wear the Legion of Honor, but failing in that, he insisted upon learning to dance like a marquis.

However, the spy began life very modestly, marrying an Alsatian girl named Unger and conducting jointly a provisions shop and iron-mongery. His income was also derived from a very brisk trade as a smuggler. Being an Alsatian, he saw no reason for living so close to the frontier without making that circumstance help to support him. And his immense popularity among all classes of society suggests to us that the smuggler—or contrabandist, as he would have described himself—then had a certain harmonious relation to public habit or desire, not unlike the American rum-runner.

It is said that Schulmeister was already an accomplished smuggler at the age of seventeen, and he was never ashamed to admit it, since he maintained that it called for unusual resource and daring in that locality. And though he achieved note and great wealth in Napoleon's service, he never so long as he lived ceased entirely to participate in smuggling enterprises. In 1799 he had become acquainted with that Colonel Savary who, as Duc de Rovigo, was one day to be Napoleon's Minister of Police, succeeding the famous Fouché. By 1804 Savary, a general now and one of Napoleon's favorite officers, had definitely enlisted Schulmeister, the smuggler, as a secret agent. Schulmeister was charged by Savary with the task of luring into France that remarkably harmless Bourbon prince, the young Duc d'Enghien, then living modestly in Baden upon funds supplied by the British and taking no interest whatever in French politics. But Napoleon wished to intimidate Royalist partisans all over Europe, and believed that the execution of an innocent relative of the proscribed Capets was just the terrifying stroke he required.

The Duc d'Enghien was accustomed to visit a young woman of Strasburg to whom he was deeply attached. Shulmeister learned of this and straightway sent his assistants to remove her to Belfort, where she was detained in a country house near to the frontier upon the pretext that local French authorities considered her a suspicious person. Schulmeister now forged a letter in her name and sent it to Enghien, entreating him to effect her release from this unjustifiable internment. Her lover responded immediately, believing that he could bribe her captors to allow him to convey her the short distance from Belfort to the territory of his protector, the Margrave of Baden. Schulmeister was ready, and before the prince himself had actually set foot on French soil, he was seized and hurried to Strasburg, and thence to Vincennes. Six days after his lawless arrest, as a Bourbon forbidden to return to France he was condemned by a preposterous court-martial. One of his last acts was to write a letter to his mistress, explaining why he had failed to assist her. But she, having served Shulmeister's purpose, had already been released, pathetically unaware of her part in the intrigue. That same night Enghien was shot, his executioners compelling him to hold a lantern so that they might see to take aim.

Savary, it is said, paid Schulmeister a sum equal to 30,000 for arranging this matter. Talleyrand observed that the killing of the young Duc d'Enghien "was worse than a crime—it was a blunder." And largely for this epigram has the savage incident been remembered; not because it exposed Bonaparte's barbarous conception of internecine politics, or because it marked the debut in European secret service of a man who was soon to become one of the most formidable espionage agents of modern times.

Schulmeister was the type for whom conflict on a Napoleonic scale was made to order. He was also that devil of a fellow for whom phrases such as "clever rascal" and "plausible rogue" and "lying imposter" must have been coined. If not so great an organizer as Stieber, as an active spy operating within the enemy's lines during hostilities he attempted and achieved stratagems which the Prussian—if he ever had conceived anything so superb and hazardous—would have divided with a subordinate, reserving the credit for himself and the dangers for his hireling.

47

Savary, who, with the murder of the young Bourbon, had again moved nearer his goal of a ducal estate, said when presenting Schulmeister to Napoleon in the following year: "Here, Sire, is a man all brains and no heart." The Emperor and his favorite appear to have chuckled over this, as though they had specialized in all heart, but could endure the difference in a smuggler and paid spy. Napoleon was himself fond of saying: "The spy is a natural traitor." He often mentioned it to Schulmeister during the next four years. Yet there is no record of Napoleon ever having been seriously betrayed by a military spy in any of his campaigns; and in contrast he disbursed large sums to corrupt more distinguished gentry, who might be persuaded to sell out to the conqueror and spare French armies from greater costs.

Descriptions which we have of Stieber are uniformly repellent, portraying him as swarthy and hard in countenance, with eyes almost white in colorlessness, and with manners at once arrogant toward his inferiors and servile, acquiescent, ingratiating in the presence of any authority greater than his own. But even the enemies of Schulmeister could not deny his personal bravery or charm or extraordinary physical endurance. The spy is said to have had a face like a mask, but probably none noticed this before his triumphs in secret service; he was broad of shoulder and imperturbable, not tall but very muscular, with a deep chest, and such manner and assurance that he passed for an officer and gentleman at the Austrian court, and could impress and captivate women and children, and generals and nobles alike.

Napoleon's campaign in 1805 against Austria and Russia was one of the most perfectly timed and maneuvered military disasters ever contrived in Europe, and that Schulmeister initiated his career in military espionage during this same campaign is significant. Napoleon had always endeavored to study the character of the commanders his royal foes were sending against him. In 1805 the Austrian hopes rested upon Marshal Mack, a general of no striking ability but great family influence and a special desire to atone for his previous defeats at the hands of the French. Mack, a confirmed monarchist, would not allow himself to perceive that the Corsican usurper was really popular in France, or that the nation generally supported him as its heroic sovereign; and Schulmeister prepared to prey upon this dull, simple-minded, and easily led officer in terms of his own astigmatism. He first appeared in Vienna as a young man of noble Hungarian ancestry, who had lived in France, but had lately been exiled across the frontier because Napoleon believed him to be an Austrian spy. In advance of his journey to Austria, Schulmeister had addressed a letter to Mack, describing his plight, his hatred of the French tyrant, and offering him some measure of vengeance. Meeting the alleged exile and hearing how much he seemed to know about the military and civil condition of France, Mack gladly availed himself of such fortuitous espionage. He introduced the spy as his protégé into the best army clubs of Vienna, obtained him a commission, and in the fateful autumn of 1805 attached him to his personal staff as chief of intelligence.

Schulmeister's operations at this time appear to have been almost fantastically deceptive. He was in constant communication with Napoleon, keeping the French command advised of every Austrian move and receiving for his expenses large sums of money which he seems to have spent lavishly but to good effect. Like most educated Alsatians, he spoke German as fluently as French; but more than merely linguistic gifts were required to make him the favorite he became in the exclusive Viennese society of that day. He found two officers of ability, Wend and Rulski, who let themselves be bribed by him. When he gave Mack false information, it was confirmed by the presumably independent report of one or both of these traitors; so that Mack understood that all his monarchist expectations of French disunion were actually coming to pass. Schulmeister was provided with letters written to him by supposed traitors in the armies of France, depicting civil turbulence, military disaffection, and kindred national ills that would seem to make a vigorous foreign campaign impossible. Mack read these joyfully, and also a newspaper that Napoleon had arranged to be printed especially for Schulmeister and dispatched to him with elaborate furtiveness, in which items supporting his mischievous intelligence were inserted to convince the Austrian marshal.

Mack was not a blunderer, not an elegant old idiot of exalted connections and unfit to command a guard of honor. He was an experienced leader of fifty-three, and determined to succeed, hence over-anxious, and all too ready to believe what he wanted to believe—an easy target for the sharpshooter from Alsace. Schulmeister caused Mack to feel sure that France tottered on the brink of civil war, with Napoleon having to recall his forces to the Rhine frontier; whereupon Mack marched out of the strategically pivotal city of Ulm with thirty thousand men, intending to pursue Marshal Ney and the retiring French vanguard. Instead he found Ney still at the head of an advancing army, ready for battle, which was surprise enough; but then Marmont, Lannes, Soult, and Dupont appeared on his flanks, and the cavalry of Murat closed the ring of steel. Three days later, on October 20, the still bewildered Austrian surrendered.

Schulmeister was not captured, but returned to Vienna and there boldly intruded upon the war councils presided over by those disquieted imperial allies, the Tsar and the Austrian Kaiser. Astonishing though it may seem, the military leaders of Russia and Austria listened to him and pondered his suggestions of strategy that would discount their losses at Ulm. Mack was thought to have been treacherous. He was subsequently deprived of his rank and imprisoned in disgrace until the truth of his betrayal was established by his friends. But in November, 1805, there was hardly a rumor discreditable to Schulmeister and, again equipped with forged documents which seemed to prove his points, he led Napoleon's foes astray while maintaining constant communication with the Emperor. The result—on December 2—was Austerlitz.

But directly after that majestic victory, persons in Vienna who had mistrusted the engaging spy caused his arrest. Undoubtedly he would have been tried and executed had not the French advancing upon Vienna moved so rapidly that they took the city and set him free with dramatic timeliness. Schulmeister's character was unpleasantly regarded after this signal success because of his boasting. He had received a small fortune from Napoleon and, said he, nearly as much for his services to Austria. It would, of course, have been impossible for him in his loyal disguise to refuse payment from Mack or the Emperor Francis for the intelligence with which he imposed upon them; but his pride in these gains reveals the small and criminal mind. Napoleon, with perhaps the feeling of the professional soldier, seems never to have valued Schulmeister as Bismarck valued Stieber, nor ever to have rewarded him in proportion to the titles and estates he showered upon adventurers of no more consequence. Schulmeister was permitted to risk his life, not only in espionage—when he went as an observer into hostile countries, even undertaking a mission to England and Ireland—but also in battle where he proved himself a man of action and of soldierly courage.

At Landshut he captained a troop of hussars, led a charge,

and captured enemy positions. Acting for Savary, whose confidence he always retained, he went back to Strasbourg to investigate civil disturbances and in the course of an open revolt again distinguished himself by shooting the principal agitator, thus eliminating the mainspring of trouble with one pistol ball. Upon Napoleon's second occupation of Vienna, Schulmeister was appointed censor of newspapers, the stage, publishing houses, and religious establishments; and with this opportunity he displayed another sort of sagacity, causing to be circulated broadcast among the races of Austria-Hungary the works of Voltaire, Montesquieu, Diderot, Holbach, and Helvetius, which thus far in that land had enjoyed prominent reservations upon the Index, both religious and political. For a time in 1809 he was Commissary General of the imperial forces in the field. Regardless of what benefits he may have hoped to gain from the lucrative dispersal of army contracts and commercial favors, he was soon returned to secret service duty; but he was already rich, having purchased some years before the splendid Chateau Le Meinau in his native Alsace and in 1807 another large estate near Paris—the two having an estimated value of more than a million dollars today.

He had frequently directed a corps of spies, though never with Prussian thoroughness, or without being responsible to Savary, and perhaps making some reports directly to the Emperor. In short, though he might style himself M. du Meinau and live as generously as a lord, he was just an adroit and daring secret agent to the imperial military caste. He begged his humorous friend, Lasalle, that crack commander of light cavalry who perished at Wagram, to persuade Napoleon to confer upon him the Legion of Honor. Lasalle came back to say that the Emperor refused, believing that gold was the only suitable reward for a spy. Nothing would seem more clearly to expose Napoleon as an upstart and parvenu himself than his treatment of one whose duplicities he had been guiding and profiting from extensively ever since the tragedy of young d'Enghien. Fouché, disreputable, ruthless and disloyal, as Minister of Police had been created the Duc d'Otrante. Fouché—as Steiber afterwards did—was not above having his own men devise dangers from which he breathlessly "rescued" his beloved Emperor. And even greater scoundrels, like Radet, paraded the ribbon which Schulmeister was loftily denied.

The spy's last chance came at the Congress of Erfurt,

where through the representations of Savary he was chosen to direct the French secret service. It would appear that he outdid himself in the substance and variety of intelligence he conveyed to Napoleon each day, for there were many notable persons to be spied upon, and the Emperor had a villager's dread of missing any choice bit of gossip. The Tsar was there, enjoying himself with Russian abandon; and Goethe—whom Bonaparte had always professed to admire—was there also, in a diplomatic mood which caused his fellow genius some concern. Schulmeister wrote Savary that Napoleon asked him every morning: Whom has Goethe been seeing? and, with whom did the Emperor Alexander stay last night? Another job of Schulmeister's to which Napoleon repeatedly alluded was keeping watch over the lovely Queen Louise of Prussia. The Russian autocrat had shown himself disposed to admire and befriend this greatly humiliated lady; Napoleon wished to continue to humble her by blackening her character to the Tsar if he could, and his chief spy—unimpeded by the Legion of Honor—was expected to supply the smut.

By 1810 Napoleon's domination over Vienna, which Schulmeister had helped to assure, culminated in the marriage that brought an Austrian empress to Paris and such Austrian influence with her that the spy was driven into retirement. Ironically enough his intrigues before Ulm and Austerlitz had never been forgiven, though the one gaining the most from them, who had been raised up to equality with the proud Hapsburgs after Austerlitz, was being accepted as the husband of Maria Louisa. Schulmeister, avoiding vain resentment, retired but not into the camp of Napoleon's enemies as many another of his kind would have done, and as Fouché did do with infinitely less provocation. He appears to have been grateful for his riches and estates. He was still the postgraduate smuggler and backer of smuggling projects, so that he went to live at Le Meinau where his hospitality and charities won him the sincere homage of his fellow Alsatians.

The Austrian vindictiveness lasted until 1814. After Leipzig and the defeat of the French, Alsace was invaded and a regiment of Austrian artillery was detached to bombard and demolish Schulmeister's home. During the Hundred Days he rallied to the Emperor; but when Napoleon left Paris for Belgium the former spy was one of the first to be arrested and he only saved himself by paying an enormous ransom. This seriously crippled his finances. He attempted to rehabilitate them with speculation and lost all that he had. For five years he had known a steadily rising fortune; for ten he had enjoyed wealth and considerable authority. He might have kept something of both, for most of the really unscrupulous Bonapartists managed to, but instead chance brought him down even as the meteoric pageant of empire came to an end. Presumably Schulmeister retained besides his good nature the regard of his Alsatian neighbors; perhaps he still danced like a marquis, though the estates to match had slipped into other hands. He was destined to live nearly four decades more, until 1853, a poor but not unhappy man, granted a tobacconist stall to tend in Strasbourg. And it is recorded that another Bonaparte who came to be Napoleon III, with ever a politician's eye for neglected henchmen of his illustrious uncle, sought out the former secret agent in 1850 when making a tour as President and warmly offered him his hand.

It is possible to write of Schulmeister with a degree of sympathy, not only because of his final failures, but also on account of the quality of the man. His successes seem now so personal, and have not that systematized and Juggernaut certainty that made much of Stieber's spying a road-roller demonstration. Schulmeister was treacherous when treachery was expedient; but whatever his practices, he never preached a debasing philosophy of patriotism which honored the impostures, bribes, and betrayals of espionage as national virtues. Schulmeister had engaging characteristics that were both French and German, in keeping with his geographical origin. Stieber was all Prussian.

It is worth noting that of all those who served Napoleon and described him in letters at the time or afterward, in memoirs, Schulmeister alone took notice of the conqueror's voice. He reports it as being crisp and strident, rather high pitched, and adds that the Emperor's habit of speaking through his teeth gave a hissing effect to nearly everything he said. Perhaps the spy lacked the one deceit of flattery to make him an appreciated courtier. More probably his notorious talents arrived upon the imperial scene too late, when Napoleon, engrossed with dynastic foundations, was growing tired of the parvneu aristocracy his victories had elevated. He would call the spy "Karl," but he treated him like a lackey, and apart from the generous expense allowance, never conceded any merit to Schulmeister's audacious and fearfully effective performances in espionage.

Mr. Rowan, the outstanding historian in the field of espionage, has given a vivid and true portrait of a "double spy." Most certainly Schulmeister helped Napoleon win many battles. The Emperor was never content to base his strategies on statistics alone but relied largely on the emotional characteristics, personal strengths and weakness, romantic inclinations and especially the ages of the military leaders who opposed him. He held little or no awe of a general over forty, but he greatly feared young commanders.

WILHELM STIEBER, KING OF SLEUTH HOUNDS

by Richard Wilmer Rowan

STIEBER, celebrated spy-master of Prussia, has been called "the father of Prussian spies" and "the father of espionage service." He was really neither of these, for Frederick the Great was the former, while the latter was assuredly Oriental, and very likely prehistoric. But Wilhelm Johann Carl Eduard Stieber was one of the greatest spies and secret-service organizers of modern Europe. Prince Bismarck called him "my king of sleuth-hounds," and honored him accordingly; and as there seems to have been a lavishness about his christening which suggests royalty, the title the Iron Chancellor conferred may be allowed to stand. Schopenhauer said somewhere that Germans are "remarkable" for the absolute lack of that feeling which Latins call 'verecundia'—sense of shame." This may have grieved the philosopher and inconvenienced a number of his countrymen, but it has accounted for many startling developments in espionage. Steiber from youth was afflicted with that "absolute lack": it proved a continual boon to his king and country, helping to make them respectively emperor and empire, and immensely improved his own standing with influential officers and gentlemen that otherwise might never have heard his name. Stieber enriched the records of European treachery and intrigue for nearly four decades with the pride of a pioneer and the zest of a fallen archangel. He was one of those fortunate malefactors who are able to serve the State without putting any tiresome curb upon their own criminal inclinations; and, though in time he uncovered for patriotic use all the more subterranean talents of a Metternich, Mazarin, or Machiavelli, his singular ability was displayed from the first, in being able to enlist himself among the Prussian police before anything he had done could be charged against him.

With Napoleon banished to St. Helena, his spies and armies scattered, and reaction strong in Europe, on the 3rd of May, 1818, Wilhelm Stieber was born, the son of a petty official of Merseburg, a small town in Prussian Saxony. A few years afterwards his father removed to Berlin, and the boy was soon being educated in the general direction of the Lutheran ministry. Sundry minor geniuses of secret service and espionage have come from the clergy, but Stieber seems to have altered his own course toward the legal profession, and upon becoming a lawyer to have turned at once to criminal cases and the inevitably congenial police work. In 1845 he was already a spy, for he denounced to the Prussian civil authorities a man named Schloeffel whose offence was alleged to be liberalism and labor agitation, but who also happened to be the uncle of Stieber's own wife. After this demonstration of ethical atrophy, his progress was rapid. The year 1848 found Europe in a very disturbed state, with Continental Kingdoms and their autocrats likely to be swept away by revolution. France was again republican and the recent advances of industrialism had aroused a new kind of agitator whose leader was Karl Marx and whose doctrine was called Socialism. Stieber needed just this intense political situation to set him apart as a useful man, a loyal monarchist, and an informer fit to whisper into the ear of the King himself.

The evidence he had given against Schloeffel was not strong enough to convict that relative by marriage, but he so managed his own participation in the case as not to endanger his contact either with the government or with the suspected radicals. Stieber posed, of course, as an ardent liberal, chum of the workingman and champion of Socialists. Whenever radical sympathizers were brought to trial he volunteered his professional aid, and "defended" them floridly and without charge, thus winning his way into the very directorate of Prussian liberalism that his friends of the police were scheming to suppress and imprison. King Frederick William of Prussia was about as timid a ruler as the ascending House of Hohenzollern had thus far enthroned. He lived in terror of mob violence, and Stieber quickly contrived to turn the royal agitation to his own account. As an *agent provocateur* it was desirable that he frequently show off his partisan ardors and reassure the radical leaders and the turbulent rank and file. One day he put himself at the head of a particularly riotous throng and in the guise of its spokesman penetrated close to the quaking person of the king. But at once he revealed to Frederick William that he was Stieber the spy and whispered that all would go well, since His Majesty was safely surrounded by him and his assistants. With those few words the young lawyer literally welded himself to the secret service of Prussia's timorous sovereign.

A sublimated stool-pigeon and simultaneously a radical plotter and defender of the oppressed, he yet had time to build up a very lucrative law practice. It is a matter of record that in the five years of his young manhood, between 184 and 1850, Stieber had no less than three thousand clients for whom he appeared in court, and this among a conservative people to whom age and experience meant everything. The bulk of his many cases had to do with crime, and he directed his amazing energies almost invariably in the criminal behalf. Since Prussia was never lawless to the extent of a modern American crime wave, Stieber must have been virtually legal adviser to the whole underworld of Berlin. And then, when his success had excited much envy or admiring notice, its basic secret was exposed. Stieber had still one other employment—as editor of the police periodical. This excellent inside connection, a part of his reward from the grateful and dependent King, he was using to acquaint himself with whatever evidence the police had gathered to produce in court against any one of his clients. It was, therefore, hardly remarkable that he could achieve his rapid fame as a criminal lawyer, the magical confounder of prosecutions, and one who, concocting impregnable pleas and alibis, was never to be overthrown by surprise testimony in the midst of a trial.

Revelations concerning the documentary source of his brilliance caused a great scandal, but nothing came of it while the faint-hearted Frederick William, who never forgot the riots, governed from Potsdam. Stieber in 1850 was even appointed Commissioner of Police, a job so much to his liking that, being unable to foresee the future with its sweep of imperial conquests, he must have believed himself, at thirty-two, to have achieved the very pinnacle of his aspiration.

The following year he set forth for England, attended the World's Fair, and eagerly spied upon Marx and the radical groups of expatriated Germans then in London. He reported to his superiors that the British authorities would not cooperate with him in a scheme to harass these subversive

lements of his own race. He began to feel snubbed and
rossed to Paris; but there he contrived to emerge as an
xile and was befriended by Socialists and liberals, so that
ie obtained a list of the radical sympathizers still resident
n Germany and at once hurried home to supervise wholesale
rrests. Thus he caused hundreds more to flee from Germany
nd seek refuge overseas; and we may reflect that Stieber
lirectly influenced much of the best immigration to America in
he decade before the Civil War, including such desirable
yp⸱⸱⸱ ⸱⸱⸱ ⸱⸱⸱ Schurz, Jacobi, and Franz Siegel.

Thus far the "king of sleuth-hounds" was only a kind of
nongrel dog in the manger. The Prussian throne had be-
ome his altar, the favor of its royal occupant his household
od; and if not yet a king he was both a sly and rabid royalist
ho would not cease to employ his spies and policemen until
e made every Hohenzollern subject a submissive copy of
imself. Presumably the army of Prussia at this period meant
o him no more than a force which might be used as *gen-
'armerie* should insurrection ever again threaten the govern-
nent. He was pleased when Louis Napoleon's adherents con-
ived the *coup d'état* of 1852 establishing an empire in
'rance, simply because it promised the wiping out of a
adical haven and all those French headquarters of Com-
nunist agitation he had found so unpleasantly near. Stieber's
roblems were international only when a Prussian whose
berty he hoped to impair eluded him and got across the
ontier. He complained bitterly of both the liberals who
ayed and the radicals who fled. Germans having moved to
orth America disgusted him particularly by their un-
nimous and unceasing outbursts in praise of the freedom
hich that refuge offered. He could not resist intercepting
neir letters, but, reading them, fumed over the glad cries of
emocratic discovery. Any such republican recruiting he
onsidered an affront to his own patriotism; he was right-
ously inflamed when German-Americans published opinions
etrimental to autocrats and their secret police.

It was now five years since the social tumult of 1848.
aving contradicted by force the assailants of absolutism,
tieber and his kind could proclaim their gift to the German
eople. He collaborated with a police official of Hanover in
reparing a book that depicted their battle with the dragon
' Marxian revelation. And it was very characteristic that he
ould include in his publication a list of dangerous radicals
nd Socialist or Communist agitators then at large, so that

conservative authorities everywhere might know whom to be on guard against and join him and his German colleagues in refusing asylum to persons whose liberal ideas were worse than cannon. But another five years and the reward of autocracy's good and faithful servant came in the form of dismissal. Stieber could strengthen King Frederick William's throne but not his wits; and when the Prussian monarch was recognized to be imbecile, he was relieved by an obstinate relative, afterward the Emperor William I, who considered that the feeble-mindedness of his predecessor had never been more abundantly exposed than in conferring upon such a man as Stieber the powers of the police.

No sooner was it understood that the Regent thought Stieber a detestable and needless functionary than the troubles of the tireless *Polizeirat* began in earnest. For all his subtle efforts he had never been popular, not even when he was posing as a public defender and offering his legal services free to the deserving. He had then come up for election to the Landtag—of course, as a liberal—and had been signally defeated. But now the many enemies he had acquired in the thirteen years since he began as a spy gathered together their charges and grievances and were successful in having him brought to trial. Sieber, badly cornered, saw no chance of retaining any position in the government or at the bar, and that counted terribly with him; yet he had not defended three thousand persons of doubtful innocence without learning all the devious routes to acquittal, and the record shows that he handled his own indictments magnificently. By proving that he had done his plotting and spying and betraying with royal authority, by showing that, however numerous and grave the offences of which he was accused, he had never acted thus except by the King's command, Stieber maneuvered the court and his foes entirely out of position. To convict him they had to condemn publicly the ethical standards of a royal Hohenzollern and a very pitiful one now imperfectly resting within the confines of an exclusive sanitarium. It was impossible to prove that Stieber's conduct ever had been disloyal, privately vindictive, or, within narrow monarchical limits, unpatriotic. He was subsequently deprived of his office, but in court he was acquitted.

In view of his place in the history of secret service it is informing to study this notorious spy in the years between 1858 and 1863, when private life was curtly thrust upon him by the Regent of Prussia. He was not idle but busied himself in helping to organize the secret police service of the Tsar. He had once been able officially to arrange the suppression of a scandal involving the wife of a Russian attaché in Berlin; and for his light touch in that instance he was remembered at a time when foreign employment was welcome to him. However, he did not remain in St. Petersburg, but was assigned to concentrate on a noble device that would henceforth enable the Tsar's agents to trace and apprehend criminals even after they had vanished from Russia. He had a sweeping commission, as well as generous pay and allowances, being expected to run to earth not only ordinary malefactors, forgers, and counterfeiters, robbers, and the like, but also political offenders and suspects, demagogues, and all manner of dangerous malcontents. So that he ally founded that system of external and nearly world-wide veillance, the foreign branch of the *Okhrana*, which tinued in operation until 1917. And in further proof of eber's unyielding if perhaps curiously deformed patriotism, is known that, though disgraced as a police official at me, he never ceased spying for Prussia and gathered aluable information all the while he was in the employ of e Russian crown.

Military items were still an unimportant matter with him, is most notable tricks of espionage having to do with the uppression of democratic tendencies; until there came that momentous day in 1863 when the course of his whole life was tered and the outcome of two European wars began to be determined years in advance. He was introduced to Bismarck. newspaper proprietor, Brass, the founder of the *Nord-eutsche Allgemeine Zeitung*, took it upon himself to present e spy to the statesman, and to recommend him, too, in ite of Stieber's unpopularity with the Regent who had ecome King. Two born conspirators thus brought together ere never again to leave off a congenial dependence upon ach other till the one had died and the other been thrust ide. Bismarck was contemplating his first broad move on the eutonic checkerboard. He had decided that overthrowing ustria would get him all the other stage effects he required r his imperial production. The new Prussian army was fit d finished; but it seemed a commendable project to try learn exactly everything about the military readiness of ustria. He suggested to Stieber that he undertake to man-

age this preliminary incursion. The spy eagerly accepted an
said he could do it alone.

In his own day a repellent and menacing personage, Steibe
seems almost a humorous figure now, not because of an
inherent wit or irony, for he was intensely serious, but becau
of his absolutely cynical realism in appraising human natur
With a horse and wagon he proposed to drive about an
investigate the Austrian military establishment while appa
ently devoting himself to commonplace transactions. H
wanted to go everywhere and be welcome, so he loaded h
wagon lightly—with cheap religious statuettes and obscer
pictures! He could be blandly commercial and seem to enjo
driving a bargain. Though he trusted nobody, he was
"good mixer." And so he travelled for months, gathering suc
data that von Moltke is said to have marvelled at its minu
accuracy.

The Prussian conquest of Austria in 1866 was one of
shortest and most decisive campaigns of modern histo
Thanks to the intelligence supplied by Bismarck's spy, t
army staff had been able to draw up practically a timetab
of victorious advances. The soldiers of Prussia and its all,
were better trained and equipped than their adversarie
and had no difficulty in reaching all objectives according
schedule. The one important battle at Sadowa ended host
ities and also the major influence of Vienna in the politics
Germany. In this glorious spree of invasion Stieber playe
his first conspicuous part in eight years, having been place
in command of a new squad of political police designed
the Chancellor for field service. But he seems to have push
himself forward a bit too suddenly around general hea
quarters. Arrogant staff officers resented it and refused to ha
him seated at their mess. Whereupon Bismarck rebuke
them by inviting Stieber to lunch with him privately, a
later urger Moltke to decorate the spy on account of t
thoroughness of his work in Bohemia. Moltke yielded up
medal, but also apologized to his aristocratic associates
having honored one whom they despised. Bismarck counter
by having Stieber appointed governor of Brno, provinc
capital of Moravia, during the Prussian occupation.

Social friction may have dismayed Stieber, who co
plicated his sinister attainments with every aspiration of t
parvenu, but his secret service activities smoothed the w
for all the uniformed nobility. He was specifically charg
with the full protection of the Prussian headquarters.

nd his agents had to guard the persons of the King and
sismarck and generals like von Roon and Moltke, and see to
that no enemy spies were allowed to approach near to any
recious secrets of the army. Thus Stieber did institute the
rst German counterespionage, but his innovation had been
nticipated by French imperial guardians sixty years before.
lowever, as always, he added those systematizing touches
eculiarly his own, and then went on to create the novelty
f an exacting military censorship which covered examination
f all dispatches, telegrams, and letters from the front. Since
ie Austrian forces were on the defensive from the beginning
nd Stieber's own observations had disclosed their weapons to
e obsolete in comparison with the new Prussian rifles, it is
robable that he established himself as censor mainly to
nlarge his own authority. For what was there now to be
ritten or telegraphed which would have bogged the steam
oller of Prussia or even disturbed its engineers' schedule by
o much as one day? While reviewing this condition of enemy
elplessness and despair, Stieber came to his next invention—
nilitary propaganda.

It occurred to him that the spirit of the German army, and
the civil population as well, would mount upon wings of
own manufacture if he spread from day to day the
noicest news of Austrian losses and panic, sickness, shortage
f supplies, divided counsel, depression, and disaster. He
ally discovered a tonic cure without having had the disease,
r both civilian and military morale on the side of the Prus-
an alliance must have been all that could be desired in a
ctorious conflict lasting a little more than forty-five days. But
ieber suggested to Bismarck that there be organized a
entral Information Bureau with himself in charge, and
sing what he called this "unobtrusive title" he began pouring
rth the first unadulterated samples of one-way war corre-
ondence. Subsequently he shut out the powerful Reuters
legraphic news agency, and detected the subterfuge when
subsidiary of Reuters began to flourish in Berlin. He ex-
uded this and invited Dr. B. W. Wolff to start the semi-
ficial Wolff bureau as a rival organization. In the public
lebration following upon the triumph over Austria, Stieber's
erits were not neglected. He was appointed a privy coun-
lor; and the King, who had formerly joined with the fore-
ost in disliking him and mistrusting all his works, now pro-
unced him a misunderstood and invaluable fellow, and as

a spy deserving not only the customary cash rewards but honor also and the public distinctions of the soldier.

Beteen 1866 and 1868 Bismarck and Stieber pondere the coming war with France. Napoleon III had been badl informed, as he usually was in external affairs, and believe that Austria would defeat the new army of Moltke an Roon. As soon as Prussia had finished dictating terms of peace the French Emperor wanted either to attack the victor of else extort an unearned share of the spoils. Bismarck, remen bering Sadowa, presented a bold front. Napoleon's arm chiefs advised patience, reminding the great politician an unwary diplomatist that his soldiers were in need of mor modern weapons. Union infantry in the last year of th American Civil War had taken the field with Enfield repea ing rifles, which the wondering Confederates described a magazine implements loaded on Sunday and fired all th rest of the week. Military attachés must have reported upc these highly educated muskets; but in Europe the Prussia bree -loading needle-guns were still the best availab arms for riflemen, and France had nothing so good. Co recting this omission produced the chassepot and th mitrailleuse, at once believed to surpass every other type rifle and machine-gun then in use. Stieber, in 1868, visited t French to ascertain the deadly virtues of their new equi ment.

But before his most destructive tour of secret service b gan there occurred an incident that, if not illustrating ar remarkable piece of espionage, will show how he endear himself to a conspirator of Bismarck's gauge. Through one his formerly numerous Russian connections he had obtain information concerning an attempt to be made upon the li of Tsar Alexander II while that autocrat visited Paris. As tl guest and potential ally of Napoleon III, the Tsar was attend a grand review in his honor at Longchamps and he the Polish assassin would try his hand. Stieber, after co sulting his astute master, withheld a warning of this revol tionary plot until just before the afternoon of the review. He French police officials been informed far enough in advan they could have so completely exploded the affair that would have attracted almost no attention. Stieber's intention delay—which was made to seem like a last-minute discove and sprint to aid the French and save their reigning guest forced the Parisian officers to alarm the Tsar and his sur and then seize the plotters with sensational quickness. B

o crime had been commited; Stieber's warning was no
vidence; and according to the French law a severe penalty
as impossible. Suspicion of intent to kill Russia's ruler was
ot a charge grave enough to get the alleged assassin and his
ccomplices transported or sentenced to prison for long terms.

The Tsar, as Stieber had anticipated, declined to see the
dicial nicety in this, his host's dilemma. The Napoleonic
pstart, he maintained ever after, had cared so little about a
al emperor's life that he did not trouble to punish a mur-
erer who had all but succeeded. The result was estrange-
ent between the Tsar and Napoleon III, and this was pre-
sely what Chancellor Bismarck needed, if the French ruler
d his marshals were presently to be led to the slaughter.
aving done so much for the next war, Stieber proceeded
do ten times more in making certain of German victory. He
d his two assistants, Zernicki and Kaltenbach, now spent
me eighteen months in France, spying, recording, measur-
g, and also boldly placing whole battalions of resident
ies to await the expected invaders. During this fruitful trip
e three sent any number of secret and coded reports to
erlin announcing their patriotic progress; yet when at last
ey returned home they brought with them additional data
ng three trunks, which they checked through like ordinary
ggage in an express car attached to their train.

Stieber afterward boasted that he had nearly forty thou-
d spies in the invasion zones of France when, on August 6,
0, the defeat of MacMahon at Worth predicted the shat-
ing of one empire and the fabrication of another. Dr.
opold Auerbach has conveyed the impression, that, if
allenged, he would supply names and even addresses. But
ere is no good reason for believing that the spy-master had
exaggerate his strength or his thoroughness. The imperial
cret police of France—who might have opposed him with
unterespionage—were instead devoting themselves to the
me internal quakes and recoils which had nagged Louis
apoleon and his ministers, until declaration of war seemed
e only dynastic refuge in a country overfond of its tradition
foreign adventures. And if this last diversion proved tragi-
lly domestic, Stieber's prodigal secret service must be
unted first, since it came first, in the array of German arms,
ganization, strategy, and preparedness that guaranteed
ench surrender.

It seems strange that in all that has been written about the

Franco-Prussian War, so little of it—outside of a few speci
treatises, should relate to espionage and Wilhelm Stiebe
France was still the most warlike nation of Europe. It was tl
customary thing for French troops to be brave and well le
and, on the Continent, generally victorious. The giant strid
of Moltke and Bismarck, the incapacities of Napoleon and h
henchmen, would scarcely account for the whole bewilderir
reversal. Worth on August 6, Sedan twenty-five days late
and a formidable military power had vanished from the co
test! Auerbach quotes Stieber, writing home proudly to h
wife at this time, upon the thrilling topic of his intimacy wi
the Chancellor. He and his two lieutenants were comman
ing twenty-nine other officers and one hundred and fifty-sev
subordinates, a magnified force of field police, who operate
just as he and a much smaller squad had done during tl
campaign against Austria. But Bismarck kept the chief s|
within call and chose him as a confidant on successive occ
sions while the disaster they had plotted together was mar
festing itself with spectacular punctuality.

Stieber had known, when he went into France to study tl
chassepot and mitrailleuse, that should he report them grea
superior to German arms, the Chancellor would wait
try to adjust his carefully trained war provocation to w
ever indefinite time it might take to deliver improved weap
to their regiments. In short, Stieber's admiration for the ne
French guns could have embarrassed Bismarck and obstru
his plans as German politics or foreign diplomacy n
had done. But again, if Stieber had underestimated the p
sible resistance of the empire—blundering as, in fact, Germ
secret agents during the (first) World War repeatedly d
when trying to judge morale, resources, and potential fighti
power of an impending opponent—the effect upon Germa
in the critical year of 1870 would have conferred a kind
suicide on the Prussian leaders. The spy-master, therefo
declared for war upon his own responsibility. And he anti
pated his own faults of military observation of judgment
preparing to encounter much less advantageous odds th
his near view of the sagging imperial régime entitled him
estimate. Overconfident and habitually slack, Napoleo
ministry of war would have intoxicated a less methodi
spy. One of its spokesmen assured an anxious Chamber tl
the French Army was ready "with not even so much as t
button of a gaiter wanting." Stieber, hearing that, might ha
justifiably telegraphed the Prussian army to join him in Pa

or at least urged his superiors to attack before the imperial incompetents could be found out and replaced by able men. But, no doubt possessing encyclopaedic knowledge of gaiter buttons, Stieber merely consulted his notes and went diligently on.

He was the first spy ever to work as a census enumerator. Roads and rivers, bridges, battalions, and fortified places were, of course, his foremost consideration. But he added an intensive interest in the population, in commerce and agriculture, in farms, houses, inns, and in local prosperity and patriotism—in anything at all which seemed to him likely to expedite an invasion or provide for the invaders. When the Prussians came, with Stieber's data, foraging and civil requisitions were made easy. The village magnate with a hundred hens could expect to be called upon for so many dozen eggs. If the hens were not laying and had been going to market in person, Stieber's nearest resident spy would probably report the change in accounting for maximum local provisions. While if the villager refused to contribute eggs or fowls or whatever else he was known to have on hand, he would be taken before a provost with a hanging warrant in blank on his table.

More than one good burgher fainted when the cash assessment demanded of him showed a quick understanding of his fortune as exact as a lifetime acquaintance with it. Because of Stieber and the horde of agents he had ready to report to him, privacy in France was the first casualty of the war. But though this omniscient kind of intelligence has seemed admirable to many and the method of it in military preparation supremely crafty and unique, Stieber's manner of gaining his victorious ends was always lawless and often possessed of a cold ferocity. His own men mercilessly punished anything suggesting French espionage, and disregarded the circumstance of war being waged entirely in the enemy's country with a dense population inevitably hostile and curious. Peasants were strung up and slowly tortured to death when they had done no more than peer out at an ammunition train or cavalry column. Bazaine and his best troops were shut up in Metz; Paris had been invested soon after Sedan saw the surrender of Napoleon himself and another army. There was nowhere in particular for the trained French spy to take his information. But even very doubtful cases of spying were handled by Stieber with unwavering severity. In a celebrated instance the victim was obviously no spy at all, but a young man, M. De Reynal, who had just returned to Versailles from his honeymoon. With a pardonable indifference to the national calamity, this bridegroom not only ventured back into a city which had become the German headquarters during the siege of Paris, but also he kept a diary recording daily events of the occupation. And with his diary in court Stieber, who said he "needed an example," convicted him of espionage. Prussian officers, detesting Bismarck's police agent and convinced of De Reynal's essential innocence, endeavored to intercede for him; but when told that the young man had recently been married, Stieber observed, "That only makes my task the more painful."

De Reynal was executed.

In Versailles Stieber and his assistants occupied the mansion of the Duc de Persigny. He had conducted himself with intolerable insolence throughout the campaign, but here, in September of 1870, he began treating Germans and French alike to the nasty condescensions of an upstart whose authority comes from obscure and lofty places. He always acted independently of the military chiefs; though the existence of martial law increased his tyrannical powers, he obeyed only Bismarck and the Prussian King, and none of the generals dared to interfere with him or his agents. It was his favorite boast to them that his army had entered France six months ahead of theirs, and though repeatedly snubbed and insulted, he grew in the arrogance of the rascal who has learned how to make others fear him. For some trivial disorder he threatened to hang ten members of the municipal committee of Versailles, and wrote to his wife describing the terror he had inspired with much gleeful satisfaction. It is said that he engaged ten thousand of the poorer citizens for a franc a day to gather in crowds and cheer the Prussian ruler and other German princes whenever they appeared in the streets. And when at last the negotiations for the surrender of Paris commenced, he accommodated Bismarck by posing as a valet.

Jules Favre came to Versailles early in 1871 to treat with the besiegers. He was escorted to the house that had been Stieber's secret service headquarters; and all during his stay inside the enemy lines he was there waited upon so expertly that he had occasion to compliment his German hosts upon the service accorded him. Stieber often candidly explained that he depended upon Zernicki for any useful display of courtesy and kindliness, since he himself cared only for action and results and wasted no time upon formalities. In dealing with the Parisian envoy, Stieber elected the role of servant, and discharged his menial duties with a certain relish since Favre was utterly deceived and every letter he received, every telegram, every secret document in his possession was exposed to by ransacking patriotism of the indispensable valet. Favre slept in Zernicki's bed, in a house staffed exclusively with Prussian police agents. Stieber claimed that the terms of capitulation Bismarck dictated were solely in accord with the information derived by him in this final triumph of espionage. But even his contemporary admirers found this exaggerated, since the Chancellor knew what he wanted and intended to get, no matter how many confidential messages came to the French negotiator.

The French General de Cilley in 1875 was serving his second term as Minister of War. France was already lifting its head, the German Empire was still very new, and in both Paris and Berlin there was much thought of a war of revenge. General de Cilley had been a prisoner-of-war in Hamburg and had there been intimate with a charming woman, the Baroness de Kaulla. Stieber, ever well informed, now contrived to enlist the services of this not very fastidious lady. He gave her a large sum of money and sent her to Paris to awaken in the Minister of War those ardors which so often unlocked official secrets. The Baroness was not obliged to exert herself, for the General seems to have been disengaged at the moment of her arrival and to have eagerly renewed the pleasant relationship that had ameliorated his captivity. Whatever scandal followed was due to the General's verbal indiscretions. Paris, never more than fashionably interested in the mistress of a minister, could be profoundly stirred by anything endangering the new republican military policies. After an all-night secret session of the Chamber, De Cilley would hasten to have breakfast with his Baroness, whose Teutonic connections were more readily discovered than Stieber had expected. In the ensuing public commotion the General went from office, and the Baroness from France, but not before he had prattled to her of many matters never intended to reach Berlin.

The Baroness de Kaulla was a Jewess and her notoriety did much to nourish the anti-Semitic suspicions complicated with fear of Germany and counterespionage that boiled to a culmination after the arrest of Alfred Dreyfus. Stieber had died before the misfortunes of Dreyfus overtook him, but the shadow of the Prussian spy-master lay darkly upon the famous treason trials. The new corps of resident agents that he had begun to distribute throughout France as soon as the Franco-Prussian War came to an end did not include any great number of Germans as had the legions imported before 1870. He understood the antagonisms of the French after their humiliating defeat—chiefly at his hands, and he therefore enlisted French-speaking Swiss, but also other nationalities of the Continent, so that almost any alien might be mistrusted as his possible hireling. French counter-spying was not for more than a decade to become sufficiently organized or forceful enough to battle with this veteran on even terms; and Stieber, meanwhile, found a new reservoir in the populations of Alsace and Lorraine, getting either pro-Germans or persons of the sort easily controlled by the police as valuable recruits for his spy service. In 1880 he informed the old Emperor that, so thoroughly had he worked this vein, he could count upon more than one thousand Alsace-Lorrainers whom he had sent into the employ of the French railroads, paying them only twenty-five percent of their regular wages as a kind of secret retainer. Should another war come, at a word from him these trusted agents would begin destroying locomotives and rolling stock to paralyze French mobilization the very day it began.

Spies of his not in the public service he planted as shop keepers or as employees in hotels. Stieber rightly discerned that if German capitalists erected luxurious hotels in foreign countries, he could insert many of his own secret service creatures into their staffs, and thus not only spy upon mysterious travelers but also upon the rich and distinguished persons who would come to reside in them. His hotel spies he expected to obtain for him information eventually useful in blackmailing enterprises abroad; nor was he blind to their chances of actually stealing important private documents from the dispatch cases of notable guests. Stieber had so formidably organized imperial espionage and counterespionage that he could command a huge slice of all German military appropriations. Some of this money he poured into the international hotel industry; so that for years the best hotels everywhere were largely German-owned and predominantly German in personnel; and not all the attentions they rendered were itemized in the bill. Stieber next tried to extend his influence by way of subsidies to banking and other international businesses, always with the idea of enlarging an already overgrown intelligence system. Undoubtedly in some cases he succeeded, or established concerns that were simply masked bureaux of the secret service.

Having instigated the Wolff telegraphic news bureau and determined the growing power of the press, Stieber maintained a special service section that watched over all foreign publications. He made it a point to learn what motive or grievance lay in back of any anti-German editorial or article. If a publisher or writer seemed to hate Germany, he sought to know the reason for it; and if any sort of cash transaction would correct this enmity he was ever inclined to buy liberally in the right places. It is understood that he purchased newspapers in nearly every neighboring country to popularize simultaneously anti-militarism, the ideals of pacifism, and pro-German sentiment. But even without his natural inclination toward every new form of political domination or deception, Stieber would have been forced to institute government propaganda. Both before and after the proclamation of the Empire, the Prussian yoke had rested heavily upon the smaller German states; and Hanover especially caused much disquiet in certain quarters. Stieber had agents continuously assigned to look out for and counteract dangerous internal resurgences. Bismarck would not permit him to dispose of German hostility with the same harsh measures he had taken against the French noncombatants. Yet he proudly records having received from the Chancellor a bonus of two hundred thalers for having managed to suppress a bitterly anti-Prussian article before it sprang from the Hanoverian press.

Stieber's sharp abilities as a plotter did not rust no matter how peaceful the horizons of Europe became; he was always inventing new jobs for himself, and, if he could not recover the raptures of invasion in '70, he could continue as Minister of Police to delve into sundry dark crimes and conspiracies. After the imperial machine began running smoothly, he habitually saved William I and Bismarck from cunning assassins and divers other perils, many of them now believed to have been instigated by his own agents. On the surface it was a great day of German unity and patriotism and of stirring acclaim for the war-born Empire and Fatherland. Stieber grafted his espionage schemes upon *"Deutschland über Alles"* and made it seem a good citizen's privilege to undertake some secret mission which to the private individual acting for himself would have meant contemptible deceit and deserved ostracism. He knew how to handle the zealous rank and file with unscrupulous appeals to patriotism and duty. Yet he had learned that the rich and influential, the minor royalty and nobility had always a much more worthwhile access to the impressive secrets than any spy he might train or hire; and this led him to the concluding innovation of his long and artful experience in mingling underworld methods with government.

He opened in Berlin the notorious Green House as a resort for people of consequence, where every form of vicious indulgence and excess was sumptuously encouraged, under the pretense of offering notable libertines an almost providential privacy. But since they came there to forget themselves, Stieber arranged to remember for them; and while there was no limit put upon his clients' behavior, if they were prominent persons the memory of it would be made to last forever. Every event at this rendezvous was, in short, known to the police because their agent conducted it, and its history was hidden away in a private file which Stieber used to extort co-operation, even from royalty, so that the imperial secret service when operating in the highest places might never mov ineffectually.

Social ambitions persuaded Stieber to promote himself and his family through the same kind of blackmail as always had been used by him in behalf of the government. He was wealthy now and the confidential adviser of Bismarck, who really ruled the empire; but whatever pressure he exerted as a police official, it seems not to have carried him far in society. Dread opened some doors to him, but apart from the affairs of state his intimate acquaintance was as parvenu as himself. Yet if he received only inferior invitations, he had been decorated twenty-seven times, and had diplomas and medals to prove it; and so when he lay mortally stricken with arthritis in 1882 there is no doubt but that he deemed himself great, his official life a useful and honorable one. Useful it surely had been. Bearing witness to that and to his long devotion to the Prussian throne, or to the fear that had died with him, a throng of distinguished men, including personal representatives of the Emperor and of the other rulers of states, attended his funeral.

Wilhelm Stieber made himself a giant in his sinister profession; his career will be studied and imitated so long as there are spies and secret agents as an integral service of government.

PRISONER IN THE LEGATION

IT WAS a typical autumnal evening in London, rainy and foggy, that 1st of October 1896, when a young Chinese stepped out of the train at Euston Station. Only a few hours earlier he had disembarked from the *Majestic* when it docked at Liverpool. Throughout the ship's voyage from New York this passenger had kept more or less to himself.

In his early twenties, the young Chinese resembled the type of serious student from the Orient frequently seen in London. He wore a well-cut suit, had a neat little moustache and kept his black hair extremely close slipped. His walk was firm and springy, with a deliberately erect military carriage.

For such a young man the Chinese visitor had had an extremely adventurous career. In fact, he had circled the world, fleeing from his native country and the wrath of its emperor. He had eaten the bitter bread of exile in Macao, Hong Kong, Singapore, Yokohama, Batavia, Honolulu and San Francisco. And now he was in London, facing still more adventures. He hailed a hansom cab and asked the driver to take him to Haxell's Hotel in the Strand.

This new chapter in his life certainly seemed to be opening in a propitious manner. His hotel room proved very comfortable, the atmosphere of the hotel congenial. In spite of the fog and rain the young Oriental went out for a stroll in the city streets. The stream of carriages, the crowds, the mood of London, all struck him as pleasant. On the strength of these happy impressions he decided to look up a former teacher of his, Dr. James Cantlie, formerly head of the Medical College in Hong Kong and now back in London.

The Cantlies greeted their young visitor with warmth. Their home at 46 Devonshire Street, a typical London house with a small garden in the rear, struck him as charming. They had a great deal to talk about. The Cantlies were especially eager for the news of some of their mutual friends who seemed to have dropped out of existence in Imperial China. On hearing of something of the young man's recent experiences, and the circumstances which had brought him to London, Dr. Cantlie looked grave. "You know we don't live very far from the Chinese Legation," he said. "Don't you think you should pay your respects to the Chinese Government?"

Mrs. Cantlie, who did not always recognize her husband's jokes, demurred. "You'd better give that place a wide berth as long as you are here," she said. "They are quite capable of kidnapping you and shipping you back."

As a matter of fact, the Chinese visitor fitted into London almost as though it were his native city. His way of dressing was completely European, and his English was faultless. London gave him a feeling of exhilaration and it seemed that, for the time being, he had reached the end of his wanderings.

The following day he paid a call on another of his former teachers, Dr. Henry Manson. Here again he was warned to keep away from the Chinese Legation. The young man did not take these words too seriously. He might be wanted back in China, but here in London, half a world away, he was perfectly safe. He had by now moved from the hotel, and with the help of the Cantlies had found suitable lodgings in Gray's Inn Road. Eleven days after his arrival the young Chinese left his rooms and started out for Devonshire Street, where he was to visit the Cantlie family and accompany them to church. He had reached Oxford Circus, when a thought which had troubled him crystallized into certainty. He knew he was being followed and that, in fact, he was not far from the Chinese Legation at Portland Place, a thoroughfare which he had up to now studiously avoided. Glancing behind him, he saw a Chinese in mandarin attire standing only a few yards away. Nor was the man's proximity accidental, for now the Chinese quickened his steps and caught up with the student just as he crossed the road. With a polite smile the older man addressed the student:

"Are you a citizen of Japan or China, sir?" He spoke excellent English.

"Of China," said the student, glancing at his unknown interrogator.

"Of what part of China, may I ask?"

"Canton."

"That makes us compatriots. We speak the same dialect. I, too, am from Canton," said the unknown, slipping into Chinese.

The two strolled on together now, talking in their native language. They reached Cavendish Street and here suddenly another compatriot, also in mandarin clothing, made his appearance. Quietly, as though it were the most natural thing in the world, he joined the party, walking on the left side of the Chinese student.

The conversation rippled on, still in the politest Cantonese. The new member of the party invited his two countrymen to his room for tea.

"I'm very sorry to have to refuse your invitation," the student excused himself. "I am on the way to meet some friends, and then we're going to church. Another time, perhaps."

Hereabouts and seemingly from nowhere a third Chinaman appeared, also in mandarin gown. The face of this man was distinctly unattractive; he looked capable of any brutality. Now the student's new friends dropped their pretence of politeness. They seized their victim by his arms, steered him around a corner, and there it was—49 Portland Place. A door opened as though they were expected. The student was hustled up the stairs and into the hallway.

He had not yet completely grasped the situation. It had all happened so quickly, in broad daylight and in the calm of a London Sunday. Could it be that the Chinese Secret Service had finally caught up with him, after he had put half the world between them and himself?

A few minutes later he knew. He had been brought to a huge room full of costly furniture, locked in and left alone.

There was an iron bar across the h.... .me door and he was no longer in any doubt—he was being held captive in the Imperial Chinese Legation. Back in Devonshire Street, his friends the Cantlies would be waiting for him. Would they realize what his absence meant, or would they think he had simply forgotten his appointment? And what did the people at the Legation have in mind for him? He took refuge in a stoic calm which came easily to his Oriental temperament. He would find that out soon enough.

Two hours later he was led to another room. He realized he was on the second floor of the Legation building. Of this latter fact there could be no doubt, since the only persons in the corridors were Chinese, some in official dress. Two Chinese, who maintained an obstinate silence, now came and searched him. Most of his belongings were taken away, even the watch in his pocket. He was now transferred to yet another room, this time on the third floor. The small windows were heavily barred. The view was of rooftops, chimney pots, fog and smoke.

Sunk in thought, the prisoner was considering and marvelling at the speed and smoothness with which the kidnapping had taken place, when the door was unbolted. A

73

tall, white-haired Englishman entered the "cell." Much later the student learned that he was Sir Halliday Macartney, a barrister who worked for the Chinese Government as counsellor and adviser.

"My dear young man," he began, "you are now on Chinese territory. To all intents and purposes you are in China, under Chinese law. May I have your name?"

The exile gave him it.

The Britisher smiled faintly. "We know better. Your name is Sun Wen." It was the name the student had used signing petitions for reform, political pamphlets and manifestos. "No sense beating about the bush, my dear young man," the Britisher continued. "We have been fully informed of all your movements. We had a message from the United States telling us that you were arriving on the *Majestic*. The Chinese Minister has requested your arrest."

"May I inquire why?"

"You know only too well. You have displeased your Emperor and your Government, haven't you?"

The prisoner remained silent. He had acted on deep convictions, knowing that to do that, under an absolutist Government, was a crime.

Meanwhile the Britisher continued his accusations. His heart was evidently in the case, and for a man so thoroughly western in appearance and demeanour he was certainly a loyal minion of his Chinese employer.

"Sun Wen, you drew up a petition calling for widespread reform and sent it to the Tsung-Li-Yamen in Peking, with the request that it be presented to the Emperor."

"I did."

"We in London have been ordered to detain you until we find out the Emperor's personal wishes regarding you."

The prisoner could only too vividly imagine what form the Emperor's pleasure would take. He saw a headsman and a gleaming sword blade.

"May I inform my English friends of my presence at the Legation?"

"No, this you cannot do. You may, however, write a letter to your landlord instructing him to release your belongings, which will then be at your disposal."

The prisoner complied. That was all Sir Halliday cared to say to him for the present, for he strolled out of the room and left the young man to his thoughts.

In the notes he made on his imprisonment, he recorded this comment on the incident:

"It was very evident that my interrogator was playing a crafty game to get hold of my effects, and more especially my papers, in the hope of finding correspondence, whereby to ascertain who my Chinese accomplices were."

An hour later he was startled by a fearful noise. Carpenters were installing a second lock on his door. In addition to this, he gathered that two guards were being ordered to stand in front of his door to maintain an unceasing watch. Hearing the guards conversing in Cantonese, the prisoner tried to speak to them through the door, but they did not reply and instead entered the room and again searched him. This time they took away his keys and pocket knife. However, they failed to find a wad of banknotes he was carrying.

The day passed without further incident. In the late afternoon the guards asked him what he wanted to eat. Physically exhausted and psychologically drained, he asked only for a glass of milk. At seven, two English servants came to clean his room and bring coal and wood for the fireplace, but evidently they had strict orders and ignored his presence as though the room were empty.

He passed a restless night. Though the room was provided with a comfortable bed, he did not bother to undress. He could hear the guards talking, and from outside the windows the night noises of the city, the sound of trotting cab horses, the clatter of hoofs and rolling of wheels on cobblestones. Unwelcome thoughts crowded his mind. He was not afraid to die, but not this way—in an ignoble trap like this. Why did Macartney, an Englishman of high position, care to serve a feudal tyranny?

The next morning found the prisoner looking pale and peaked. His mind, however, was sharper than it had been the previous day, and he was determined to overlook no possibility for escape. He would try bribery. Above all, he must play for time. His friends had cautioned him not to go near the Legation. When they realized that he was missing, they would know where to look.

His first visitor that day was Kidnapper No. 1, the man who had engaged him in conversation on the street. He gave his name as Tang and identified himself as one of the many secretaries of the Imperial Chinese Legation.

The diary preserves this conversation. "Our first meeting," Tang said, "was more or less in line with official duty. I now come to talk to you as a friend. You had better confess that you are Sun Wen. There is no sense denying it. All arrangements have been made for your return to China."

Tang could not resist being sarcastic and said: "You are well known at home. The Emperor and the Tsung-Li-Yamen are acquainted with your activities. Just think what a wonderful chance you'll have to distinguish yourself, what a beautiful ending for a career, what an example you will be able to give of a courageous death. In that way you will become a real hero."

"Why do you assume I am going to die?" asked the prisoner, trying to sound out his captors' plans. "After all, I am not in China, but in England, a free country. What can you do to me here? Of course you could have me done away with right here in the Legation. That is certainly something you could easily do. But without a trial, such an act would be considered murder here, and these things have a way of leaking out. You wouldn't want any trouble with the British authorities. Then again, you might try to have me extradited, but such a procedure takes a long time. Besides, the British Government would learn of my illegal imprisonment. I don't think the English would turn me over to you anyway—this country has a tradition for providing political asylum."

A sneer appeared on the face of the Legation secretary.

"Naturally we won't ask for extradition—that would be a very stupid thing to do. A freighter is waiting for you in Southampton right now. We will have no trouble at all in pacifying you and transferring you from the Legation building to the ship—after which you will of course be put in chains. Before the ship reaches Hong Kong it will be met by a gunboat which will take you aboard for Canton. That is where your execution will take place."

"Without a trial, I suppose," the prisoner said dryly.

"The proper formalities will be observed. We are not barbarians, you know. First the trial and then the beheading," the middleaged official answered politely and with equal dryness.

"Don't you think you are running a risk? What if the British police should get to know of this thing? I might get word through or try to escape. Then you'd all be in hot water."

Tang assured his prisoner that these eventualities were extremely remote. He was well guarded here and there would be no slip-up.

"Have you forgotten about the officers and crew of the ship which is supposed to take me back?" asked the prisoner. "They will all know something is going on. The docks are teeming with people. They're bound to notice something and make a stir."

Tang seemed unmoved. Everything had been thought of, he said. The owners of the ship were close friends of Sir Halliday Macartney. They were interested in trade with China. He had their word for it that no untoward incident would occur.

The more the prisoner talked with Tang, the more he would learn of the plot, he realized, and this could certainly be useful to him. Tang seemed not at all averse to discussing the arrangements, so perfectly sure was he that the situation was under control. For example, Tang told him that he would "travel" on one of the Glen Line steamers during the coming week. The Minister had not been willing to charter a ship exclusively for the purpose of conveying him to justice.

The prisoner pointed out that the enterprise looked rather difficult and complicated. One mis-step and the whole thing would fall through. Hadn't they better change their minds and set him free?

Tang did not seem to appreciate this kind of humour. Not a muscle of his face moved as he replied: "You understand the problem very well. You are a clever man. Too bad you are not loyal to us and dream only of revolution. As it happens, you are right. We are not very pleased with this plan. If we had our way, we would dispose of you here in the Legation. That is a far more practical way of doing it. But our orders are to have you sent to China. The Emperor wishes it."

The prisoner's diary records more of this fateful conversation:

"For my edification and consolation, Tang then cited the case of a Korean patriot who, escaping from Korea to Japan, was induced by a countryman to go to Shanghai where he was put to death in the British concession. His dead body was sent back by the Chinese to Korea for 'punishment,' and on arrival there was decapitated, while the murderer was rewarded and given an important political post. Tang was evidently fondly cherishing the belief that he would be similarly promoted by his Government for arresting me and securing my death. I asked him why he should be so cruel, to which he replied: 'This is by order of the Emperor who wants you captured at any price, preferably alive.' "

The prisoner refused to lose his calm. As detachedly as if someone else's life were at stake, he continued to discuss various possibilities. "If the British Government should get to know of this it may declare all members of this Legation *persona non grata*? In which case you would have to return to China. My people in the province of Kwang-Tung would be on the lookout for a chance to revenge me. I hate to think what they would do to you and your entire family in payment for your act of treachery."

As the prisoner had guessed, this blow found its mark. Family feuds and bloody acts of revenge were very real concepts in the mind of Tang. He suddenly became apologetic and anxious to prove to the prisoner that he was only obeying orders. He was but a minor official—he had to do as his superiors commanded, no matter how personally repugnant it was to himself. . . . He asked for understanding and forgiveness. In fact, he became quite conciliatory and ventured to offer the young man a helpful suggestion.

"As I see it, you still have a small chance for life. What you must do is to deny that you had anything to do with the Canton plot and the reform plans. Accuse your accusers. Say that the whole thing is a trap sprung by the mandarins. Declare that you came voluntarily to the Legation to clear yourself and to ask for a review of your case."

It seemed a rather servile line to take. However, since no other course was open, the prisoner agreed to write such a letter. Perhaps it would soften the hearts of his kidnappers after all. Tang took the letter with a peculiar smile. It was the last the prisoner ever saw of him.

As the days went by, the young man had time to realize that he had fallen into a trap. He'd been foolish to write such a letter and acknowledge that he had come to the Legation of his own accord. This would clear the Legation with the British authorities, at least to some extent.

In despair as time ran out, he was ready to try anything, futile as it might seem, to reach the outside world. On two occasions he tried to smuggle notes to his friends, but none of the servants could be bribed. He wrote short notes on tiny bits of paper and threw them out of the window in the hope that some passer-by would find them. The first ones were caught in the wind, tossed up and whirled about for a moment. He watched them fall into a drain pipe on an adjacent roof.

He wrote other notes and weighted them with copper coins to make sure they would fall to the street. One fell into the garden of the adjoining house, No. 51 Portland Place, the home of Viscount Powerscourt. Another note fell on the roof of No. 53. The third and last fell on the street and was spotted by the Legation guards.

That was the end of the prisoner's attempt to draw attention to his plight. Some servants entered his room and fastened wooden boards over his windows. The room was now in total darkness.

"I was now worse off than ever," wrote the young man who had dared to defy an Emperor, "for my sole means of communication with the outside world seemed gone."

The prisoner had been raised as a Christian and he found consolation in prayer. He spent many hours praying, at least it seemed so, for he no longer had any way of estimating the passage of time. He didn't know whether one day went by or many. It was perpetual night in his room and blackest night in his soul. His only light came from the fire.

He had one last chance and that was to appeal to the two English servants who appeared daily to clean his room, bring him food and tend the fire. They performed their duties like machines, never speaking nor even seeming to see him. However, the younger of the two had a sympathetic face. His name was Edward Cole. So one morning the prisoner summoned up all his resolution and spoke to the man.

"Sir, will you not do something for me?" he asked.

To call a servant "sir" was sufficiently unusual for the man to start and look at the prisoner as though seeing him for the first time. "Who are you?" he asked in low, frightened tones. "And what do you want of me?"

"I am a political refugee from China. I came to England to seek the protection of the British Government. I am a Christian just like yourself. You must have read in the newspapers that the Sultan of Turkey is massacring the Armenian Christians. Well, the Emperor of China wants to kill me because I am a Christian, too. I belong to a political party that wants good government and democratic freedom for all in China, the way it is in England. I have done no harm to anyone—I was brought here by trickery and am being held under duress."

It was rash of him to say as much as he did, for the guards

might be listening outside the door. But he felt it was the only way to win the man's sympathy.

Cole did not answer immediately. He busied himself sweeping the floor and hearth. At last he said in a whisper: "I don't know whether the British Government would want to help you. After all, you are a foreigner and these people are your own countrymen."

Desperation sharpened the prisoner's wits and urgently he replied: "The British Government would surely help me. That is why I am being kept here by force. Otherwise, don't you see, the Chinese Government would have to ask for my official extradition."

The impassve servant went on with his work. There was no way of telling whether he felt sympathetic, or whether the prisoner's plea fell on deaf ears. "My life is in your hands, sir," the prisoner pleaded. "If the proper authorities are informed of my confinement I shall be saved. Otherwise it means death for me. Is it not better to save a life than to see it destroyed? Doesn't your duty as a Christian come before your duty to your employers?"

One thing was certain—Cole had never been appealed to in such terms before. He had always been a good, conscientious servant and discreet enough to realize that he was not concerned in the business of his superiors.

With the calm impersonality of a perfect servant, he finished his work and withdrew.

It was another sleepless night for the prisoner. Had he won Cole over—or would Cole go to his employers and reveal all he had said?

In the morning Cole brought him his breakfast. He deposited it on a table and left, avoiding the prisoner's piteous eyes. Returning in the evening with a scuttle of coal, the servant again did not utter a word. Instead he pointed towards the scuttle he had brought in, and left the room.

Tucked in among the coals was a scrap of white paper. The prisoner snatched it up and read:

"I am willing to bring a letter to one of your friends, but not to the police. You must not write at the table as the guards can see through the keyhole. If you write on your bed, you cannot be seen from the hall."

The prisoner lay down on his bed and faced the wall.

With a tiny stub of a pencil he wrote a message on an old and dirty visiting card of his. From this message, preserved for reasons which will be clear later in the story, we learn that the prisoner's written English was not as good as his speech.

His note read:

> "To Dr. James Cantlie
> 46 Devonshire Street
>
> "Please take care of the messenger for me at present, he is very poor and will lose his work by doing for me. I was kidnapped into the Chinese Legation on sunday and shall be smuggled out from England to China for death. Pray rescue me quick? A ship is already chartered by C.L. for the service to take me to China and I shall be locked up all the way without communication to anybody. O! Woe to me!"

But the note was not delivered as its writer had written it. Cole waited until October 17th, a Saturday and his day off. Ever discreet, he did not deliver the prisoner's note, but sent one of his own by express messenger. It read:

> "There is a friend of yours imprisoned in the Chinese Legation since last Sunday. They intend to send him out to China where it is certain that they will execute him. It is very sad for the poor man and unless something is done at once he will be taken away and no one will know it. I dare not sign my name but this is the truth, so believe what I say. Whatever you do must be done at once or it will be too late. His name is, I believe, Lin Yen Sen."

The Cantlies were enjoying a typical Saturday night at home, reading by the fireplace when this letter arrived. They had of course been aware of the defection of their Chinese friend, but they knew that Orientals often acted oddly by English standards and did not take his absence much to heart. They were sure he would turn up soon, with a perfectly good explanation for his behaviour.

Cantlie knew that he had to act quickly. A professor of medicine, he knew little about investigations, spies, kidnapping and politics in general. But he knew that Sir Halliday

Macartney was the legal counsel for the Chinese Government, so he decided to see him first. It never occurred to him to apply directly to the police. He happened to know that Sir Halliday lived nearby, at 3 Harley Place, in an impressive four-storey building of grey stone. But the house was closed, the shades pulled down and the high iron gate locked. Perhaps its owner had gone to the country for the week-end.

A constable on duty in nearby Marylebone Road informed the anxious-looking gentleman that the house had been closed for at least six months. It was at this point that Dr. Cantlie decided to go to the nearest police station. There an inspector listened to his story and advised Cantlie to go to Scotland Yard.

The officers at police headquarters were extremely polite. But the story was so fantastic, so implausible and un-English, that they began to imagine that the doctor must be a crank or a bit potty. They listened and took down the facts. They would they assured Dr. Cantlie, report the matter to their superiors. That was as far as Dr. Cantlie had got when, around midnight, he left and walked home.

There was not much he could do at that hour of the night, Cantlie decided. But he had no intention of leaving the matter there. At eight o'clock the next morning he was out of his house, consulting a friend. The two men deliberated a long time, and decided that if Scotland Yard failed to act it might be advisable to get someone to make a private approach to the Legation.

Once more Cantlie stopped at Harley Place, where he hoped to find at least the caretaker, who would tell him how to get in touch with Macartney. The place was completely deserted.

Finally Cantlie went home, exhausted from his long tramp across London. He found Cole waiting for him in the living room, and heard the "wild story" from the man's own lips.

Cantlie mentioned his fruitless visits to the Macartney residence. Cole raised his eyebrows. Sir Halliday was living in town and paid daily visits to the Legation, he said. In his opinion Macartney had a large part in the incident.

Cantlie immediately saw that this complicated the matter. A man of Macartney's standing had great power and influence. At this point Cole volunteered further information. Macartney, he alleged, had passed word around the Legation that the prisoner was a dangerous megalomaniac, who was being kept under lock and key for his own good. He was due to be shipped home on Tuesday. A captain and some sailors had come to the Legation to discuss the matter.

That gave them, Cantlie saw, forty-eight hours in which to act. He set off immediately to see his medical colleague, Dr. Manson. Together they went to Scotland Yard to make another appeal for help.

The officer on duty listened to their story. He consulted the records. "You were here on Saturday night," he said. "No new facts have turned up since to confirm your story."

In desperation the two doctors decided to go directly to the Foreign Office. It was not far, but gaining admittance was another story. They were politely informed that the clerk in charge could not see them before five in the afternoon.

They decided to wait and in due time were ushered into the office of this personage. He heard them out and with a shrug of his shouldrs regretfully informed the gentlemen that since the day was Sunday, no action could be taken. He would report the matter to his superiors early next morning.

The doctors were dismayed. What if the Chinese should change their plans and ship the prisoner out a day earlier? They expressed their indignation: the entire British law enforcement system seemed to be in a state of paralysis because it happened to be Sunday.

The Foreign Office official tried to explain that this was a delicate matter involving foreign relations, diplomatic privileges, immunities and international law. He personally was not empowered to deal with such a problem. The doctors would have to wait as he had suggested.

The doctors, however, were not easily discouraged. They stood together outside the Foreign Office debating the next move and Cantlie suggested that although he was too well known to go to the Chinese Legation, there was no reason why Dr. Manson should not be admitted. He must go and take the bull by the horns. If he were not back within an hour, Cantlie would inform Scotland Yard.

It was already 6:30 p.m. when Dr. Manson rang the bell at No. 49 Portland Place. An exemplary English footman opened the door. Dr. Manson was led into an anteroom which was beautifully furnished with silver and gold brocades, bronze Buddhas and a huge portrait of the Emperor.

Dr. Manson had asked to see one of the attachés on an

urgent matter. He had not long to wait before Tang entered the room. Bowing and smiling, the Chinese greeted the flustered Englishman who, waiving the usual formalities of greeting, stated the reason for his visit.

"A friend of mine, one of my former medical students in China, is being held prisoner in this Legation. I demand to see him."

Tang's face became cold, stony and cruel.

"We have no prisoners in this Legation. What is the name of this young man you seek?"

"Sun Wen."

"No man of that name is under this roof."

"I know he is being held here, and so does Scotland Yard and the Foreign Office."

Tang remained imperturbable. He assured his excited visitor that it was all a great mistake. Perhaps someone was playing a joke on him. So convincing was the official's manner that Manson ended by believing him. When he rejoined Dr. Cantlie thirty minutes later, Manson told him that the story really was a bit preposterous. The people at the Legation knew nothing of the matter.

Dr. Cantlie, however, was more disturbed than ever. He could not subscribe to his friend's interpretation. In fact, he was convinced that the danger for his Chinese friend had increased as a result of the visit to the Legation. Something must be done quickly or the prisoner would be bustled on board the boat, which would perhaps leave earlier than planned. Then and there Cantile decided to put a private detective on the job—to keep watch on the Legation in case an attempt was made to remove the prisoner. But then he remembered it was Sunday, a Victorian Sunday, and knew that nobody would be available.

Cantlie went back to Scotland Yard and implored them to set some detective to watch the Legation. He was told that the place was out of their zone; he was advised to go to the appropriate West End Police Station.

There the good doctor experienced his usual trouble in making the officers see that this was a real emergency. In the absence of concrete evidence the police had no authority to place a guard over the Chinese Legation. As a last resort, Cantlie offered a substantial sum to any constable off duty who would undertake the surveillance as a private job. The officers at the station were on duty all night; they were kind enough to recommend a chap who lived in Islington, a retired member of the force, who was usually glad for a job of some sort.

On his way to Islington Cantlie had to pass Fleet Street. Here he had an inspiration. He walked into the offices of *The Times* and asked to see a member of the editorial staff.

Nobody showed any eagerness to help him. The clerk in the front office insisted that the gentleman state the reason for the desired interview. Fuming with impatience, Cantlie took the slip of paper the clerk offered and wrote these words:

"Brutal kidnapping at the Chinese Legation; immediate danger of death."

The receptionist looked quite dumbfounded. It was, apparently, not every day that visitors came with such messages. But the person in question would not be available until ten in the evening. "Come back then," the clerk said.

"I will," Cantlie said grimly.

At Islington the doctor discovered that the retired member of the constabulary had something else he had to do that night. He promised, however, to find a substitute.

By this time Dr. Cantlie was dead tired, having spent the whole day on his quest for help. He was not a young man, but he returned to *The Times* office, where a vigorous-looking veteran journalist listened to this story. That it was an astonishing story he was the first to admit. Still, it was of such importance and delicacy, having regard to the circumstances, that he would be unable to do anything until it was referred to the editorial board.

Dr. Cantlie left in utter disgust. He had knocked at every possible door and been turned away. His efforts, it seemed, had failed completely.

It was eleven-thirty when he arrived home. Tired as he was, he was in no mood for sleep. His wife tried to calm him; together they discussed what else could be done. "Perhaps something will suggest itself in the morning," Mrs. Cantlie suggested. But this only made the doctor more restless. He couldn't go to sleep while that good young man might be being murdered. He was a medical scientist; his life had been devoted to teaching and research, and in the course of his work he had learned the value of persistence. One had to go on trying.

Operating on this assumption, Dr. Cantlie decided to skip sleep for one night. He put on some warmer clothes and set out for the Chinese Legation; he would watch it himself, he decided. He stayed there until the following morning and then paid a visit to Salter's Detective Agency as soon as it opened. There he engaged a number of agents to watch the Chinese Legation day and night.

His next call was to the Foreign Office, where he told his story once more, this time in the form of a sworn statement. The reaction here was not too encouraging. Officials pointed out that the only evidence was the alleged prisoner's own note claiming that he had been kidnapped. The rest was hearsay and could be very regrettable, diplomatically speaking, if it turned out to be a hoax.

The Foreign office, however, asked Scotland Yard to investigate whether the Chinese Legation had made a charter or similar arrangement with any of the shipping lines.

Scotland Yard could work fast if it wanted to. The answer came promptly that such a charter had been drawn up with the Glen Line for a ship due to leave on Tuesday. The vessel had been chartered for a mixed cargo to China. There was also to be one passenger; his name was not given; he was merely identified as a Chinese national.

. . . .

In the meantime the young man held behind the windows of the Chinese Legation was dying all the deaths which uncertainty can provoke. He had no idea whether Cole could be trusted sufficiently to have passed his message on to Dr. Cantlie.

The first real gleam of hope came when Cole brought in the usual evening scuttle of coal. Tucked into it was a note: "Be hopeful," it said, "we are working for you."

Still, this was no assurance that the rescuers would make it in time. Meanwhile Cole sent another note to Dr. Cantlie informing him:

> "I shall have a good opportunity to let your friend out on the roof of the next house in Portland Place tonight. If you think it advisable to have someone there waiting to receive him, and I am able to do it, find means to let me know."

Cantlie seized on this suggestion. He hurried to Scotland Yard again with a plea to have them put some police officers on the roof of the neighbouring house. But the police decided against it. Such a procedure was beneath their dignity; the proper legal steps had been taken and soon the order would come through for the Legation to open its doors for inspection.

On October 22nd, England's great contribution to the rights of man, the writ of habeas corpus, was requested on behalf of the unknown prisoner, but unfortunately the judge before whom the application was made refused to grant it.

Nevertheless it brought England's newspapers into the fight. A reporter from the *Globe* called on Cantlie for a story and the doctor gave him the facts and also spoke of his visits to *The Times*.

That was the turning point. Other newspapers became interested in the prisoner in the Legation and soon reporters were swarming outside the house in Portland Place. They demanded to see the prisoner. Secretary Tang came out of his private office to talk to the reporters. Polite, smiling, utterly urbane, he assured the gentlemen that the story was a gigantic hoax put across by some joker with a wild imagination.

The reporters warned Tang that if the prisoner were not released within a day citizens might storm the Legation and free the hostage.

Tang went on smiling his subtle Chinese smile, seeming to imply that the journalists were surely joking, although he understood their flair for humour. It was apparent, though, that he failed to gauge the temper of the people of London, or the influence of the national Press.

Finally newspapermen tracked down Sir Halliday Macartney to Midland House. It was the *Daily Mail* which pulled off the scoop and printed the first interview with the legal representative of the Chinese Legation.

INTERVIEWS WITH SIR HALLIDAY MACARTNEY

Sir Halliday Macartney, Counsellor of the Chinese Legation, visited the Foreign Office at 3:30 yesterday afternoon. In conversation with a Press representative Sir Halliday said: "I am unable to give you any information beyond what has already appeared in print." On being informed that the Foreign Office had just issued an announcement to the effect that Lord Salisbury had requested the Chinese Minster to release the prisoner, Sir Halliday admitted that this was so, and in answer to a further question as to what would be the result of the request, replied, "The man will be released, but this will be done strictly without prejudice to the rights of the Legation involved."

In the course of a later conversation with a representative of the Press, Sir Halliday Macartney said: "Sun Wen is not the name of the man whom we have in detention upstairs. We have no doubt of his real identity and have been all the time fully informed of all his movements since he set foot in England. He came of his own free will to the Legation, and was certainly not kidnapped or forced or inveigled into the premises. It is quite a usual thing for a solitary Chinaman in London to call here to make casual inquiries or to have a chat with a countryman. There appears, moreover, to be some ground for suspecting that this peculiar visitor, believing himself unknown, came with some idea of spying on us and getting some information. Nobody knew him by sight. When he called he got into conversation with one of our staff and was afterwards introduced to me. We chatted for a while and some remarks he made led me after he had gone to suspect he might be the person we were having watched. These suspicions being confirmed, he was on returning the following day detained, and he is still under detention pending instructions from the Chinese Government."

Speaking of the international side of the matter, Sir Halliday said: "The man is not a British, but a Chinese subject. We contend that for certain purposes the Legation is Chinese territory where the Chinese Minister alone has jurisdiction. If a Chinaman comes here voluntarily and if there are charges or suspicions against him, we contend that no one outside has any right to interfere with his detention. It would be quite different if he were outside this building, for then he would be on British territory, and we could not arrest him without a warrant."

Answering further questions, Sir Halliday mentioned that the man was not treated like a prisoner, and every consideration had been paid to his comfort. Sir Halliday ridiculed the statement which had appeared that the captive might be subjected to torture or undue pressure. He added a statement that a letter of inquiry had been received from the Foreign Office on the subject, which would receive immediate attention.

The Central News says Sir Halliday Macartney, on his return to the Chinese Legation from the Foreign Office, proceeded to the bedside of the Minister Kung Ta Jen, and explained to him that Lord Salisbury had insisted upon the release of Sun Wen.

British newspapers came out with a rash of editorials, waxing indignant at the uncivilized breach of international law by the Imperial Chinese Government. Scotland Yard posted guards outside the Legation. The harbour authorities, too, were alerted. By October 23rd the incident was having repercussions at the highest level; Lord Salisbury, Britain's Foreign Minister, issued a note of protest to the Chinese Minister demanding the immediate release of the prisoner. Two hours later, the Legation guards came to "Sun Wen" and told him to put on his shoes, coat and hat and to follow them downstairs. Was this the last act of his kidnapping? Were the Chinese ready to ship him out? Or was he going to be transferred to a cellar, where he could more conveniently be shot?

"Where are we going?" he asked his impassive Chinese guards, and received no answer.

The prisoner was led downstairs into a small reception room. Three men were waiting for him, and lo and behold! One of them was a friend. He had never welcomed the sight of a man's face as he did the friendly visage of Dr. Cantlie. Accompanying the doctor was Inspector Jarvis of Scotland Yard, and a clerk from the Foreign Office. Neither Tang nor Macartney were in the room, nor any member of the Legation staff.

The doors were open; the four men walked out of the Legation, where a huge crowd was massed to greet the prisoner. Newspaper men from all parts were there to give him a hero's welcome. The young man who had landed on England's shore so unobtrusively three weeks ago was now bombarded with hundreds of questions. The chief question everyone asked him was: How had he managed to communicate with the doctor? But this was one question the ex-prisoner would not answer. He had an obligation to the quiet, colourless servant who had saved his life.

After a visit to Scotland Yard and a happy dinner at the Cantlie home, the freed man wrote a letter of gratitude to every London newspaper. No editor could know that this letter was written by the man who was later to become the first President of the Republic of China and founder of China's native democracy even though his friends had helped him to compose it.

The text of the letter has made history:

> "Will you kindly express through your columns my keen appreciation of the action of the British Government in effecting my release from the Chinese Legation? I have also to thank the Press generally for their timely help and sympathy. If anything were needed to convince me of the generous public spirit which pervades Great Britian and the love of justice which distinguishes its people, the recent acts of the last few days have conclusively done so.
>
> Knowing and feeling more keenly than ever what a constitutional Government and enlightened people mean, I am prompted still more actively to pursue the cause of advancement, education and civilization in my own well-beloved but oppressed country.
>
> Yours faithfully
Sun Yat Sen."*

* Sun Yat Sen became China's great Socialist leader dedicated to overthrowing the Manchu régime and establishing a republic. He was the son of a poor Chinese farmer and as a student became associated with a secret revolutionary society. The failure of a plot led to the execution of several of the conspirators, but Sun Yat Sen escaped. At one time a reward of $300,000 for his capture was offered, but in 1912, on the onset of revolution, he became provisional President of the new republic. He died in 1925.

THE MATA HARI LEGEND

I'M SORRY to disillusion you. But she wasn't beautiful. She was no great shakes as a dancer. She wasn't much of a spy. Yet Mata Hari will be remembered when Mademoiselle le Docteur, Alice Dubois, Irma Staub, Louise de Bettigny, Maria Sorrell, Judy Coplon and a score of others far her superior, are forgotten.

During her lifetime, legend was busy to create a fabulous

creature who combined the beauty of an Aphrodite with the cunning of a Machiavelli; and since her death, that fable has gained credence until it is accepted as the truth.

More than anything else, her profession established this woman as a spy of the first magnitude. She danced wholly naked, delighting Europe's war centers the while she shocked them with the display of unlimited corporeal charm. Such a sensational abandonment to unrestricted nudity furnished her exploiters with blurbs and photographs that few newspapers would refuse to print. News agencies scattered them throughout the world; and when the time came for her intrigants to disclaim this plaything of politicians and spy-masters, the material for her perpetuation was in the files of every newspaper worth the name.

She had been promoted as a sensational dancer. She was proclaimed a modern Delilah who had shorn a hundred Samsons. She died before a firing squad while her bureaucratic lovers and espionage overlords ducked for cover and renounced her.

Mata Hari died as she lived—an inconsequential demimondaine transformed into an insidious spy; and, fact to the contrary, this she is bound to remain. . . .

When Adam Zelle's good Vrouw Antje presented him with a daughter on August 7, 1876, he was the happiest man in Holland. The worthy pair christened her Margarida Gertrud, never thinking but what she would grow up like any of the stocky, square-headed youngsters with whom she played. So she might, too, for she was put to school in a religious institution with every intention of mating with some substantial Leeuwarden burgher, when a vacation at the Hague crossed her path with that of Campbell MacLeod. She was eighteen, and this captain in Holland's colonial forces was a broken-down roué of forty-odd. He drank deeply, loved savagely and sought bitterly to regain the vanished pleasures of desire that women and liquor had long since sapped from him.

But with all that, this hard-bitten scoundrel, fit to qualify for the Foreign Legion, awoke an amorous response in the little Dutch maiden schooled in a cloister. They were married and 1895 found them in Java, where MacLeod was in command of a colonial army reserve. Two children—boy and girl—were born to them. Liquor and island skies got in their work, and MacLeod reverted to type. He beat his young wife unmercifully; he threatened her with a loaded revolver.

As much as he was able, he betrayed her, not once but many times. So in the end she left him and returned to Holland.

Six hectic years in the islands had unfitted her for the quiet of a Friesland provincial village. She left her daughter with relatives—her son had died in Bali—and headed for Paris and adventure. A brief experience in vaudeville ended when the MacLeods clamped down, proclaiming her a disgrace to the clan. But a short respite found her back again, taking the second step toward her tragic death.

Paris this time received a personality far removed from the amorous Dutch girl who had sailed away to the Orient in 1895. Years in Bali made her acquainted with the dances of the tiny Javanese *bayas* from whose posturings came her inspiration. She boned up on the literature of Buddhist temple rituals, and from this half-digested material framed a new life and a new personality.

No longer was she Margarida Gertrud Zelle, daughter of a substantial business man of Leeuwarden. She was Mata Hari, "The Eye of Dawn," born in southern india to a family of sacred Brahmin caste. Her bayadere mother had died in giving her birth, and the temple priests of Kanda Swandy dedicated her to Siva, and schooled her in temple dances to replace her mother. How she came to Paris was glossed over, but there she was, exponent of rituals never before disclosed to unbelieving eyes.

The caterpillar was twenty-nine when it metamorphosed into the butterfly that was Mata Hari. Even then she was far from beautiful. Her jaw bordered on the prognathous, and the animalism that was her was evidenced in her face. Her dark brown skin encouraged the fable of her Oriental ancestry, and there was a dampness about it that might have been oil or perspiration. Her beauty lay in her eyes and arms—arms that some avowed were the most beautiful in the world. But her flat breasts were pendulous and flabby. It was this that discouraged her attempts at modelling, and it was the only part of her person she did not expose during her public exhibitions.

As "The Eye of Dawn" she became the darling of Parisian night life, and the mistress of more than one prominent politician and plotting spy.

Unlike Aphrodite rising from the foam, Mata Hari did not emerge to public gaze in all her uninhibited nudity. Guimet Museum was devoted to Oriental collections; and there, appropriately enough, she made her debut in a mist of diaphanous veiling. From this it was but a step to drop veil after veil until only her breast-plates remained.

She was a sensation. Lovers found her waiting with open arms—for a price. She was put up in the Champs Elysées. She acquired jewels and costly clothes and rode the fashionable boulevards and entertained as befitted a dancer-courtesan surrounded by a mob of eager millionaires.

Two years later she was ready for a change. Off she went to Berlin. The Crown Prince was her first conquest. He took her with him to the military maneuvers in Silesia. The Duke of Brunswick shared her favours. Von Jagow, the Kaiser's foreign minister, was her avowed lover. Vienna saw her exhibitions. So did Rome and Madrid . . . London came later.

It is believed that in 1910 she attended the espionage school at Lorrach for a term. That may have been so. Again, it may not. There is nothing in her life to warrant the assumption, since every move she made was publicized and her private life consisted only of such conquests as she could keep under cover. There was nothing secret about her travels. Her departures and arrivals were functions attented by a train of admirers. As to nationalities, she played no favorites, French, Spanish, Germans, each shared equally in the privileges of admiration. Later, on trial for her life, she explained:

"I am not French . . . I have my right to friends in other countries, even those at war with France. I have remained neutral."

If so, it was a neutrality tinged with a flavor distinctly *Berlinoise*. The most reasonable explanation of the woman is found in petty grafting for private indulgences. In her adventurings in Germany she accepted the attentions of bureaucrats and army officers. For her favors she demanded the highest market price; and the man, not the woman, had to pay. Money was to be had from funds earmarked for undercover work, and from its very nature some of it could be juggled to cover petty deficits. So these men shared Mata Hari and paid her from this secret fund.

Once ensnared in the toils of her own avarice, she became a not unwilling agent of spy-masters. For the greater part, her duties consisted of picking up information confided to her by her dupes. A barmaid in a seamen's grogshop often did exactly the same thing with drunken sailors celebrating shore leave. But this difference marked the two women: Mata

Hari's information could be depended upon. It came from high places, and bore the stamp of authenticity.

Even at that, however, nothing in the record goes to show that Mata Hari possessed an aptitude for espionage. There is little or no evidence that any of this information possessed an important significance. Yet rattling back and forth between Berlin and Paris, she attracted sufficient attention to warrant her being watched. It may be that some of her lovers realized that they had spoken too loudly and too often, and were only too glad to cover up for themselves.

During the first year of World War I, there is no record of her activities. But when she came to France in 1915, a telegram from the Italian Secret Service had preceded her.

"While examining passenger list of a Japanese vessel at Naples, we have recognized the name of a theatrical celebrity from Marseilles named Mata Hari, the Famous Hindu dancer, who purports to reveal secret Hindu dances which demand nudity. She has, it seems, renounced her claim to Indian birth and become *Berlinoise*. She speaks German with slight Eastern accent."

Duplicates of this message were filed in espionage headquarters of each of the allied powers; and by this act, Mata Hari was branded as a German spy. French operators were put on her trail. They followed her day and night; yet nothing definite could be pinned on her. But at last they found that she was sending messages with the help of diplomatic intimates. Attachés of the Dutch, Swedish and Spanish legations were giving her the privilege of enclosing letters in their diplomatic pouches, which of course were despatched sans censoring.

Now Dutch and Swedish pouches were opened and Mata Hari's letters appropriated. They were harmless enough, and the Black Chamber could not discover any secret code. But the letters played an important part in her trial.

A visa was granted her for Vittel, where, she said, she wished to visit a former Russian lover, Captain Maroff, blinded in the war. An important airport was being established there, and France had been warned of German spying. But her trailers were disappointed. She devoted every hour to the wounded Russian, and returned without any untoward action.

Her deportation was decided upon. Had she accepted it, Mata Hari might have survived the war. She was vehement in her denials of ever having worked for Germany. She declared herself unqualifiedly for France. She boasted of her intimacies with many German leaders, and volunteered for the French secret service.

The offer was accepted, and she was sent to Brussels to victimize General Moritz von Bissing, one of her conquests. Six Belgian agents were made known to her. Not long after, one of them was executed by the Germans. British counterspies reported that he had been betrayed by a woman. Mata Hari's next venture found her headed for Spain via Holland and England. In London, she was escorted to New Scotland Yard and questioned by Sir Basil Thompson. She readily admitted she was a spy—but for France, ally of Great Britain. Sir Basil advised her to quit her espionage duties—excellent advice, too—and sent her on to Spain. In Madrid she teams up with the German Naval attachés Captain Walter Wilhelm Canaris, Captain von Kalle, and the military attaché Major von Kron. All three tapped the espionage fund to meet her demands.

This final escapade marked the beginning of the end. German headquarters were clamping down. Too much money was being spent on wine, women and song, with insufficient returns in the way of information. Liquidation is the fate of spies who lose their worth, and Mata Hari was one of little value at the best. Captain Canaris received his orders. (Canaris became chief of all German espionage during World War II).

"H.21" was to proceed to Paris. She was given a check for fifteen thousand pesetas for services performed in Spain, payable through a neutral legation. Mata Hari swallowed the bait. She went to Paris, and registered at the Hotel Plaza-Athenee in the Avenue Montaigne. She was arrested the next day before she had time to cash the check.

The message to Captain Canaris had been an overt statement (they used an outdated code, known to the French) that the betrayal and liquidation might be more certain. (Or did Captain Canaris want to get rid of her for personal reasons?)

It all ended with the arrest of Mata Hari. They took her to the prison of Saint-Lazare and assigned her to cell No. 12, which she was to vacate only at her death. A spacious room with two windows and three beds it had housed Mme. Caillaux, who shot down Gaston Calmette, editor of *Figaro;* and Mme. Steinheil, who had accorded President Francois

Faure similar ministrations; and Margueritte Francillard, who was executed as a spy.

On July 24, 1917, Mata Hari was brought to trial by court-martial. Her fate was a foregone conclusion. Semprou, president of the court, believed her guilty. Massard and Mornet, his associates, were of the same opinion. Maitre Clunet, her counsel, was convinced of her innocence, and so were many who thronged the streets awaiting the verdict. Proceedings were secret. Sentries guarded all doors, and none might approach within ten paces. There was much wisdom in this secrecy, for Mata Hari told all.

She told of viewing army maneuvers in Silesia, France and Italy; of receiving thirty thousand marks from von Jagow after being with him when war was declared; of other payments of similar amounts.

"They were the price of my favors," she announced. "Thirty thousand marks? My lovers never offered me less."

She admitted corresponding with Germans. But they were her lovers, and she communicated nothing but private endearments. The diplomatic pouches were used to send letters to her daughter. She emphasized she had been a spy for France, but could present no information that she had gathered for them. Her fate was decided when she was unable to produce the list of six Belgian spies which had been furnished her. Nor could she explain what had been despatched to the German officials in Amsterdam before she left France.

But Mata Hari summoned witnesses: Jules Cambron, chief of the permanent staff of the Ministry of Foreign Affairs, former Minister of War, Messimy, and others.

"I am not French," she declared. "I have the right to have friends in other countries, even among those at war with France. I have remained neutral. I count upon the goodness of heart of you French officers."

The members of the court filed to a retiring-room to consider their verdict. They were back in ten minutes with the decision: Mata Hari was to be shot as a spy.

There are any number of soft spots in this prosecution. It had been contended that she was responsible for the torpedoing of fourteen French transports in the Mediterranean with great loss of life. But nobody names the ships; nor is there any record of their loss.

And if she did furnish information that led to this destruction, what of the members of the ministries of marine and commerce and war who gave her this information? It seems quite evident that Mata Hari was a German spy; that her activities were of limited account; that she paid more for her favors than for her information; that she lacked ordinary horse sense in acting as she did; and that her betrayal was certain whenever German spy-masters decided it was time to abandon her.

Whatever her life may have been, Mata Hari died bravely. When the findings of the court-martial were read to her, she heard her sentence with a smile. The stubborn courage of her Dutch ancestry proved itself in her bearing. An enigmatic smile lightened her face, and the only tension evidenced was a nervous biting of her lips as she turned away.

Back in cell No. 12 in the prison of St. Lazare, the two nuns sought to comfort her. She thanked them for their kindness and assured them that all would be well. For by this time those she had favored were coming to her rescue, seeking a commutation of sentence, at the worst. This did much to bolster her courage—for, supreme egoist that she was, Mata Hari could not see why their influence would not work to her good. Her first days were filled with temperamental outbursts. After a bit she became philosophical and wholly tractable.

In that welter of mingled fact and fiction surrounding her last days, Pierre de Morrisac plays no minor rôle. Younger son of a prominent French family, this Parisian roué had turned to the dancer after an abandoned life of degenerate dissipation and reckless love affairs. He loved her truly, and taking a page from the opera *Tosca*, he planned a mock execution with blank cartridges for the firing squad. This plot was worked out in detail, and no doubt may have accounted for the woman's composure.

She had much time to prepare for the end, since the findings of June 25 were not executed until October 15. The hour was fixed at 5:47; the place, the rifle-range at Vincennes. She accepted the glass of rum prescribed for the condemned by law; wrote three letters, one to her daughter; made a final inspection of her toilette; and announced her readiness.

Guards and official witnesses waited without. A procession of cars made its way to the execution spot, where the troops waited, drawn up in three sides of a hollow square. On the fourth side stood a bare tree, stripped of leaves and branches.

The death warrant was read. They tied her to the tree— she refused to have her eyes bandaged; and nuns and priest withdrew. The firing squad snapped into readiness. Major

Massard barked a terse command. There was a volley of shots, and Mata Hari sank slowly to earth, her body pierced by twelve bullets. . . .

In the once quiet cloister of the Carthusian monastery Aula Dei, a solitary monk huddled above a machine-gun one late September afternoon in 1936. He was awaiting the next advance of Spanish-Loyalist troops.

For eighteen years he had sought the refuge of the monastery, hiding his identity from the world, trying to forget. His companions fled the place at the first approach of danger, but he chose to remain.

For hours he held the Loyalists at bay, decimating their ranks until his last cartridge was spent. When the troops entered the building, sixty of their number lay dead.

Infuriated that one man should have caused such havoc, the Loyalists placed him against a stone wall, and eight bullets ended his life.

Eight bullets—four less than tore through the breast of Mata Hari eighteen years before—ended the life of him who had been known to the world as Pierre de Morrisac, lover of the Eye of Dawn, who as a youth of twenty-two fought desperately to save her from the firing squad, believing to his last hour that she was innocent of the crime for which sh[e] died.

TREBITSCH-LINCOLN, ADVENTURER ON THREE CONTINENTS

by W. Lüdecke

IGNATIUS TIMOTHY TREBITSCH-LINCOLN, the international adventurer and spy, may justly lay claim to the doubtful glory of being acknowledged as the greatest political charlatan and humbug of his time, for he managed to take a hand in an extraordinary number of notorious scandals and disturbances in public life. His versatility in the province of political crime and the chameleon-like gift he displayed in changing his coat bordered on the marvelous. He was an actor, or, to speak more accurately, a quick-change artist with the talent of a professional in the performance of all the parts demanded by his dangerous game, while the scenes of the amazing dramas in which he appeared embraced the continents. We find him not only in Europe, but also in

America and Asia, as a journalist, political agent, priest, member of parliament, forger, double-spy, Buddhist monk, and mandarin. What led him to adopt this many-colored kaleidoscopic sort of existence? Was he merely cool and calculating, with an irresistible thirst for wealth acquired anyhow and at any cost? Was he impelled by morbid ambition to attain political power, and skillful enough, for a time, to choose the easy path opened to him by unexpected but favorable opportunity? Was he possessed by the love of adventure, the desire for exciting experience, the exhilarating enjoyment of danger? We cannot tell what it was that brought this remarkable Hungarian, for a brief period, into such a prominent position upon the political stage. This only we know, that his meteoric career was run on bluff; that it was as full of sensation as an American film; that it came to a sudden end, after all its brilliance, falling to earth like an exploded rocket.

Lincoln, or, to give him his real name, Trebitsch, was born in the Hungarian town of Paks, situated on the Danube. It was not a big place, but its trade was prosperous. There his father, in comfortable circumstances, had a thriving boat-building yard. Ignatius was a younger son, and as he was destined for the profession of rabbi, he received a very careful and thorough education. His chief intellectual interest was the study of foreign tongues.

When he reached the age of twenty years he set off on his travels, and presently arrived in London. Here he took a rather unusual step for a budding rabbi: he joined the Anglican church. After a certain lapse of time he returned home and found his father very naturally indignant at the conduct of his renegade son. Ignatius, therefore, found it advisable not to postpone too long his second departure. In fact he left the house of his parents with all possible speed, and betook himself to Hamburg, where, in 1899, he changed his religious denomination for the second time, on this occasion going over to the Lutheran church. By his brethren of his persuasion he was sent to Canada, as a missionary to the Jews. But, strangely enough, he had not long exercised his new functions when the mission was transferred to the Anglican church, with the result that Trebitsch promptly changed his faith again. For some years he remained in that position of Anglican missionary, earning a reputation as a sound and able preacher. Then we find him on furlough in Germany. At his own request he was appointed by the authorities of the church in England to the living of Appledore in Kent. However, the worthy villagers in this parish appear not to have taken very kindly to this ex-Hungarian Jew as a pastor, and the latter, after remaining with them for some fourteen months, decided that his best policy was to leave his flock to their own devices. He went to London, where he discovered a talent for journalism, and contributed for a year or two to several newspapers.

The year 1906 brought with it a decided turn in the affairs of this man. He went in for politics. He made the acquaintance of Mr. Seebohm Rowntree, the well-known Quaker who was also a distinguished member of the Liberal Party. The young Hungarian was undoubtedly capable and gifted, and Mr. Rowntree was so much attracted to him that he made him his private secretary. It must be admitted that Trebitsch had a strange way of showing his gratitude, for he rewarded the trust of his patron and friend by relieving him of the handsome sum of seven hundred pounds: he forged his signature to a bill. His crime was not discovered till years after, but it was paid for.

His efforts to win political laurels were crowned with success, for, in 1910, he made his entry into the House of Commons, as member for Darlington. The House did not take him very seriously, however; he was a stranger, and his foreign pronunciation often excited noisy mirth. He was sent at various times by his Party on tours of investigation, for the purpose of studying economic conditions on the continent of Europe, and was thus brought into touch with eminent politicians and diplomatists. But these continual journeys began to excite a certain degree of suspicion. When he lost his seat in Parliament at the last election before the War, he found himself in a financial situation that was anything but favorable.

Then came the War. His civil status, as an alien and really a subject of one of the hostile belligerent powers, made his position decidedly more difficult. However, there were influential people to supply him with credentials, and he applied to the War Office for employment as censor of Hungarian and Rumanian correspondence. And he actually received such an appointment! He was not maintained in it very long, for his colleagues naturally looked askance at him, considering him as an enemy within the gates and suspecting him of double-dealing, although, possibly, he had not yet been guilty of any conduct that would have justified their attitude. In any case, he was obliged to give up his post in the censorship. Once more, then, he found himself in difficulties. In the club which he frequented people began to turn the cold shoulder to him, and it seemed evident that his expulsion was merely a matter of time.

It was then, so far as we can judge, that the thought entered his head of avenging the insults he had suffered at the hands of Englishmen, by betraying them; and he did not delay long in taking the steps necessary to achieve this purpose. Trebitsch became a German spy. He immediately got into communication with the British Intelligence Service, and, again with the aid of influential persons who could not believe the late M.P. capable of any evil design, he succeeded in obtaining an interview with responsible officials of the secret service, to whom he intimated his desire to assist in the work of counterespionage. But Trebitsch did not present himself empty-handed. He was in the unexpected position of being able to submit to the British naval staff a plan, a really ingenious plan already fully worked out, which, in his opinion, would prove of the utmost value and importance to Britain. This fantastic scheme was, in a few words, as follows: Britain was to send out into the North Sea a small squadron, and he would then inform the German Admiralty of the fact. The Germans would send out a more powerful fleet and annihilate the British ships. But that would have enabled him to gain the confidence of the Germans. After this maneuver had been repeated two or three times the great affair was to follow. The British would have a mighty fleet of dreadnoughts in waiting, and thus the whole German navy would be wiped out. That was Trebitsch-Lincoln's plan—far-fetched and stupid at one and the same time.

But somehow the British did not show any great appreciation of the naval strategy evolved by this zealous ex-M.P., for they saw through the sly proposals of the crafty Hungarian. They understood what he was after. Had such a project been realized, he would have acquired very reliable information concerning the station and distribution of the British naval forces, and would then have passed it on to the Germans. After ten days of futile expectation, he was told very drily that his suggestions could not be accepted, as the authorities had no intention of letting him know anything of the whereabouts of British ships.

Trebitsch was never at a loss, however, and he had another proposal to lay before them. He offered to go to

Rotterdam. He would pretend to place himself at the disposal of the German espionage service, and so be in the best possible position to serve the interests of Britain, by procuring information at first hand. The British authorities affected to approve of this scheme. He was given his passport, and in December he went to Rotterdam, where he at once made advances to the German consul-general. What he did not know was that his every step was being most carefully observed by agents of the British counterespionage, who, before long were quite convinced that it could not be Britain that he was working for. The information that he brought back from Holland was examined by Sir Reginald Hall, the chief of the naval intelligence staff, and proved to be utterly worthless. He was kept hanging about for a week or two, and was then summoned to appear before the chief, bringing his passport with him. Sir Reginald Hall had no doubt whatever of the fact that he had been playing the dangerous part of double spy, and gave him clearly to understand that the sooner he turned his back upon England, the better it would be for him. He realized that the game was up so far as his stay in England was concerned; and, very much relieved at not finding himself under arrest, Trebitsch did not wait to be told twice. The very next day he sailed for New York on board the steamer *Philadelphia*.

He arrived at New York on the 9th of February. The first thing he did on landing was to present himself to the German secret service, but they refused to have any dealings with him. Apparently they, too, distrusted him. So Trebitsch resumed his journalistic activities and contributed articles to the pro-German American press.

In the meantime his act of forgery had been discovered in England, and the British Government made application to the American authorities for his extradition. This was granted only after protracted negotiations. On the 4th of August, 1915, Trebitsch was arrested and was at once conveyed to England, where he was tried and sentenced to a long term of imprisonment. His time expired during the summer of 1919, and on coming out of prison he was to be deported to Hungary. But it happened that Bela Kun's reign of terror was just then raging in Budapest, so Trebitsch-Lincoln's expulsion was delayed for some weeks. In September of that year he was sent out of England, and found himself once more in the capital of his native land, where, however, the atmosphere proved, after a short stay, rather uncongenial.

He therefore quitted Hungary and went to Germany where there were then brighter prospects of fishing in troubled waters.

He made some attempt to approach the ex-Kaiser Wilhelm, in the palace of Amerongen in Holland, but had no success in that venture. That did not stand in the way of his being taken up by the reactionary and monarchist circles of Berlin, who had grouped themselves round Kapp. He managed to win the confidence of men like Colonel Bauer and Captain Pabst; and, his journalistic ability once more standing him in good stead, he became the director of the press campaign that was being carried on in preparation for Kapp's abortive insurrection, in the execution of which he also played a considerable part. After the failure of this rising a warrant was issued for his arrest, but he fled with the other bravoes to Munich, where their new headquarters were established.

Here Trebitsch succeeded in doing what Major Stephani had failed to do, that was, to induce Pohner, the chief of police, and Kahr, the Bavarian Prime Minister, to join the new project of the conspirators, who were planning to bring about the simultaneous action of Bavaria against Saxony and of Mecklenburg against Berlin. But as money—a great deal of money—was absolutely necessary for this purpose, Trebitsch received from the chief of police in Munich a false passport and went twice to Berlin, to interview Ludendorf or some other member of the initiated, who had control of the funds required. The Berlin detectives were on the lookout for him, and were occasionally close at his heels, although the Bavarian police had expressly warned him to be on his guard against them. On the occasion of his second visit to Berlin, he happened to come across Captain Pabst, who was still in possession of a large sum of money remaining from the treasury of the original conspiracy in Berlin, and who also knew Ludendorf's secret place of abode—a lonely house in the forest, in the neighborhood of Rosenhain. The two of them went to call on Ludendorf, where Major Stephani also put in an appearance. It was resolved, for reasons of personal security, to transfer the headquarters to Budapest. The idea was, that the Hungarian and even the Russian monarchists should be persuaded to interest themselves in the movement, and that the revolution should be organized and directed from Budapest and Vienna. On the 8th of May a monarchist congress was to be held in Berlin. Trebitsch, therefore, betook himself once more to the German capital, but, for some reason or another, he was not very warmly received by the other partisans, who advised him that the police were after him and that he should make himself scarce. He followed their advice and disappeared, at least for the night, finding shelter in Trebbin, a little town near Potsdam, in the house of a governess who had once been employed by him. Next day he was standing on the platform, waiting to get into the train for Berlin, when he was recognized and stopped by an official of the criminal police. Trebitsch got the latter to allow him to go back, under escort, to his own quarters, in order to pack his things. The attention of his warder being distracted for a moment, the prisoner took advantage of the fact to jump through an open window, and so he made his escape.

But the police did have something to show for their trouble. One valuable piece of booty fell into their hands: a trunk containing the secret correspondence of the conspirators.

Trebitsch remained concealed for a short time in Potsdam, being sheltered by a political sympathizer. Then he made his way by Frankfort to his friends in Munich. Pohner, the chief of police, gave him a note of introduction to the Hungarian counsel-general in Munich, who was so well satisfied with his initiation into the immediate plans of his fellow-countryman that he supplied him with a guardian angel as far as Vienna, in the shape of a consular official. In Vienna his difficulties threatened to become serious, for he noticed that he was being followed by detectives.

However, he found Gratz, the Hungarian ambassador in Vienna, quite willing to have a new passport made out for him, and he arrived without further molestation in Budapest hoping to obtain congenial employment. Without any loss of time he made the acquaintance of the deputies Gombos and Eckhardt, and of Colonel von Pronay, the chief press-agent of the Hungarian Government. To them he unfolded a plan that was comparable in value to the one he had proposed to the British Admiralty during the War. A large number of German soldiers, dressed as civilians, were to be smuggled into Hungary, and there to receive their military equipment, after which they were to be sent against Vienna and Czechoslovakia. Colonel Bauer, who had accompanied Trebitsch, had actually received from Ludendorf plenary powers to conclude a preliminary treaty with Hungary. But Colonel von Pronay did not look with approval upon this mad project which struck him as being risky in the extreme. The whole scheme ended in smoke.

Trebitsch now understood that there was no further opportunity of using his talents in Germany and Austria, so he moved to Italy, trusting that, among the Fascists, there would surely be scope for his activities. And he was not disappointed. There is still a dark veil of mystery surrounding the intrigues in which he became involved as a Fascist, and perhaps this is not incomprehensible, if it be true, as has been alleged, that he had some connection with the murder of Mateotti.

Then, for a fairly long time, nothing more was heard of him, until people concluded that he was dead. But it was not so. He had certainly shaken off from his feet the dust of an ungrateful Europe. The astonished world heard through the reports from an American correspondent in China, that were being published in the New York *World*, of a certain Chilan, said to be the political adviser of Wu Pei Fu, and to have organized the anti-British propaganda in China. At the same time we learned that this Chilan was no other than the notorious Trebitsch-Lincoln, who had found a new outlet for his energies in the turmoil of the Far East. With cynical frankness he had related to the American newspaper man the vicissitudes of his adventurous life, making no effort whatever to conceal his employment as a double spy during the World War. It will hardly astonish anyone who knows his previous history to hear that in China he had once more changed his religion and gone over to Buddhism.

The last news of this incorrigible adventurer, that had interest for the world, was the announcement that he was returning from China to England. His son was under sentence of death for murder, and Trebitsch wished to see him once more before his execution. The British Government was magnanimously willing to put no obstacle in his way. But as a matter of fact the father was too late. During the course of his checkered career he had many a time had vast sums of money placed at his disposal for various purposes of conspiracy and underhand work. To mention only one case, Lieutenant-General Krauss had once opened for him a credit of 230,000 dollars. On this occasion, however, by the time he reached France, his financial resources were so completely exhausted that he was not able to pay the fare that would have brought him over the last short stage of his journey to London. He never saw his son again in life.

Since that last melancholy appearance, Trebitsch-Lincoln has faded completely from public notice.

Trebitsch-Lincoln died October 7, 1943 in Shanghai. His friends buried him as Abbot Chao-Kung.

THE ADMIRAL WHO NEVER WORE A UNIFORM

On the historic morning of September 1, 1939, a neatly dressed little man of most unhistoric appearance walked down Berlin's Wilhelmstrasse. World War II was but a few hours old; at dawn German troops had poured across the border into Poland. The Berlin police had closed the Wilhelmstrasse against all traffic. They wanted no demonstrations, patriotic or otherwise, in front of the government buildings. But the little man walked through their lines without hindrance toward the grandiose and impious Reichschancellery.

He entered the building, passing Hitler's personal guard, who was obviously a high officer, with many ribbons and cords bedecking his dark blue uniform. The officer stiffened his arm and cried, "Heil Hitler, Admiral."

The privileged little man in civilian dress was, of course, no civilian. He had just been promoted to the rank of admiral, and he had come to thank Hitler for the promotion. He was the new chief of all German espionage, the head of the German Secret Service.

Admiral Wilhelm Canaris was the mystery man of German espionage. He himself may well be judged by future historians to have been the greatest spy of our time; certainly he was the greatest *organizer* of espionage the world has ever known.

Since 1945 the Germans have indulged in hero worship of Canaris. To them he is the man who dared to turn against Hitler midway in the dictator's mad war of world conquest. He allegedly was the man who knew and helped in the plot to assassinate Hitler, the man who, like Faust, had sold his soul to the Nazi devil and then turned against Mephisto until Mephisto destroyed him.

The British have said that "without being on our pay roll, Admiral Canaris helped us to destroy Hitler."

But Canaris' own friends saw in him the German patriot who never deliberately teamed up with Britain. This would have been considered "treason" and Canaris to them was never a traitor.

What is his real story?

Canaris was one of the most unusual figures any secret service in history ever produced. More than any other important Nazi, he cultivated obscurity. Deliberately he reduced his personality to a cipher. Few cameras ever caught his likeness. He was never seen at any of the great Nazi mass meetings in the Berlin Sportpalast. He never spoke on the air. Though one of the mightiest and deadliest men of Hitler's Germany, he was never mentioned in the German press.

His headquarters, however, could not be concealed so successfully. He shared quarters with the war department at 74 Tirpitz Ufer, in the very heart of Berlin. But of the thousands who frequented this enormous building, only a few ever saw him face to face. Those who caught a glimpse describe him as small and slight with colorless skin like that of men who work at night, and with prominent cheekbones which gave his face a Slavic cast.

His home address during the war was a close secret. A handful of his assistants knew that he lived somewhere in the south part of Berlin, and that his house was surrounded by a flower garden of which the admiral was very fond.

One might have trudged down every corridor in the building at Tirpitz Ufer without finding a door bearing the admiral's name. Indeed, few could have directed you even to the part of the building where his offices were located. In March 1935, Canaris had a private entrance constructed, and he entered and left by a staircase exclusively his. A big Mercedes with bullet-proof windows brought him daily from his home.

Canaris' career as an intelligence officer started back in 1914. At the age of twenty-five years, he was a naval officer of great promise, already the captain of the cruiser *Dresden*. The outbreak of the war found him on the high seas. With no hope of returning to a German port, he brought his ship to neutral Chile, where he and his crew were interned.

A German secret service officer in the guise of a Red Cross visitor made contact with him in the internment camp. He outlined a plan for a daring escape that would enable Canaris to go on serving the Fatherland. Once free, Canaris was to enter the imperial intelligence service. He would then go to the United States and work under Franz von Papen, organizing anti-American espionage and sabotage.

The escape was managed with ease. And in 1916 an unprepossessing, smallish man with prominent cheekbones came to New York. He called himself Otto Seliger, a Polish Jew. The American and Canadian intelligence services possess huge dossiers on Otto Seliger, who was in charge of dangerous sabotage assignments under the leadership of the reckless spies and saboteurs of the imperial German secret service, headed in America by Franz von Papen and Franz von Rintelen.

The American dossiers also mention the alias of Moses Meyerbeer. Under this name Canaris gave his occupation as music dealer and even dared to pretend that he was a nephew of the famous composer Meyerbeer.

A few weeks before the United States entered World War I, Canaris received orders for precipitate action. He was to leave the United States, go to Spain and there organize a naval espionage unit. He crossed the British blockade in a daring enterprise, in which he posed as a Chilean merchant, Señor Reed-Rosas, passenger on a British ship.

He reached Spain safely and his first secret assignment was to bring unrest to the French colonies of Africa. His orders were to incite Arab tribes in North Africa, to hand out subsidies to these tribes and to start revolts against France and Great Britain in both Morocco and West Africa.

In the German and British secret service files is the entry: "Canaris blew up nine British ships from his base in Spain."

It was in Spain that he met a woman whom he would never forget, a woman who was to give her life to purchase advancement for the career of Walter Wilhelm Canaris.

For her charm alone she was unforgettable, as many have testified. Her name was Margarete Gertrude Zelle. She was dark, exotic, fascinating, a passionate and inspired dancer. Born in Java of Dutch parents, she had taken the stage name "Mata Hari," Arabic words meaning "Eye of the dawn."

Canaris' meetings with Mata Hari have been denied by his family and by some of his biographers. But in the archives of Allied intelligence offices is evidence showing that Canaris and Mata Hari knew each other well. According to these reports, young Canaris first saw her at the famous Madrid night club, the Trocadero. As he entered she was dancing an authentic Javanese temple dance. Afterward Canaris invited the dancer to his table. Though he was never good-looking, his Prussian formality and the forcefulness of his vaulting ambition gave him power over women. It began as a light-hearted flirtation, with Canaris coming to the Trocadero night after night, but soon it developed into a passionate love affair.

The passion did not last long. Canaris had other uses for Mata Hari. His immediate superior, the German ambassador to Spain, Baron Eberhard von Stohrer, who was later to hold the same post in World War II, wanted a woman spy to be sent to Paris as soon as possible.

Canaris was ostensibly a naval attaché to Spain. His real duties, however, were not so ornamental. What he was actually doing was preparing bases for German submarines along the neutral Spanish coast, conducting harbor espionage against Allied shipping, and planting agents at the Spanish court to offset Allied influence over the Spanish royal house. Above all, Canaris' job was to smuggle German agents into France across the Pyrenees.

Mata Hari was to go to Paris on a Dutch transport, dance at the Moulin Rouge, and become Canaris' key agent in France. It was anticipated that her charm and artistry would conquer all Paris, especially—and this interested Canaris most —high-ranking officers of the French army and navy. Mata Hari was reluctant to go. But Canaris promised that he would see her soon and that she would become the greatest dancer in Europe.

Canaris' prediction came true. Mata Hari fascinated Paris. The most sophisticated roués worshiped at her feet. Money poured in, and Mata Hari loved money. She purchased a small estate near the Bois de Boulogne. There she held open house every Sunday evening. Forty or fifty men would come to vie for her favors, among them members of the French general staff.

In Spain, Canaris grew negligent; his letters became less frequent. His duties were too pressing to allow time for romantic attentions. After all, the girl was not a German, so marriage was out of the question. For him, Mata Hari became only Agent No. H-21. In that capacity she did satisfactory work. She learned the secrets of troop movements, of new offensives, of fortifications and defense plans. She made occasional trips to Holland, where she reported her findings to German officers.

In 1917, Agent H-21 made one of her courier trips via Holland to Cologne. There she had a prearranged meeting in the loge of the opera with one of the highest officers of the German general staff. She had come to inform him about important troop movements from England to France and to give him details on the Allied defense lines. By chance, French intelligence agents saw her talking to the German.

The mission accomplished, Mata Hari set out for home. Without the slightest trepidation she took a boat which was headed for France via Denmark and England. She was about to leave it when a British customs official came up to her and whispered: "Don't touch French soil. You'd better stay on this boat. It goes to Spain."

Mata Hari thought swiftly. She instantly realized that someone had discovered her. She was fortunate in being on a neutral boat and she decided to stay on it and flee to Spain.

Her frequent and apparently aimless trips to Holland had aroused the suspicions of the British and French intelligence services, and she had been under observation for several months. But the German counter-espionage was also on the alert, and the British customs official was, in reality, a German agent.

In Spain, she went to the German Embassy. She asked for Walter Wilhelm Canaris, the man she still loved, but he was disgruntled at seeing her. He had no business here; her place was in Paris. She tried to tell him what had happened, but he interrupted her with a fearful scene about her *affaires d'amour* in Paris. After a reconciliation and a week together, Canaris broke the news: she had been so valuable that she *must* return to Paris, *"mag es kosten was es will,"* at no matter what price.

Mata Hari knew that she would never see Canaris again, but there was no way out—a spy could not desert.

The inevitable happened. Mata Hari was arrested by the French and court-martialed: in the fall of 1917 she was shot. But it was not the French who really sentenced her to death. It was the German secret service. When Canaris ordered her back to Paris, he informed the German intelligence service in Amsterdam of her whereabouts, deliberately using a code which had been discarded for the transmission of vital information—for the French intelligence service had broken it. The French intercepted the message—and that was the end of Mata Hari, mother of a young daughter.

Then the German revolution broke out. The Kaiser went, though the generals remained. Many conscientious military men found themselves out of a job. Canaris emerged from the war with the rank of lieutenant commander—but jobless.

During the next few years he appeared and disappeared. It is hard to say what he did in those unfavorable times. We do know that on his own initiative Canaris was extremely active in organizing counter-revolution against the Weimar

Republic. He helped to conceal the arms the Inter-Allied Control Commissions were hunting for. He helped to establish the various Free Corps which were in the forefront of the numerous *Putsches* that shook the German republic. In fact, he planned several of them. He was one of Hitler's collaborators in the famous Beer Cellar Putsch of 1923, and had that conspiracy been successful, Canaris was to have "taken over" the northern seacoast of Germany.

Around 1926 Wilhelm Canaris, in title still a member of the nonexistent navy, sank out of sight of the general public. Only a few insiders knew that a man like Canaris would not disappear for good. Obscurely but patiently he was working in a tiny office in the War Ministry. The lettering on his door read "Department for Naval Transport," which meant exactly nothing. In these cramped quarters Canaris toiled away at naval intelligence, preparing for *"Der Tag."*

In 1927 the limelight was suddenly turned upon him, to his very great annoyance. At that time one of Germany's largest motion picture companies, the Phoebus Corporation, went into bankruptcy. The company had produced a number of pictures glorifying the gallantry of the nonexistent German navy. These movies were nothing more nor less than militaristic propaganda for the navy and merchant marine. The bankruptcy proceedings turned up the embarrassing evidence that they had been financed by Canaris.

The German public was curious to know where Canaris had secured the necessary money, for the cost of the pictures had come to some seven million marks (roughly two million dollars). Canaris answered, "Secret funds." But he would not tell the German court anything further. His excuse: to say more would give away important defense secrets. That was enough for the nationalistic judges. He was excused from further questioning. The financial crookedness not only was never punished; it was never prosecuted.

Nevertheless it created a scandal: the German navy packed him off to Spain, where much of the secret German armament was going on. He saw to the building of U-boats in the Echeveria shipyard. Although the treaty of Versailles prohibited Germany from having any submarines at all, construction went on quite brazenly.

In Spain, he was a frequent guest of the well-known Spanish munitions king, Juan March. They discussed purchasing weapons for the German army and storing them in Spain. Canaris' connection with Juan March turned out to be highly useful during the Spanish civil war. For some time, it will be remembered, the Germans did not have to come openly to the aid of Franco, since they were already established in key positions in Spain.

Canaris' reports from Spain were invaluable to the German naval intelligence. He set up an espionage system directed against British and Italian shipping which was to be of immense advantage to Germany.

In 1929, Franz von Papen, who had been Canaris' superior when they worked in the United States, introduced him to Hermann Goering. The characters of Canaris and Goering had much in common, since both men were the Prussian type of *Junker* officer, and they liked each other from the start. Both had actively participated in the Munich Beer Hall Putsch, but had never chanced to meet. Canaris told Goering that he, Canaris, could bring some of the intelligence facilities of the Weimar Republic's army to the aid of the Hitler movement. Goering agreed. Canaris was the very man to head an espionage apparatus for the steadily growing Nazi party. He had proved in World War I that he was one of the best pupils of Colonel Walter Nicolai, then the head of the German secret service. He had excellent connections in the navy, too. Moreover, the information he could bring in was supremely marketable; certainly Fascist Italy would be glad to buy it, and that would help swell the party's finances.

Canaris' first job for the Hitler gang was a simple personnel report. Hitler asked for a file on all German officers, indicating their political leanings, their financial situations and their moral attitudes.

It is well known that Canaris and Von Papen were instrumental in deposing Chancellor Kurt von Schleicher, thus leaving his post free for Hitler. The deposing came about because Canaris was able to obtain interesting documents from Schleicher's private desk.

Schleicher had been secretly dallying with the idea of a new legislative measure that would cut off the *Junkers'* subsidies and break up the vast East Prussian estates into small farms. Certainly the measure would have eased somewhat the dangerous unemployment problem in Germany. But Schleicher knew well that the time was not yet ripe for risking such a great reform; the reactionary forces in the country were still too strong. Quite probably Schleicher himself was none too eager to have such a law passed, but the economic predicament of the country was driving him to it.

After Canaris succeeded in getting a copy of this secret document, he immediately turned it over to Hitler. A photostat of the stolen document was presented to President von Hindenburg, along with what amounted to an ultimatum from Hitler. Hitler accused Hindenburg of harboring Bolsheviks in his government. He threatened to arouse industry and the landowners. The doddering Hindenburg was embarrassed and dismayed. He wanted to avoid a scandal, and above all he wanted to protect his *Junker* friends.

The upshot was that he dismissed Schleicher from the cabinet. Germany received Hitler as her new chancellor and Fuehrer, the world in due time received a second world war, and Wilhelm Canaris, the clever master mind, received his high position.

Those who have indulged in praising Admiral Canaris as a most important instrument of the Germany military underground against the Hitler dictatorship love to gloss over the man's past. They like to forget the ingenious, devilish, brutal, and cruel spy plots conceived by this master of world espionage.

When the Allies marched into Berlin at the end of World War II, they were able to seize many of the Nazi files intact. It took years to assort and evaluate the findings, but in the offices of German *Abwehr* (counter-intelligence III F) were documents and memoranda telling of a meeting between *Luftwaffe* and armament production chief Hermann Goering with Admiral Canaris.

It was revealed at this meeting, what Count Ciano later admitted frankly, that Germany had given 500 million marks to General Franco to help Fascism in Spain. It was an outright gift, admitted Italian Foreign Secretary Ciano: "Hitler gave it unconditionally."

But the Germans were clever. They had another plan as well. It was decided that the Nazis should deliver arms not only to Franco—but to the Republicans also.

Now, fifteen years later, I have found out how naive I was as a foreign correspondent when I had convincing "evidence" that the Germans in 1937 were delivering guns to both sides, to the Fascists and the Loyalists. I thought I had a scoop when I met Krupp's representative in Stockholm, Sweden, who was selling these guns through a Swedish senator to the Spanish Republican Government.

Today I know the rest of the story. It was one of Canaris' most fantastic plans. Canaris helped to sabotage the Spanish

Loyalists' war potential by sending rifles, ammunition, carbines, grenades, to the Republicans. But it was defective war material that he sent. His plan succeeded. He helped Spain become a Fascist dictatorship.

Admiral Canaris, to those who followed his actions from the very beginning, was the man who helped to murder the democratic Republic of Weimar. He was the same man who now helped murder the Republic of Spain.

In the confiscated German secret service dossiers, Allied intelligence found the files of Canaris' chief armament dealer, Josef Vetjens. This man had helped both Canaris and Goering to sell German weapons abroad at the end of World War I. Those armaments the German nationalists refused to give to the Allies as reparations in accord with the Versailles peace treaty.

Vetjens had his own stooge armament companies in Czechoslovakia and Romania. The weapons were stored all over the Balkans, in fact. They were naturally outdated when the civil war started in Spain, but the guns and grenades were still usable. These old weapons were partly and effectively sabotaged and sold to the Spanish Republicans, while Hitler and Mussolini equipped Franco with the most modern war material.

Canaris was often in Spain during this period. He met General Franco and toured the Spanish front with him. He met Franco's chief of staff, General Mola. He was seen in Cadiz, Cartagena, and Gibraltar. There was a deep friendship between Franco and Canaris. Later, when Canaris was in trouble with Hitler, Franco invited him to escape to Spain, but Canaris declined. After the end of the war General Franco invited Frau Canaris and her daughter, who had been sent to school in Spain earlier, to live there for the rest of their lives.

Canaris' next historic master stroke was to bring confusion to Soviet Russia. It was his idea to behead Russia's military staff in order to bring about a weakening of the Soviet's military machine.

It is today an open secret in every war department in the world, including the Kremlin, that the head of the German secret service—"His Excellency," as they called Canaris—forwarded ingeniously forged documents to Soviet agents, proving that Marshal Tukhachevski and seven other Soviet generals, as well as many small functionaries, were engaged in a plot to assassinate Stalin and grab the state with German help. The Soviets fell for it. On June 12, 1937, Marshal Tukhachevski and seven generals were executed. But the real executioner was sitting at Tirpitz Ufer in Berlin.

It was after this bloody incident of the Soviet military purge that Canaris got a new villa for his family, and was decorated by Hitler, who said: "I do not want men of intelligence. I want men of brutality."

There is no doubt that Canaris was one of the most brilliant men on the German general staff and in the war department. But his dramatic end was inevitable—he was pro-British as so many Germans were. He wanted war with Russia; he hated Communism; he perhaps was never a Nazi deep inside his heart; but he gave the Nazi salute and wanted panGerman glory as did thousands of non-Nazi German officers before and after Hitler. His intelligence reports had informed him that Germany could lose a war with Britain as the enemy; he was sure Germany would lose if America came in. He also knew Roosevelt would not remain neutral.

Admiral Horthy, the former dictator of Hungary told Ian Colvin, author of a most remarkable book about the German intelligence chief: "Canaris and I agreed in 1939 that if America entered the war against Germany then Germany was finished."

Canaris knew that Britain's and America's fate could not be separated. He, who had meddled in Spain and even inside the Soviet Union, decided now to find out the most minute details of British and American plans. Would both countries accept aggression in Czechoslovakia, Austria, Poland? Would they dare to fight back?

He had to find his way first into the British secret service, then into America's G-2 service—*and he did*.

He arrived in London on January 21, 1938, and stopped at 28 Cleveland Terrace, Bayswater. The exact day he left is not known.

Though Canaris entered on a false passport, the British intelligence service knew of his presence almost immediately. The information had been secured from another German agent whom the British had arrested, a man with two names and two passports, a certain Ludwig, alias Winkler.

Canaris spent January and part of February trying to lay his hands on certain items, including a new Vickers-Wellesley model about which he was most keen. The items were a new 14-inch gun, a new depth charge, a new detonator testing apparatus, and a confidential bulletin on explosives used in naval warfare. The gun, the depth charge and the testing apparatus were produced in the Woolwich arsenal. Canaris had a number of agents planted there.

British intelligence knew pretty well what was going on. It knew, for example, that one man had met Canaris through a certain woman—for that woman was a British counter-espionage agent. The dossiers always alluded to her as *Miss X.* Her real name cannot be mentioned.

The purpose of Canaris' trip was the delicate work of laying the ground work. Later that year, Canaris and an agent met in Holland. Also present was an Englishman named Kelly. The rendezvous took place in the office of the German military attaché at the Hague. Kelly was an employee of the large Euston Shell factory in Lancashire. Canaris offered Kelly thirty pounds a week in return for gathering valuable information.

Kelly, however, had been under surveillance before he left England. A Scotland Yard man followed him throughout his trip, and upon his return he was arrested. He proved quite amenable to the proposals Scotland Yard laid before him. He would go on playing his part for the Nazis. He would supply them with bogus material which the British authorities would give him, and he would let the British authorities know everything he could discover about German espionage.

This channel between the British and German secret services was to make history because Admiral Canaris discovered that his own agents were British counter-spies. He did not arrest them; he kept his doors open. The war had started and he knew within a few months that America would enter the battle scene. Then Germany would lose.

It was through this secret channel—to which Canaris deliberately closed his eyes—that the British received most valuable information of high level German planning.

Canaris, the master mind, almost became spy chief for two countries. The British knew that it was Canaris who did not stop the flow of certain information after 1943. Canaris, seeing the disaster of Hitler ahead, hoped to save Germany by keeping open these undercover channels to Britain. He did it for Germany's future.

Those in Britain and Germany who indulge in hero worship for this strange man Canaris try to prove today that he sabotaged Hitler's orders and saved Churchill's life. This might or might not be true; we will never really know. But the fact remains that Canaris received orders to plot and execute a plan to shoot down Churchill's airplane on his return from Washington, D.C.

Ian Colvin describes this incident in his book, *Chief of Intelligence*. He tells how Mr. Churchill set out from England to the White House and returned via Algiers after the second Washington Conference, meeting Anthony Eden in North Africa on May 30, 1943. There, naturally, his presence was reported to Berlin by German agents, and the *Luftwaffe* was alerted to intercept his aircraft. It is probably to these circumstances that we owe the loss (so Colvin believes) of the British Overseas Airways liner that was shot down at sea by the *Luftwaffe* on June 1, 1943, on its return flight to London. The thirteen passengers and the crew all lost their lives, and the Wehrmacht communiqué of the day claimed it as a "transport aircraft." Leslie Howard and Mr. Alfred Chenfalls, a financial expert who bore a certain resemblance to Mr. Churchill and smoked cigars, were on board this aircraft and lost their lives with the rest. Mr. Churchill believes that Chenfalls, crossing over the airfield to the B.O.A.C. plane, may have been mistaken for himself and so provided a motive for this singular crime—for the B.O.A.C. airliner carrying freight and some diplomatic correspondence to and fro had been allowed to run unmolested by the *Luftwaffe* all these years.

Did Canaris deliberately "get" the wrong plans, as his friends claim?

We will never learn the truth. Though it is claimed Canaris saved Winston Churchill's life, he had at the same time employed the agent Cicero (Daniello) to steal the minutes of the Yalta and Teheran conferences from the British Ambassador in Turkey.

It was in 1943 that Canaris first felt sure that the Nazi war was hopeless. But before that his secret service planned the disaster at Scapa Flow, the landings of the Nazi spies from submarines on American shores, the weather station and radio wave espionage at Greenland and Spitsbergen, the world system of harbor espionage, and the work of agents in the Middle East, Latin America, France, Burma, and Indo-China.

Then the peace feelers came. Canaris became a part of these moves. He had contacts with the pope. His channels were open to Britain. He told them that the Russians were scouting for a German military group to make a separate peace—and this perhaps was the real reason for the many Western concessions given to Stalin at Yalta and Teheran.

Then the Stauffenberg-Gisevius bomb plot was organized against Hitler. After the bomb explosion, Stauffenberg called Canaris to tell him Hitler was dead. Canaris only asked, "Who did it, the Russians?"

Hitler was sure that Canaris was a part of the plot. In any case, an intelligence chief who could not protect the life of his Führer was better than useless to Hitler. Two days later Canaris was arrested in his villa at Schlactensee.

His wife knew nothing of his real activities, which he never officially confessed to. But the Germans—now losing the war —were jumpy. The Russians were at the Oder; the Hitler-Herren-Rase dream was almost over. In the prisons with Canaris were men like Schacht, Goerdeler, generals and gauleiters. The end of everything was near. Who would survive?

Then Canaris' successor, S.S. General Schellenberg, found some secret documents in Canaris' office: the record sheets of Corporal Hitler; a psychiatrist's report on him; a diary detailing the worst Nazi atrocities; and, most important of all, copies of secret correspondence with the pope's secretary in behalf of possible peace moves.

It was evidence enough that Canaris was critical of Hitler and believed he had lost the war. There was no evidence for the bomb plot for which he was imprisoned, but it was enough suspicion to hang him.

At the Flossenburg concentration camp, he was interrogated again and again. After the Nazis found Canaris' secret diary and atrocity reports, which they suspected he had sent also to the Vatican, Canaris was put into irons. Fellow prisoners reported he accepted his sufferings stoically.

By now the war was almost over. Italy had capitulated but Hitler still controlled the power of the Nazi storm troopers. On April 8, 1945, Canaris came to trial. S.S. Judge Thorbeck presiding, found him guilty of high treason. In totalitarian fashion, counsel was denied to the admiral, and he was returned to Berlin for speedy execution.

The list of victims was large and Canaris had to wait his turn. On his last night in the cell he knocked against the cell wall to his neighbor, Colonel Lunding, a Scandinavian secret service chief, and said:

"Das ist das Ende . . . schwer misshandelt, Nas gebrochen." (This is the end . . . badly mishandled, nose broken.)

He tapped out a last message to his wife and daughter. Then came his last hour. It was five in the morning. The execution guard had received extra rations of liquor and sausages—and Admiral Canaris died naked on the gallows with the words:

"I die for my fatherland. I have a clean conscience. I only did my duty to my fatherland when I tried to oppose the criminal folly of Hitler leading Germany to destruction. Long live Germany."

THE SPY CHIEF WHOM KHRUSHCHEV
KILLED

THE FOUR most powerful men in the world of espionage in our generation have been Russia's Lavrenti Beria, Germany's Admiral Canaris, Britain's Sir Percy Sillitoe, and the U.S.A.'s Allen Welsh Dulles.

Such men are men of almost limitless power, men who write the secret history of our age. In their sphere of political intrigue, military defense, and internal security they all are geniuses, men of imagination, brilliant men who have dedicated their lives to the grim profession of espionage.

These four spy masters, who have much in common—as secret service leaders the world over—represent two completely opposite ideologies, and the differences reflect in their methods of operation. The totalitarians have always accepted the techniques of the Inquisition: torture-forced confessions and assassination. The democratic nations' intelligence chiefs, however, have never forgotten their mandate from the people and their ultimate civilian control.

The most dangerous spy chief in the world was Lavrenti Pavlovich Beria, the chief of all Soviet intelligence. After the death of Joseph Stalin he was the uncrowned crown prince of world Communism and the No. 2 dictator of the Soviet Union, until he, too, was executed on the same charges with which he had condemned others, to make the road free for Nikita Khrushchev.

Lavrenti Pavlovich Beria looked oddly like a mild old bear and was certainly not the type one expected to find as chief of the famous MVD or of the NKVD. He smiled readily. He was by no means the man of cruel eyes and rapacious mouth whom the anti-Communists have tried to paint.

Beria worked in a cheerful office on Lubianka Street. Thousands of people worked under him, all of whom praised his friendliness, his amazing capacity for work (he often worked sixteen to twenty hours a day), and his consistent fairness to his associates. Legends have, of course, sprung up in wild profusion around the Ogpu (to use the initials more familiar than NKVD to the English-speaking world). The truth is much more sober. The Ogpu (*Obejedinenonnoe Gosudar stennoe Politicheskoye Upravlenie*) is no doubt one of the world's most efficient espionage and counter-espionage organizations.

Beria ruled over a global espionage network of 200,000 trained men and women of whom about 15,000 had received special expert training. His yearly budget ran up to one hundred million dollars. No Soviet espionage project from Klaus Fuchs to David Greenglass, from Richard Sorge to Ernst Wollweber, was organized without his knowledge of approval.

Because of his reliability and his long-standing personal friendship with the late Joseph Stalin, he held office longer than any of his predecessors—a good many of whom are no longer among the living. Soviet spy chiefs such as Yagoda and Yezhov, designers of the various Soviet purges, finally became victims and were themselves liquidated, too. Beria alone had survived, a Georgian from Stalin's and Malenkov's own home state. Now, in 1953, he, too, has known the relentless purge.

Edward Crankshaw, one of the most brilliant British journalists who served with the British military mission in Moscow during World War II, described Beria as

> . . . shortish, bald today, thick-necked, the face pallid in the Kremlin manner, the nose a little like a duck's bill, but sharp, the mouth tight and thin, the manner gentle and coldly, abstractedly benign—the whole effect of that pedantic aloofness which makes people think of scholar when they should really think of fanatics of the most dangerous kind.

Crankshaw even called him a "genius."

Beria gave the impression of being disillusioned and a little sad about his own disillusionment. In his early youth in Czarist Georgia he was a confirmed, God-fearing idealist who wanted to redeem the world and cast out all evil. Later he became an agnostic on philosophical grounds. But he speculated much and he stopped far short of militant atheism. He was well educated, spoke many languages, and quite casually quoted Persian poetry or bits of Heinrich Heine, Longfellow, and Elizabeth Browning.

He claimed to despise women, and contended that a man succeeds in socially useful work in the measure he is able to eliminate women from his life. He liked to refer to the story of Samson, interpreting it to mean that the Philistines sent the woman spy Delilah to destroy Samson. One suspected that Beria was really very shy and rather afraid of women. But there were a few women who were his good friends, and Beria set friendship very high in his scale of values. He could also be ruthless and cruel, however, to a degree which might have made even the Gestapo falter. The cruelties in the North Korean prisoner of war camps and the hardship experiences of German prisoners of war came under Beria's jurisdiction. He would often abstain from killing a woman agent or from beating her; but on the other hand, he subjected women to hearings lasting fifty hours without a pause.

Beria was born in Tiflis in 1899, of good family. In his student days he became infected with the prevalent spirit of revolution. In 1915, a Czarist court martial sentenced him to death for the crime of spreading revolutionary propaganda within the Caucasian army. While in prison awaiting execution, he managed to escape. He took to the mountains and lived the hard life of a fugitive. Then he became a partisan, and kept in steady contact with the leader of the Russian underground—Stalin. He studied the treatises of Lenin, and read Pushkin and Karl Marx. He obtained weapons from the army and took a hand in getting money for the Communist party. Like Dostoevski, he cried for abstract justice and truth in Russia. With the Bolsheviks, he prepared for the coming revolution.

Finally the great storm broke. Beria joined the workers in the Baku oil fields. After some time the private detectives of the Nobel Oil Refinery discovered what he was up to, and to stay would have meant death. Beria dressed in the cumbersome costume of a Tartar woman, sneaked through the enemy lines, and escaped death a second time. He reached the ancient Balkan city Albana, the old capital of what is now Albania. There he met other revolutionaries who helped him. One was a young Communist who, like Beria, thirsted for adventure and was willing to stake his life, if the cause were high enough. He was a handsome, bold young man named Josip Broz, who today is known to the world as Marshal Tito.

In his wanderings through the Balkan cities, Beria discovered how easy it was to fake a passport whenever he needed a new one. It could be counterfeited or else bought from some poor worker or farmer. Armed with a new passport and a new birth certificate, Beria returned to Russia to take part in Lenin's revolution. In his travels he used various aliases, such as Vanno Tcheshivili and Garabet Abamalek. After all, aliases were the fashion among revolutionaries. The names Lenin and Stalin were aliases, too.

As Garabet Abamalek, he commanded a group of five hundred Communists, former Austrian prisoners of war, in their fight against the White Guards. While engaged in this, Beria-Abamalek hit upon the scheme of sending some of his men as deserters to the Whites. They were to join up with the enemy and win confidence by giving them fake information about the Reds. These "deserters" were Russia's first military intelligence officers.

His work did not go unnoticed. The Moscow government decided that such a man should be given greater responsibilities.

We find Beria in 1920 in Prague, ancient capital of Bohemia. He was a member of the Ukrainian Embassy in the newly established nation of Czechoslovakia. His secret business was espionage. With Prague as his seat of operations, he organized a Russian counter-espionage system which covered the continent of Europe. Every White Russian *émigré* was listed and the more dangerous ones shadowed. All the Czarist officers were carefully watched, for the Russians at that time seriously feared the Czarist clique.

The legend spread around the world that this master mind of Cheka spy activities was a mild-mannered, understanding Communist who was different from all the other terrorists. This misconception could be easily exposed even in early phases of the Russian revolution, but it still prevails.

The man whom the Kremlin had sent to the Baku oil fields, who had to carry out the harsh orders of mass collectivization, irrigation, control of the Moslem element, and disciplining the mountain peasants, was anything but a mild man. The Kremlin had chosen the toughest man available, a man who knew the mild approach but also used the Bolshevik whip as a weapon if he were disobeyed.

The Soviets always feared resistance inside their country, whether it was during the Hitler war in 1942 or in 1924 when Moscow faced a full-fledged civil war in Georgia. It was Lavrenti Beria who had to suppress the 1924 rebellion of the Kuban Cossacks and the hundred thousand small landowners and poor farmers who were called—in party jargon—"kulaks." They were shipped or deported like cattle in box cars to the far-off ice deserts of the Arctic or the vast Siberian plains.

Beria returned to Moscow a total victor. He was Stalin's loyal servant who had secured the power for the state and the Communist party. Stalin rewarded him with party leadership in Georgia. Later he asked him to set into practice some of the Communist International secret service ideas. Beria was sent abroad.

Nine years later, when Beria was attached to the Soviet Embassy in Paris, he was also one of the department chiefs of the Foreign Department of the Ogpu and had to report to Stalin personally on his foreign observations.

In France, Beria accomplished a masterpiece of espionage. So far as the French authorities knew, this man was in France officially on diplomatic business. Unofficially he was virtually reborn. He cast off the old-fashioned pince-nez he ordinarily wore and even gave up his beloved cigars. He took daily walks down the broad avenues of Paris. He did this with a stately air and he invariably dressed in a Czarist uniform. He was seen at the Café de la Paix and the Champs Elysées, again always in uniform, and wearing an arrogant expression which went well with his new identity—Colonel Yenonlidze, who had lost his fortune in Russia and was an arch-hater of the Bolsheviks.

As Colonel Yenonlidze, Beria indicated his interest in cooperating with anyone who would overthrow the Stalin regime. He met Ukrainian Fascists, Japanese agents, and White Russian officers who had contacts with Mussolini and were already hand-in-glove with Hitler's young movement. To all of them, he aired his plans. He knew ways to smuggle agents into Russia by way of the Estonian border. He contributed articles to the Russian émigré press. It was not hard for him to become popular in the White Russian circles. His articles were incisive and brilliant, as was his conversation, which was interlarded with quotations from Persian poetry. He came to be looked upon as quite a leader among the émigrés.

It was here that Beria laid a foundation for a network of Fascist agents which many, many years later would become useful to the Soviet apparatus. Later, Beria was able to utilize Fascists inside the governments of Germany (the Rote Kapelle spy ring), of Japan (through Richard Sorge), and inside Italy (through friends of Mussolini's mistress Clara Petacci). Some of these former Fascists also became willing tools for the Russian spy service during and after World War II.

But in 1931 Beria still played, to perfection, the role of the sincere Czarist officer who hated the Stalin regime.

In two years he had learned whatever there was to be known about the network of counter-revolution. It spread from Japan to Manchuria and China, to Germany and Poland and the Baltic countires. Russian Czarist officers had established themselves in the secret services of all these nations and worked for their own ends. It was Beria who exposed them—not publicly, but very privately to the Soviet secret service. His investigations, begun as far back as 1929, uncovered most of Russia's counter-revolutionary patriots.

That was why Russia was able to exterminate her "fifth column" and Stalin's personal enemies in the controversial Moscow trials, before they had a chance to strike. The archenemy Trotsky was assassinated in Mexico and Beria had advance notice. Dangerous spies and Czarist generals working from Paris were kidnaped and put out of the way. The leading spirit behind these purges was Lavrenti Beria.

From 1930 to 1937 he traveled all over Europe, inspecting and re-inspecting Russia's espionage network for possible weak links. He had come to feel that the major problem was to strengthen and safeguard Russia's military position, rather than to waste time on the complicated quarrels within the various Communist parties of Europe. He even decided that it would be wiser for the Soviets to employ non-Communist agents rather than party members in the various countries. Like most Russians, he was converted during that period from an International Communist to a plain Russian.

Beria went to Spain during the civil war to study combat espionage in action. He spirited away German models of tanks and guns, and was especially interested in their anti-aircraft guns on which a new Russian model was to be based.

In 1938 Stalin called the thirty-nine-year-old Beria to Moscow—an airplane was even sent to pick him up. He was nineteen years younger than Stalin, nine years younger than

Molotov, and three years older than today's chief Malenkov. In the Politbureau itself, everyone was older than he: Bulganin, Andreyev, Kaganovitch, Kikoyan, Shvernik, and Khrushev.

Stalin appointed him to the country's most important job: to bring an end to the megalomania and the mad purges which were weakening the army, the party, the entire country: to bring unity to the country. Enough party leaders had died, and war would come soon. Beria was to do constructive work for Bolshevism.

Beria became overnight the mightiest man in the land— next to Stalin. He was the uncrowned czar of all concentration camps, slave labor camps, corrective labor institutions, and mines; he was master of the midnight arrest, chief of the courts where men and women were sentenced without hearing, and boss of the secret forces which threw men and women into oblivion.

He became Yezhov's successor—chief of all Soviet intelligence.

Beria, however, was not presented to the country as the new police chief of world Communism but as Stalin's closest friend, a man to be trusted. A book he had once written was now re-issued. In it Stalin was portrayed as Lenin's assistant and right-hand man; Beria glorified his chief in the early days of revolution. Actually it was Beria who had started the legend that Stalin was Lenin's real and only intimate.

Stalin praised this new NKVD chief, who had been chief of the Georgian Ogpu, then for a while secretary of the Georgian Communist party and as such virtually Stalin's governor over all of Georgia—at the time the most notorious, difficult, and turbulent of all Soviet republics.

Beria had a double task at home and abroad. He continued to infiltrate foreign governments with Soviet agents. A German-Russian alliance was possible in the future; but Soviet agents had to be inside the Goering Luftwaffe Ministry, inside Hitler's Reichschancellery. The idea of organizing a Soviet spy ring inside Europe's governments—the so-called "Red Orchestra" (Rote Kapelle)— took form.

In 1938, just after he had been promoted to the head of the entire Ogpu apparatus, he summoned his ten best agents to Moscow. A conference was held at Lubianka Street. It is not known what was discussed, but it is known that in the next two months ten Soviet agents were smuggled into Hitlerite Germany. They entered from England, from Belgium, from Norway, from Italy. They had foolproof passports; some were even equipped with the names of German aristocrats. Beria had a number of tricks for obtaining passports. He could have them expertly counterfeited—a subagent of his, Rudolf Haus, had a very fine counterfeiting outfit. Another method was to get Communists in other countries to take out passports and send them to the Ogpu, which distributed them to its agents. Spain was a bonanza for passports. Thousands of volunteers who came to fight for the Loyalists from all parts of the world lent their American, Swedish, Dutch, or French passports to the Ogpu, which used them for a while and then returned them. Fascists taken prisoner in Spain carried passports which could be used, too.

These ten agents belonged to a secret section of the Ogpu, the N.O. 7, a department devoted to obtaining blueprints or models of the latest armament of the great powers.

These agents were exceptional. They went to Lübeck and to Dessau and to the other cities where Stukas, dive bombers, and fighters were being built. They had plenty of money to work with. They opened neat diners near the armament plants, where workers in the aircraft industry went to eat. They also set up shabby little saloons with "hot" shows and pretty girls to entertain the workers. They went to the hidden underground Communist cells in Germany and organized them for industrial espionage. The very same year that Hitler struck at Austria and Czechoslovakia, Lubianka Street had possession of Hitler's latest airplanes in blueprints. They were the He 70; the Ju 60; the Focke-Wulf A 43; the Junkers G 38.

Beria had not only outwitted Admiral Canaris; he had outwitted the secret services of all other countries. Beria produced results. His foreign reports were correct. Czechoslovakia was betrayed, Britain and France split, North America isolationist, and South America disinterested. Beria was right when he informed Stalin that Hitler was ready to talk terms and would offer a friendship pact which would give time for Russia's defense plans.

His former Fascist friends in the European governments had delivered the information. His "Rote Kapelle" agents inside the Nazi government had the secret news of the new alliance plans weeks in advance. In the fall of 1939, after the Molotov-Ribbentrop friendship pact was signed, Beria was appointed automatically to the inner committee on defense which conducted the war.

Beria was not ever fooled by the "friendshhip" pact. His Nazi friends, working for him, informed him of German preparations in the Baltic, in Poland, in Finland and the Balkans. Hitler would invade Russia—sooner or later. While the Soviets were speaking of friendship and delivering oil and war material as a token friendship to Hitler, Stalin knew Beria was spying on the Germans day and night.

Beria knew what a rapid turnover there is in secret agents. They are either unmasked or they are arrested and shot. He had to replace hundreds of agents. Many of them wore the Nazi uniforms. Beria calculated as follows: the Communists had received five million votes before Hitler took power. Of the five million there should be at least five hundred left who would be willing to pretend they were good Nazis while actually working for Beria in the disguise of their SA or SS Elite Guard uniforms.

The flying robot bombs which did so much damage to England were not solely discovered by British aerial photographs taken of their launching points in France and Peenemünde. Long before that, British intelligence officers had received warnings from Beria. He knew from reports of the Communist underground that Germany was building the robot planes. He knew that workers assigned to their construction were being kept in strict isolation, segregated even from their families. Beria even knew the location of some underground factories.

Beria followed the party line of world Communism in the most minute detail. He knew Russia was fighting not only Hitler and the stormtrooping Germans but also world capitalism which, after the invasion of Russia, was to become a temporary ally. He knew that Russia had to weaken capitalism and, for that reason, the world's most guarded secrets which were actually in his hands were never given to the allies. The secret of the plan and date of attack on Pearl Harbor was deliberately kept by the Soviets. Beria had received this information from his own agent inside the German Embassy in Tokyo: Richard Sorge.

The war brought Beria into the Soviet triumvirate which would succeed Stalin after his death—Molotov, Malenkov, Beria. In 1946 Beria was rewarded with full membership in the Politbureau and was called the one man, next to Malenkov, closest to Stalin. He was chosen to write the leading front page article in Pravda on Stalin's birthday and to hail and praise the dictator—a great honor and a sign that he enjoyed full confidence.

He was in complete charge of all fifth column activities, the military, naval, and scientific espionage of the country, as well as the Cominform, until his liquidation in the summer of 1953. He was chief of all atomic energy and hydrogen bomb research and production in Russia. His espionage service delivered formulas and uranium samples from Canada through Dr. Allan Nunn May; other atomic secrets from Britain through Dr. Klaus Fuchs and Bruno Pontecorvo; and invaluable scientific information from the United States through Harry Gold, David Greenglass, the two Rosenbergs, and many others.

Beria had the scientific results of atomic research on his desk when American cabinet members and generals were declaring: "Russia will need fifteen years to produce the atom bomb."

Although the Soviet atom spies caught by the Western secret service are in prison today, their findings have been put into active production.

Beria became more than a spy organizer, a brilliant master mind of intelligence work. He was a political conspirator who one day might have succeeded Malenkov, if the power conflict had not turned against him. It was his political ambitions which were his final undoing. He had said quite openly:

"Stalin has laid down a program of action for Communists. They must, he says: (1) exploit all differences and contradictions in the bourgeois camp; (2) take concrete action to unite the working classes of the economically advanced countries with the national liberation movements of the colonies and dependent nations; (3) complete the struggle for the unity of the trade union movement; (4) take active measures to bring together the proletariat and the small peasants; (5) support Soviet rule and disrupt the interventionist machinations of the imperialists against the Soviet Union, bearing in mind that the Soviet Union is the base of the revolutionary movement in all countries."

Beria's greatest value to Soviet Russia was his long-range strategy of political conspiracy. I remember that in 1940 Chinese Communists living in Europe, Swedish "comrades," Danish seamen, and German conspirators were ordered to Shanghai into a China which was to be taken over ten years later by Mao Tse-tung at a moment when the West was divided, ill-advised, and confused, and could not stop the conquest of the Communist International.

Beria's agents were planted everywhere. The vanguard of his dark war of invaders operated inside governments, embassies, police corps, unions, colleges, schools, and churches. It also worked inside factories and through "peace" movements. The intelligence machine Beria inherited in 1938 was monstrous, but it was really an amateur outfit compared with the scientific, military, and political organization Beria later developed. His machine had one dominant purpose: to bring to the world the dictatorship of the proletariat under the leadership of the Communist party of the Soviet Union. His own power grew by the day. Then suddenly, on July 9, 1953, the Moscow radio announced: "The Central Committee of the Communist Party of the Soviet Union held a plenary meeting . . . as regards the criminal, anti-party, and anti-state actions of L. P. Beria . . . as an enemy of the Communist Party and the Soviet people."

The purger was purged. Beria was eliminated and liquidated as the result of a long-standing feud with the Krushchev faction, and his fate had been decided long before Stalin died. Beria had too much power. His ambitions had menaced the balance of the Soviet power structure. The security chief was not saved by Stalin's death; moreover in the new set-up he quickly seized more power than he had ever held before. Khrushchev felt that the need for his removal was urgent.

Beria's fate was hastened by a strange incident that occurred late on the night of May 30, 1953. According to United Nations sources, Malenkov's and Khrushchev's car was shot at by MVD soldiers as it was leaving the Kremlin through Spasski Gate. Allegedly, the chauffeur had not given the signal required of all government cars and had failed to halt to show his pass. A shot injured the driver, but Malenkov and Khrushchev were unhurt.

Beria showed great concern, and had both the chauffeur and the MVD soldier arrested. He fired even Colonel General Sergei N. Kruglov as commander of the Kremlin guards.

But this incident convinced Khrushchev that Beria had tried to assassinate him under cover of a clever stage setting. He accused Beria of trying to get Stalin's post—just as Stalin had accused Trotsky of the same crime. The party was only too happy to co-operate with Malenkov. Beria was arrested at a routine conference of the Presidium (formerly the Politburo). Taken completely by surprise, Beria had no chance to alert his personal following; and all exits at the Lubianka were barred by army soldiers. Darkness fell at noon.

The man who had sent millions of innocent people to prison and to slave labor camps became himself a doomed prisoner, accused of crimes so vast that his jailers planned no mercy for him. Not since the purges of Beria's predecessors, Yagoda and Yezhov, has Soviet "justice" been so fitting.

Colonel General Kruglov succeeded Beria. Soviet Russia's secret service continued with business as ususal. Beria had made history, a history written in blood.

VIDKUN QUISLING

MANY traitors have infiltrated governments—but few men in history have been capable of capturing whole governments.

The prototype of the master of the twentieth century *coup d'etat* was not Mao Tse-tung nor the kingpins of the Soviet satellite empire but a man who added a new word to the languages of the world: Quisling.

On July 18,1887, in Telemark in southern Norway, Vidkun Abraham Lauritz Quisling was born.

His childhood was unhappy. The boy spoke an uncouth country dialect and was teased by his schoolmates. Entering school late in the year, he was put into the second grade, although he could not yet read or write and, consequently, he was at the foot of the class for some time. As his Nazi biographer puts it, "the marks of this humiliation burnt themselves upon his memory." And "he was always homesick. He disliked the town and all it stood for. His sole desire was to go home."

Fear, loneliness, injured pride, and the feeling of being one against many, seem often to be characteristic features in the personality development of the would-be dictator.

But later Quisling turned out to be a brilliant student. He was graduated with high honors and entered upon a military career. In the military academy he was considered the most promising of the cadets, and two years later was graduated from the military college with a "recommendation to the King," a citation which had never been given before.

In 1911 he became a probationer on the general staff. He was promoted to captain in 1917 and during World War I his sentiments were pro-British. After serving as military attaché in Leningrad in 1918, he was for two years military attaché and secretary to the legation at Helsinki. Here he met the great explorer and philanthropist, Professor Fridtjof Nansen, and at Nansen's request directed the International Russian Relief Organization in the Ukraine and the Crimea during 1922-23. He also assisted Nansen in 1924-26, during Nansen's great relief work in Russia and Armenia under the auspices of the League of Nations.

Nansen was one of Norway's greatest men. He received the Nobel prize for his humanitarian work; he also won fame as an explorer of the North Pole and the Arctic regions. In him were combined the faculties of the great scientist and the spirit of the great liberal. Quisling was proud to work with Nansen, and under his influence declared that liberal democracy is the only government that can bring human happiness. For many years, too, Quisling was an admirer of Soviet Russia; he stayed some time in Moscow, and in 1923 he married a Russian girl and later had to assure his Nazi friends of his wife's "Aryan" descent.

When diplomatic relations between Great Britain and Soviet Russia were broken off in May, 1927, he was appointed secretary of the Norwegian Legation in Moscow, charged with the duty of guarding British interests in Russia. Quisling, who was to become the arch-hater of Great Britain during World War II, was awarded the Order of the British Empire for his services.

In 1928 he retired from active military service, since the general staff refused to give him further extension of his leave, and he stayed in Russia for a year.

In an autobiographical note written in 1930, he said: "My strong, and perhaps predominant, interests are politics and science. In politics it is chiefly Russia that has interested me. With this nation my activities have been closely connected for the last twelve years."

When Quisling returned from Russia in 1930 he found himself out of a job, receiving half pay as an officer in the reserve. Here was a man of high gifts and equally high ambition, who, returning from great enterprises abroad, finds that his abilities are spurned at home. Quisling soon became convinced that he was the victim of persecution.

In compensation he decided to create the career for which he believed himself destined, no matter how desperate the means. He was prepared to give himself to any political party or group that could bestow on him the role of leader.

Once he suggested to the Socialists that he form "Red Guards" and become the Trotsky of Norway. Of this there is documentary proof. He actually wanted to organize armed workers' groups to initiate insurrection and revolution after the Soviet manner.

Communists and Socialists rejected the suggestion with some fierceness. Both were positive that Quisling was a British agent; surely a man with a British service medal would not turn to radicals without a concealed motive.

If Quisling had been accepted by the left radicals he would certainly have risen to become a formidable leader. But rejected by Communists and Socialists, he had no other haven but the circles of conservative and semi-fascist elements in Norway.

When, in May 1931, the new conservative government of the Farmers' Party made Major Vidkun Quisling minister of defense, he was still scarcely known to the public. Nevertheless, he was received with a good deal of approval. For the first time in many years the ministry was to be headed by a professional soldier. Quisling's brilliant intellectual record became known, and his work with Nansen in Russia was given due credit. Moreover, he was without a past as a politician.

Quisling's function in the new government was to carry out a drastic reduction in Norway's defense expenditures. Quisling was an efficient defense minister who kept his papers in order, but otherwise it was difficult to form an estimate of him. He gave the impression of being a silent and lonely man. But all at once the dignity that cloaked his secretive personality was suddenly torn away by the famous "assault case" in the ministry. I narrate it according to his own account.

On the evening of February 2, 1932, Quisling went to his office. As he was passing through a darkened room, someone suddenly threw pepper in his eyes, stabbed at him with a knife and beat him on the head so that he lost consciousness. The culprit was never found, and the affair soon became a subject of rumor and speculation. It was suggested that the attack had been arranged in order to get publicity, or that it was connected with some love affair. Officially the case has never been solved, but the chief of police intelligence privately stated that "it was a swindle, pure and simple."

But the case received wide publicity, and everyone in Norway became aware of Vidkun Quisling, who had narrowly escaped assassination. What part Quisling himself played in the assault is equally obscure; it was not he, but an enterprising friend of his who reported the case to the police. The affair roused such a sensation that for months afterwards the name of Quisling made the headlines on any pretext.

Vidkun Quisling utilized the rather embarrassing pepper-and-knife episode as the motive for an incendiary speech he made in the Storting about two months later. The speech came as an utter surprise to his colleagues in the government. He spoke darkly of the activities of subversive and destructive forces, hinting that he possessed conclusive proofs that the leaders of the Labor Party were guilty of high treason and were on the payroll of the Ogpu. Everyone was alarmed. He was asked to produce his evidence, and a special investigating committee was appointed. The evidence proved to be certain antiquated documents from the archives of the defense ministry and the police. Quisling himself could not muster any new or plausible contribution. The committee, alas, could make only a very bare report. Not even the members of the minister's own party would commit themselves further. The scandal shook his position.

When Quisling, together with the other minsters of his party, left the cabinet, he must have realized that he would never again be invited into the government, by his party or by any other party. The dubious pepper assault was not forgotten, and public opinion had marked him as a scandalmonger and alarmist.

His only recourse was to start his own movement. There was but one man who would understand him and employ him. Quisling paid a visit to Berlin. After an interview with Hitler, the Nasjonal Samling (National Union) was born; this happened in May, 1933. It presented candidates at the general elections held in the same year. In not a single constituency did the National Union receive more than a fraction of the votes necessary to secure a seat in Parliament under Norway's system of proportional representation.

From the very beginning Quisling's party copied Nazi methods: uniforms, marches, strange emblems, espionage groups, and, above all, the "Fuehrer" principle. It never had followers among mature responsible citizens but like many other mystical and foggy political creeds, it succeeded in gathering a group of the youthful and uncritical around Quisling. For the 1936 elections the party staged such a tremendous propaganda campaign, with considerable funds from Germany and the Nordic Society, that even its opponents were surprised when the election results were published. Not even 2 per cent of the votes went to the Nasjonal Samling, and again the party sent no representatives to the Storting. After this disaster the party began to disintegrate. The few clever and ambitious men within the party now deserted it, telling Quisling that he had caused the defeat by his incompetence and inability to co-operate.

After this defeat, Vidkun Quisling vanished into oblivion. The Norwegians ignored him completely. Only his weekly newspaper, *Fritt Folk* (*Free People*), remained.

I wanted to see this defeated man. I recognized, of course, that at the moment Quisling did not loom as a danger to Norway. But I knew also that he was only a tool of Hitler's; if he had dropped out of sight for the present, it was in order to prepare secretly for the future. Moreover, I was convinced that Quisling and his men were engaged in espionage activities for Admiral Canaris.

In 1937, *Folket i Bild*, a Swedish magazine, and several American newspapers had sent me to Norway to interview Leon Trotsky. I decided also to interview Vidkun Quisling.°

When I entered his small newspaper office, I found him sitting behind a desk covered with newspapers. He greeted me with the words, "Well, what kind of lies do *you* want to concoct about me?"

I replied I would write only the truth and asked why a man like him preferred to work with the Germans rather than with the Norwegians.

Quisling showed signs of interest. He asked me whether I considered him a traitor, as everyone else did. I countered that I could answer that question only after the interview. A frown spread over his plump, swollen face, but he began to talk freely. I took notes of what he said to me and later entered them in my journal.

"To tell the truth," Quisling began, "I don't give a hang what people say about me." He explained that Norway was a small country and must inevitably remain tied to the apron strings of the great powers. Germany had entered on a period of rejuvenation. To be sure, the rejuvenation necessitated brutality and concentration camps, but if one had seen as much as he had—famine in Russia, extermination in Armenia —one was forced to believe that the majority of mankind

° See *Duel for the Northland* (New York: McBride, 1943).

were illiterates, that the people could not rule themselves, and that it was essential for a few chosen intelligent men to take over the business of government.

"I've seen the Labor Party send a charwoman to Parliament. What did she know about politics?"

Quisling was embittered. During the two hours I spent with him I did not once see him laugh or smile.

"We represent the New Europe," he said, "the Europe of Youth. We want new methods, and the methods of Hitler will bring us to our goal. If I pronounce myself for dictatorship, I do so irrespective of Hitler, simply because I believe dictatorship is the form of government that will prevail in the future. I have studied history; whenever a liberal age failed, as it did in Greece and Rome, dictators came to rescue the people. Did not Napoleon save France from dissolution?"

"But you cannot rule against the will of the people, can you?" I asked. "And the people rejected you in the last elections."

"When I come to power, and I will come to power, elections will be abolished," he declared. "Are women whose talents are limited to the art of cooking to have power over me? Are workers whom the capitalists consistently exploit to govern? No, I do not need the people."

Two months before the invasion of Norway, *Fritt Folk* became a daily newspaper. Quisling had been to Berlin and received new funds. But no one bothered much about it, nor about the fact that in the winter of 1939-40 Quisling made several trips to Germany. The purpose of these trips has since become tragically clear.

Quisling knew about the coming invasion and was even informed of some details. He himself wrote leaflets and proclamations which were printed in Berlin. The Fuehrer-elect spent the night of April 8-9, 1940, at the Hotel Continental in Oslo, where the Germans were to make their headquarters the following day. Throughout the early hours of the morning he walked restlessly in his rooms, nervously awaiting those who were to meet him there. And in the evening his name was announced over the radio as the new prime minister. This was the first great mistake the Nazis made in Norway.

Premier Quisling established himself in the Storting. He published a list of ministers, with many posts unfilled. Many of those included in the list promptly announced that they would have nothing to do with the traitor. His one official act was to issue a treacherous order canceling mobilization; it did not prevent thousands of young men from slipping through the German lines to join the free Norwegian army. He gave another order to all Norwegian ships to go to neutral ports; the order was not obeyed by one ship in a thousand.

It was not until 1942 that Hitler and Quisling decided to employ pure terrorism in Norway. Other methods had failed to pacify the country, and Nazi generals were warning him of the possibility of an Allied invasion of Norway.

Quisling could never walk the streets of any Norwegian town unguarded. In 1942 fifty men watched over him day and night. The Norwegian Nazi puppet had built for himself a new sixty-thousand-dollar "Northern Berchtesgaden" near Oslo, where he lived under the increased protection of one hundred and fifty guards who manned machine gun posts twenty-four hours a day.

He maintained one hundred and fifty storm troopers on duty constantly both at his new retreat and when he moved about the country. Fearful of poisoning, he refused to eat or drink until the food or liquid had been tasted by someone else.

His house was furnished with property confiscated from Norwegian patriots. Quisling had a number of masterpieces on the walls of his estate and a large library comprised entirely of books seized by the Germans and his own storm troopers.

In his vanity Quisling even demanded that his portrait be placed in schoolrooms and affixed to stamps; but here he was overruled by Gauleiter Terboven, who declared that Adolf Hitler's portrait was sufficient.

Quisling told the Norwegians—who hated him more than any figure has been hated throughout the heroic history of Norway—that he was the successor to the king and that Haakon VII would never return to his people.

In 1942 Quisling declared himself Fuehrer of Norway. In German fashion, he held a torchlight procession in honor of the new order. But even while he was celebrating his coronation as Norway's hangman, the railroad stations of Oslo were burned, there were bomb explosions throughout the city, and fires burst out in many important Nazi offices.

From 1940 to 1942 Quisling organized a spy machine in Norway and abroad. The Norwegian ships that had been caught in Swedish ports were desperately trying to break through the Nazi blockade in order to reach England. The spy apparatus set up by Quisling denounced these ships to the German submarines. Some were torpedoed, some forced to flee back to Sweden, and only a few succeeded in reaching England safely.

The idea of reorganizing a Norwegian secret service was Quisling's own; his suggestion was at once taken up by the Nazis. But aside from the affair of the Norwegian ships in Sweden, Quisling had little to show for his efforts. He even experimented with espionage in America, among people of Norwegian descent, but accomplished nothing.

Quisling's end was not sudden. It was bitter and dramatic, though not as spectacular as his rise to power. The last days of the Nazi empire brought total destruction and defeat to Quisling's world. Nazi officers offered him space on a small submarine heading for Spain, but he declined.

The Allies landed and very soon Quisling was arrested. What would the Norwegians do with him now? Would they shoot him without a trial?

The land of Fridtjof Nansen and Haakon the Great behaved as any democracy should. There was no military trial, no court martial, no mob aroused to kill the traitor. When the trial finally started on August 20, 1945, there were very few on the streets to watch Quisling being transported from his twelfth century Akerhus fortress-prison to Oslo's historic Logan Hall.

But the courtroom was crowded. There were a hundred and fifty newspaper correspondents from all corners of the world; there were a hundred photographers and diplomatic representatives.

Ashen-faced, trembling, anything but a Viking hero, Quisling faced Annaeus Schjoedt, the prosecutor.

The Norwegian government had made it a point to bring Quisling to trial for common and brutal murder, for desertion from the Norwegian army at war with Hitler, for stealing property and amassing a private fortune of over one million Norwegian crowns.

Quisling pleads "not guilty."

The judge turns over the state's case to the prosecutor, who is cool and legal-minded.

"Did you plan the invasion of Norway together with German leaders before it actually happened on April 9, 1940?"

Quisling denies the charge.

The prosecutor goes on. "Did you ever meet Alfred Rosenberg?"

Quisling at first denies that he had known this commissar of Nazi Weltanschauung.

But in his hands the prosecutor holds the answer. Three days before the trial, the war crime commission had found Alfred Rosenberg's diary. The prosecutor now starts to read from it, and indictment after indictment rains upon Quisling.

Rosenberg Diaries:

December 14, 1939: The step in planning the Norway action is now complete. The Fuehrer read through Quisling's proposal of the Greater German Federation.

March 6, 1940: Yesterday Hagelin (Quisling's courier) returned from Oslo with a message that Britain and France were preparing to invade Norway.

April 9, 1940: Today is a great day in Germany's history for Denmark and Norway have been occupied. Now Quisling can form his government.

Then letters are read from Quisling to Hitler and Hitler to Quisling. The would-be dictator sits down sullen and defiant, and finally admits he had met Rosenberg to discuss a plan for invasion. The prosecution has made its point. They have their evidence for charges of high treason. Quisling jumps from his seat and yells, "I cannot remember all this. I was only the Savior of Norway."

This he is to repeat at least twenty times during the trial.

Quisling, who denies he ever received any money from the Nazis, was in fact subsidized with $40,000 a week. Only a few months before the invasion of Norway he had brought a coal company to import coal from Germany. The coal barges came into Norwegian harbors and in the bottoms there were Nazi soldiers hidden, the shock troops for the invasion of Norway.

"Did you ever meet Admiral Raeder?"

Quisling cannot remember until the war crime commission presents testimony from Admiral Erich Raeder. In addition it reveals documents from the Nazi general staff proving that Admiral Raeder had been furious about the information Quisling had given for the Nazi invasion of the harbor of Narvik. The data was wrong, and the Nazi losses were heavy because Quisling's naval intelligence had been lax.

The prosecution proves that the man who "wanted to spare Norway" had drawn up plans for the invasion of Iceland, Greenland, and the Faroe Islands to give Germany mastery of the Atlantic. The prosecution has also secured the original copies of the Quisling plan for "Operation Arctic."

The next point of the indictment seems to hurt Quisling more than any other charge. As a former major in the Norwegian army he had his post assigned to a motorized unit in case of invasion. When Hitler invaded the country with his aid, Quisling did not show up at his mobilization post and could be legally charged with desertion. He, the man who always spoke about military honor and pride, is now charged with desertion. He sits trembling.

"I am not a deserter, I'm not a traitor. The King had told me he would abdicate. . . . I was the savior of Norway when King and Government were running away."

Through the Norwegian Justice Department, King Haakon declares that he had never informed Quisling that he wanted to abdicate.

Quisling is now near tears; his voice breaks. The prosecution asks, "What did you own before April 9, 1940, before the invasion?"

"Just furniture and little property."

"What do you possess today?"

Quisling refuses to answer, but the prosecution proves that he owns Gimble castle; that he has stolen valuable art pieces, and has cash on hand of 1,040,000 Kroner ($260,000).

Quisling cannot control himself any longer. He shouts, "Isn't is sufficient to impute politically unclean motives to my actions? You also try to make me out a scoundrel and swindler generally."

This is exactly what the Norwegian government wants to do. They produce a receipt for 100,000 Marks for subsidies which Alfred Rosenberg had given Quisling before the invasion. They charge him with the criminal murder of two members of the underground. (They could charge him with the killing of thousands more.) They prove that Quisling had asked the Nazis to deport two hundred and fifty Norwegian officers to a German concentration camp in order to be rid of their opposition.

He is further charged with murdering 1,000 of Norway's 1,500 Jews; they charge also that it was he who personally signed the order to arrest every Norwegian of Jewish faith.

"Insanity" is mentioned by both sides. But Quisling was obviously not insane to Hitler, or to his own followers. The leading psychiatrists of Norway blame his uncontrollable lust for power more than anything else for his behavior.

Prosecutor Schjoedt winds up his case by stating: "It may be rare luck for Norway that this man cuts such a poor figure at this moment. Instead of standing up in manly fashion and acknowledging his faults, Quisling has chosen to deny and not to remember everything detrimental to his case. Or he blames the Germans. He is so small in defeat and adversity that he is contemptible."

A weak smile is Quisling's only answer.

In his final words at the trial he says, "I have done nothing wrong. I prevented Norway and the North from becoming a theatre of conflict and here I stand charged with treason. I am innocent."

He explains that he is an idealist and patriot and that he could have had high office elsewhere. Trotsky, he claims, had offered him in Russia the post of chief of staff and he had declined it in the early twenties.

His defense attorney speaks for six hours, asking for mercy.

After proclamation of the death sentence, there are only twenty-nine persons who wait at the prison to see him.

His wife Maria is the last to visit him, before ten policemen —not soldiers—fulfill the execution order. Five men shoot blank cartridges. The witnesses of the execution are a doctor, a clergyman, and his defense counsel. The press is barred.

His last words to the world are these: "If this is treason—I hope more of Norway's sons will be traitors . . . no prophet was ever well received in his native country."

Quisling, known to the world as the greatest traitor of our century, is far less known for his spy activities. For years Quisling delivered military information to Hitler and on the day of the Nazi invasion, troops swarmed in and took over certain strategic positions which had been pinpointed by the Major himself.

THE LONG WAIT

His COLD eyes glittering, Admiral Karl Doenitz, commander of Germany's U-boat fleet at the outbreak of World War II, turned from studying a huge wall map to the young submarine commander standing stiffly to attention beside him. It was a Sunday morning in October 1939. The war was a month old.

"Everything hangs on a sudden and surprise attack," exclaimed Doenitz. "There are seven entrances to Scapa Flow. A determined submarine commander would be able to make a penetration despite the swift and treacherous currents."

His mouth creased into a thin smile. "The British Admiralty believe that the three blockships sunk here"—his finger stabbed the wall map—"in Kirk Sound are adequate protection for the capital ships lying in the anchorage."

The submarine commander, whose name was Guenther Prien, nodded understandingly. He, too, was filled with the same fanatical spirit which manifested itself in the eyes of his chief. This, he reflected, would be a daring exploit which, if successful, would win him high praise and a decoration from the Führer.

"It can be done. And I think you are the man to do it." Doenitz strode over to his desk and picked up a collection of diagrams, scale drawings and charts giving detailed information of the British naval defences at Scapa Flow in the Orkney Islands where the battleship *Royal Oak* lay at anchor. Clearly marked among other vital factors were the strategically placed blockships with their steel cables strung between.

"Take all this data and study it carefully," continued Doenitz. "The information you will find is absolutely reliable. It has been supplied by one of our most diligent agents. Analyze it, and tell me what you think, Captain Prien. Understand, you are entirely free to make a decision. If you come to the conclusion that the enterprise cannot be carried through, we shall not hold it against you. On the other hand . . ." Doenitz gave the young commander an appraising look. "You have until Tuesday to give me your answer."

For the next two days, Kapitan-Leutnant Prien studied the charts and drawings with the concentration of a scientist conducting a ticklish experiment. The more he thought about the plan, the greater became his enthusiasm. On the following Tuesday, when he reported back to Admiral Doenitz, he expressed himself eager and ready to go into action.

The sinking by submarine attack of H.M.S. *Royal Oak* with the loss of 833 lives in the early hours of October 14th, 1939, ranks among the most audacious feats of the war. No less audacious, however, were the means by which Admiral Doenitz and the German Naval Command obtained the secrets of Scapa Flow, those carefully compiled charts and diagrams which enabled the U47 to sneak in through the bottleneck of Kirk Sound and send her torpedoes crashing into the silhouetted shape of the 29,000-ton battleship. In many respects the preliminary work overshadows the audacity of the assignment itself, for a spy's persistent and patient cunning spread over years of systematic espionage enabled the order to be carried out.

In 1927, twelve years before Hitler launched his attempt at world domination, there came to Britain from Switzerland a somewhat retiring and bespectacled little man answering to the name of Albert Oertel. He told the immigration authorities that he was a watchmaker and would very much like to carry on his trade in the United Kingdom.

"There are so many watchmakers in Switzerland," he said with a disarming smile. "Here in Britain, I am told, there is room for a good craftsman. If possible, I would like especially to find work in your lovely Scotland with its lakes and mountains which would remind me of my own Switzerland."

In truth, Switzerland was not his native land. Nor was his real name Albert Oertel, though that was certainly the name on his passport. The watchmaker from Switzerland was in reality Alfred Wehring, an ex-German naval officer who had served the Kaiser with distinction in World War I. After the 1918 surrender, Germany had little to offer its former officers. Wehring spent the next four years in restless idleness. Then, in 1923, Admiral Canaris, then quietly reconstructing Germany's spy system and who held a high opinion of the young naval officer, offered him a post in the organization. It was a new line of work for Wehring, but he was thankful to become active again.

Under Canaris's orders Wehring became a respectable representative of a German watch firm. In this capacity he visited several European countries with instructions to find out details of any new naval construction work. After three years' "apprenticeship," he was sent to Switzerland to learn more about watchmaking. This would provide excellent cover for other activities and enable him, if necessary, to prolong his stay in a country by obtaining work.

Under Swiss tuition, Wehring quickly became proficient. He was now ready for a more important assignment. Equipped with a passport provided by Admiral Canaris in the name of Albert Oertel, nationality Swiss, Wehring came to Britain and in due course settled down in the pleasant, old-world town of Kirkwall in the Orkneys, not far from Scapa Flow.

At first, he worked for a local jeweler whom he persuaded to take in watch and clock repairs instead of sending them to Leith. The people of Kirkwall needed a good watchmaker, he argued. His work was excellent, and he soon earned quite a reputation. It was not long before he opened a shop of his own in one of Kirkwall's quaint, narrow streets. It was a small place, rather like that in Dickens's *Old Curiosity Shop,* where Wehring, alias Oertel sold fancy goods and souvenirs and, of course, carried on with repairing clocks and watches.

The people among whom he now lived liked Oertel. He was pleasant, courteous, apparently honest, and his business enjoyed considerable patronage. Several of his customers invited him to their homes. He made many friends. Life in the coastal town was indeed enjoyable, so much so that in 1932 Oertel completed the process of assimilation by becoming a naturalized British subject.

Local feelings might have been somewhat less effusive had the folk of Kirkwall known that the friendly little watchmaker was in fact German and had been a former intelligence officer in the Kaiser's Navy. There were many things they did not know about Alfred Wehring, alias Albert Oertel. They did not know, for instance, that every scrap of information he picked up in conversation with the naval ratings and officers who came to his shop to buy gifts or have their watches repaired was noted down in a little book kept locked away in a cupboard in his room above the shop.

They did not know that the cupboard also contained what looked like an old-fashioned radio set but was in fact a short-wave transmitter. Nor did they know that on certain nights after business hours Oertel adjusted the dials of the instrument and, in answer to acknowledgement of his call signal, tapped out certain vital information in code to the German naval attaché in Holland, Captain Baron von Bülow. Likewise, they were quite unaware that the letters he received from Switzerland were innocent-looking but cunningly coded instructions from Admiral Canaris and the Nazi secret service.

Oertel took care never to arouse suspicion either by his talk or his conversation. Even his enthusiasm for the sea and the great ships sailing in and out of Scapa Flow did not strike the people of Kirkwall as peculiar. They merely smiled and made some pleasant, commonplace remark whenever they met Oertel prowling about the waterfront or gazing through binoculars at the broad expanses of tumbling water stretching away to Pentland Firth and the mainland of Scotland. Life in Kirkwall was too peaceful and provincial for them to question the actions of the man they had come to regard as one of themselves.

The war broke out.

On that never-to-be-forgotten Sunday morning, while Britain's air-raid sirens wailed their false warning of enemy attack, the local postman delivered a letter bearing a Swiss postmark to Albert Oertel. To friends who had invited him for lunch that day he said it was a message from his aged father telling him that his eighty-year-old mother was dangerously ill and was asking to see her only son. "I must go," cried the little watchmaker with tears in his eyes. "I may never see her again. Pray God, this war will not prevent me. Poor, poor Mamma!"

Two days later, Oertel sailed from Leith aboard a ship bound for Rotterdam. With him, carefully concealed in the linings of his jacket and light overcoat, were the secret charts, diagrams and drawings of Scapa Flow which he had drawn so painstakingly at night in the room above his shop.

The letter he had received was actually a coded message from Admiral Canaris instructing Oertel to deliver the documents to von Bülow in Holland. The Nazi spy chief had already learned from his agent in the Orkney Islands that the vital papers were completed. That the letter arrived on the very morning that the British Government declared war on Germany is possibly mere coincidence. It may have been intended to reach Oertel sooner but was delayed.

On his arrival at Rotterdam, watchmaker Oertel went straight to the Hotel Commerce, where he inquired of the reception clerk for Herr Fritz Burler. Burler was agent H432 and chief of the Nazi secret service in Holland. He treated his visitor with marked deference, took him by car to The Hague, where the two men went to the private house of Baron von Bülow.

The German naval attaché glanced rapidly through the charts and drawings as Oertel extracted them from their hiding-places in his garments.

"Kapitan Alfred Wehring," he exclaimed, a ring of admiration in his voice, "I congratulate you. These plans are invaluable. You have performed a most excellent task. I will see they are passed to Admiral Canaris without a moment's delay. Heil Hitler!"

Oertel returned the Nazi salute. At that moment he was no longer the retiring little watchmaker so familiar to the people of Kirkwall. Gone were the slightly rounded shoulders and the pleasant, friendly smile. He was once again an officer of the German Navy, upright, stern-faced. All that remained of his other personality were the gold rimmed spectacles behind which his eyes shone brightly.

With such highly important documents safely delivered to his masters, one might imagine Oertel's spy mission to be at an end and that he would conveniently disappear. The Nazis were too clever to permit him to fade out. Absence might only arouse suspicion and jeopardize the plan. There was still much work to be done, much up-to-the-minute information to be obtained before the scheme they had in mind could be put into execution.

Within a week, the pseudo watch repairer, glum and wearing a black tie, was back at the scene of his exploits. He received plenty of sympathy as he told friends that he had arrived at his mother's bedside just two hours too late.

The next morning, passers-by saw a Union Jack fluttering over the doorway of the gift shop. "I'm British," proudly declared the shopkeeper. "I must show my loyalty to the Allied cause." Oertel was not only a clever spy. He was also an accomplished actor.

Diligently he set about once more unearthing the latest defence secrets of Scapa Flow and finding out what ships were using the great naval base. He already knew that shortly before the outbreak of hostilities the intricate traps and anti-submarine nets guarding the entrances to the Flow had been found weakened by erosion and generally unsound. Replacements were ordered immediately and the work given high priority. Now he must find out to what extent the work had progressed and how many of Scapa's seven entrances were resealed. It was not long before he got what he was after. Kirk Sound, one of the eastern approaches to the Fleet anchorage, was not yet roped off with underwater cables of high-tension steel. Except for the three blockships, there was nothing to stop a submarine negotiating the narrow, shallow channel!

On the October afternoon that Albert Oertel learned this vital fact, he closed his shop early, bounded up the stairs to the room above, and opened the cupboard wherein he kept his short-wave transmitter. The great moment had come! His years of "apprenticeship" and patient, methodical compilation of information was almost at an end. This was the hour of destiny.

Oertel tapped out his call signal, waited tensely for its acknowledgement, then flashed out the message which told the Nazis that Scapa Flow was defenceless.

The message was hastily relayed to Admiral Doenitz at the *Kriegsmarine* headquarters. Doenitz realised that delay would be fatal. Not only would Kirk Sound become resealed, but the two great British naval vessels which Oertel's radio communiqué said were lying at anchor, *Royal Oak* and *Repulse*, would leave their berths to add their might to the enemy's sea power. The blow must be struck within the next few days. Doenitz acted.

On the night of October 13th, 1939, the black snout of the German submarine U47 slithered through the water out of Kiel. The weather was fine and clear as the submarine, running surfaced, ploughed into the whistling wind. Captain Prien, who was in command, alone knew their tremendous target, but he was under orders not to reveal it until just before the run-in. All he told his men was, "We enter Scapa Flow in the early hours of tomorrow."

Thanks to the diligence of Albert Oertel, the young U-boat commander knew precisely where the blockships were tethered in vulnerable Kirk Sound and how the temporary cables between them were strung.

As the submarine approached the eastern entrance to Scapa Flow, a curt order crackled out: "Diving stations." Bells jingled in the engineroom and the slick, black shape submerged in a whirl of bubbling foam.

Now was the time for all Prien's navigational skill. The tide was swirling and eddying through the narrow cut. The cables laced between the blockships were waiting to trap him like a fly in a giant web. Suddenly the U47 went aground between two of the blockships and her stern chafed dangerously against a cable.

To his credit, Prien did not allow the incident to panic him. His senses were taut, but his brain was a block of ice. He rang down his orders to the engine-room: "Stop port engine. Starboard slow ahead. Rudder hard to port."

As the rhythm of the powerful motors changed, U47 floated free. The cable released its clutch. A bad moment had passed, and the commander issued his next order: "Surface."

Shudderingly, the submarine drifted upwards and her periscope was raised. Captain Prien swept the wide reaches of Scapa Flow.

"We're through," he grunted. "Now for the kill."

Peering intently ahead, Prien saw the outline of a great

battleship lying close to the shore. It was the *Royal Oak*. U47 edged nearer, nearer, until she was dead on target.

"Fire!" Prien felt the familiar shudder as the torpedo left its tube. Five seconds . . . ten . . . fifteen. Then a terrific detonation, and the bow of the battleship disappeared in a leaping foam-lashed column of water.

"Fire!" A second torpedo crashed into the *Royal Oak*, hitting her amidships. Hard on the heels of the second came a third. As their war-heads exploded on the target a huge curtain of water rose up as though the sea had suddenly lifted itself. Angry jets of fire lit the night sky, blue, orange and brilliant red. Pieces of mast, the funnels and great chunks of the bridge hurtled upwards through spray and steam as with a deafening roar the battleship's ammunition lockers blew up. It was a wild scene and a terrifying one. Pandemonium reigned at Scapa Flow that night.

Searchlights sprang into life, stabbing the sky with their fingers of dazzling white light, searching the flame-licked darkness, sweeping the surface of the water in jerky, wavering arcs. Amid the awful inferno, sub-chasers and swift-moving torpedo boats hummed into action, their lean prows cleaving the water as their commanders vainly sought for the enemy which had delivered the surprise attack.

However, the luck of the daring was with Prien. With engines racing full speed ahead to hold U47 on her course, he slipped out between the blockships to the refuge of the open sea, leaving the *Royal Oak* in her death agony precisely one hour and seventeen minutes after the first torpedo struck her.

Prien did an amazing, incredible job. But the real triumph was Alfred Wehring's. Without his patient espionage work the whole undertaking would never have been possible.

What became of these two men who played leading roles in the destruction of the *Royal Oak*? Prien died on patrol in the spring of 1941. The subsequent history of the man who posed as Albert Oertel is shrouded in mystery.

It is known that he left Kirkwall shortly after the disaster, suddenly and without explanation. He was serving in his shop one day. The next day he was gone. Some say that he was picked up under cover of darkness by a German submarine and taken back to Kiel. No record of this was found in the official papers captured by the Allies. Nor was there any indication that he was given further assignments elsewhere.

BRITAIN'S PET SPY

by Al Newman

IN OCTOBER, 1940, Franco's government requested admission to the British Isles for a Falangist who had something to do with the youth movement in Spain. He said he wanted to study the British Boy Scouts during wartime or some such utter rot. Not being such fools as they sometimes seem, the Foreign Office said "Righto," come ahead. They knew the man, of course, and were positive that everything he saw or heard went straight to Berchtesgaden and Berlin.

All the King's Men: He was our own pet spy and we loved him dearly. A few others and myself acting as Scout officials met him at an airfield and tucked him carefully into a suite at the Athenaeum Court Hotel. That suite was probably the greatest job of concealed microphones and tapped wires ever accomplished. We furnished him with a great deal of liquor and all the women he ever wanted—ours of course.

That wasn't all we did for him. There were at that time only about three heavy ack-ack batteries in the London Area. One of them we moved into Green Park, directly across the street from the hotel. They had orders to fire continuously, as fast as possible all through every raid, whether there was anything within miles or not. Lord, what a bloody row they made. Since there was at least one raid every night, our pet spy spent most of his time down in the air-raid shelter, convinced by the noise that London was thickly studded with ack-ack protection. We let him inspect the battery—a crack 3-inch outfit—and even furnished a few Boy Scouts for the occasion.

Then we took him out toward Windsor to look at more Boy Scouts. By what may have been the sheerest coincidence, but wasn't, just about the only fully equipped regiment in all the islands and all the tanks we possessed, were assembled there. Fine, tough-looking men they were. Guardsmen. We said that they were just a small force which could be spared from the defense of the island and had been detailed as a ceremonial bodyguard for the royal family. We could see how surprised he was, but he swallowed it whole.

All the King's Ships: Then we took him out to a seaport where every available fleet unit had been mustered. We hinted delicately that secret additions to the Home Fleet

148

enabled us to keep these ships as the defense of one port. His eyes popped a little at that, but there it was before him and he had to believe what he saw. We also showed him more Boy Scouts. He was beginning to get awfully sick of them by this time and so were we, but it was part of the game and both sides had to play it to the finish.

Our greatest triumph of stage management was his trip toward Scotland by plane a fortnight later. You remember how thin our air-power was at this time. A few Hurricanes, fewer Spitfires. Well, all the way up there, we ran into squadron after squadron of Spits. The sky seemed full of them. How could he know that it was the same squadron ducking into and out of clouds and coming at us from all angles and altitudes?

Then on maneuvers in the Scotland area, we showed him the same regiment of guards and the same tanks that he had seen near Windsor. I was a bit afraid he might recognize a few of the guardsmen, but he didn't. We explained that this was just a small, poorly equipped force, re-outfitting to join others training over a wide area and that the whole maneuver army was merely what could be spared from the main defense forces.

And Boy Scouts to Spare: Oh, yes, and there were a few more blasted Boy Scouts about the premises. We ran into more Spitfires—hundreds and hundreds of them—on the way back toward London. If I hadn't known what was going on, I'd have been taken in myself.

Shortly after this he left. Later I saw portions of his report—don't ask me how we got it because that is a secret. The document was just appalling. Britain was an armed camp. Any rumors of her weakness were merely attempts of a crafty foe to inveigle Germany into the inevitably disastrous invasion. All this was eyewitness stuff and apparently great weight was given to it by his masters in Berlin.

I often wonder what happened to him afterward. I suppose he's retired somewhere on half pay now. Pity too, because he was quite a presentable chap. We loved him dearly and cared for him tenderly. But I'll bet 10 pounds our pet spy still dreams of Boy Scouts every other night. I know I do.

SPIES AT PEARL HARBOR

THIS IS the story of espionage in Pearl Harbor, a battle which the United States lost, and which Germany and Japan won, but not to the extent they had planned.

Modern crazes had hit Hawaii. Jukeboxes and swing music had long ago drowned out the native music sung by the beautiful Polynesian girls. But there was a brand-new sensation for Honolulu.

Every woman on the islands heard about it, but most appreciative were the Navy wives, the American girls living far from metropolitan luxuries.

The islands could now boast an ultra-modern beauty parlor. Ruth, the store's manager, was universally liked. She gave the best permanents. She installed equipment and brought in a staff whose skill at hair-do's and facials compared favorably with the expensive treatments of Fifth Avenue.

Hundreds of women spent the whole day relaxing in the suave atmosphere of Ruth's beauty parlor.

The place, highly fashionable, soon became the clearing-house of Hawaiian gossip. Women discussed who was in town, who was leaving, furloughs, assignments, ship arrivals and departures. This was the stuff that made up the life of the islands and naturally could not be excluded from conversation.

The beauty parlor opened in 1939. Nobody on the Hawaiian Islands thought of war, and few back in the mother country thought of it. But espionage does not operate intermittently. It is a continuous business pursued in peace as well as war.

This particular plot did not originate in the German War Office and the ubiquitous hand of Admiral Walter Wilhelm Canaris, subsequently hanged, Nazi Germany's spy chief, was not in it.

All the credit is due to late Propaganda Minister Joseph Goebbels (who committed suicide in 1945).

Goebbels had held office for two years when, in the beginning of 1935, he threw a party at the Ministry for all the personnel. It was a gala affair, with everyone feeling happy and proud, inspired by the new-born strength of Nazi Germany. Goebbels, who never denied his interest in the female of the species was greater than befitted a happily married man, was in his element. His affairs with women were complicated and extensive, and this evening promised the beginning of a new one.

His private secretary Leopold Kuehn was there and with him his young sister Ruth. The girl was a stunner. Goebbels, who when it suited his purpose could be extremely charming and sociable, stayed with her the whole evening. They got a little drunk together and had a wonderful time. Any halfway intelligent girl would realize that an affair with the Propaganda Minister was a big thing.

The trend the affair took is not known. Its denouement is a secret shrouded in the mists of history. What we do know is that the Propaganda Minister hastily decided that Ruth had to leave Germany. Was it that Frau Goebbels (later killed by her own husband) interfered, or that Ruth demanded too much, or that she threatened to tell? These questions are interesting but not relevant to the main story.

Ruth Kuehn had to get out of Germany. Goebbels, who was not on really good terms with Army or Navy Intelligence —they knew too much about him—turned to another quarter. One of his closest satellites was Dr. Karl Haushofer, son of the famous general and geopolitician. Father and son were in charge of the Geopolitical Department of Berlin University. The students of geopolitics graduated into the foreign service, principally into the spy organization under Foreign Secretary Ribbentrop (who was hanged at Nuremberg). It was General Haushofer (who committed suicide in 1946) that first welded the bonds between Germany and Japan. He was indebted to Goebbels for the incomparable prestige enjoyed by himself and his school of thought. If Goebbels wanted anything in Haushofer's power to grant, there was no further question about it.

Yes, Haushofer could use the young lady Ruth Keuhn. The old general, who had visited Japan and seen the possibilities there as early as 1914, was in regular contact with that country. Very recently his Japanese colleagues had expressed a need for white men and women. This was a new kind of white slave traffic. Japan's Government through their liaison officers, the two Haushofers, requested the services of white folk to help in the Japanese espionage service and in the Kempei Tai, Japan's secret military police force. Japan, in fact, needed a good many people for intelligence work. Haushofer therefore informed Goebbels that he had openings not only for Ruth Kuehn, but for her brothers and parents, provided they were intelligent and careful, and had received a course of basic training.

It is not only theatrical blood that runs through a family. A flair for espionage may also be shared. In this case the entire family was involved and all, plainly, had a talent for it, though Ruth seemed to be the smartest. Her family background was unquestionably helpful.

The father, Dr. Bernard Julius Otto Kuehn, was born in Berlin. He was forty and Ruth eighteen. When the doctor was eighteen he had enlisted in the Imperial German Navy and served as a midshipman aboard a cruiser in World War I. When the ship was sunk in an encounter with a British battleship in 1915, he was taken prisoner and landed in England, where he quickly acquired the language. When the armistice came, he was a young man without a civilian profession. He re-entered the naval service of the Weimar Republic as an Oberleutnant. Six months later the German fleet was destroyed and he was stranded. They put his name down on the naval reserve list and he had to adjust himself to civil life.

Kuehn decided to take up medicine. He became a member of several nationalist officer organizations. Very early he espoused the Nazi cause. Early too he indoctrinated his daughter Ruth with the diabolical ideas of Adolf Hitler.

Dismissed from several hospitals and unable to make the grade as a private physician, Kuehn at last accepted a position in the Gestapo under Heinrich Himmler (also executed at Nuremberg). Himmler was his personal friend. Long afterwards Dr. Kuehn complained that the Gestapo had frequently promised him a good job as police chief in one of the German cities. Instead, through the failings of his beautiful but reckless daughter, he was exiled to Hawaii.

American athletes were preparing for the Olympic Games; Japan was a good United States customer for oil and scrap iron; the world had just come through the great depression, and peace organizations were flourishing. This was the world picture when a German family landed in the Hawaiian Islands on August 15th, 1935. They were not the usual run of giddy tourists. The father was a scientist, a trim, grey-haired professor. They were well-bred and handsome people. Dr. Bernard Julius Otto Kuehn came with his entire family, except his son Leopold, who remained in Berlin as Goebbels' secretary. With him were Frau Professor Friedel Kuehn, his six-year-old son Hans Joachim and his daughter Ruth. Ruth and the absent Leopold were not really his children but his wife's children by a former marriage.

A well-knit family, their domestic life was a joy to behold. They were here because the father was interested in the Japanese language. The doctor and his daughter were also very much interested in the ancient history of the Hawaiian Islands. They travelled around, visiting the old stone houses of the early settlers. Very soon they knew the topography of the Hawaiian Islands as well as their own coats. Ruth loved the seashore and all water sports, as did the whole family. They used to go swimming frequently, or they would hire a sailing boat or motor launch and go exploring. Friedel, the mother, was a commonplace sort of matron, but extremely helpful. She could listen and observe details of military significance when to all appearances she was simply a housewife completely bound up in the care of her family. Twice during the period 1936-41 she travelled as courier to Japan, and neither the F.B.I. nor the U.S. Navy Intelligence had an inkling.

Ruth, lithe and tall, worked according to plan. She made great headway with her English. She was a wonderful dancer and attended every important social affair. A constant guest at the naval and yachting clubs, she attracted scores of naval officers—much more handsome than her club-footed lover Dr. Goebbels.

On political questions, the Kuehns would answer that they personally did not like the Nazis. Ruth would say: "I was so young, when we left Germany." The doctor wrote a number of articles on the early German settlers in the islands. These were published in Germany. Neighbors and acquaintances had the impression that the Kuehns were very well off. Kuehn had some excellent investments in Holland and Germany. They had a beautiful home, fine art pieces, exquisite silver, all indicating a family of culture and wealth.

During the first three years on the islands, they received about 70,000 dollars transmitted through a Honolulu bank by the Rotterdam Bank Association. On one of her trips, Friedel returned from Japan with 16,000 dollars in cash.

The F.B.I. and American Army and Navy Intelligence have since ascertained that during this period the family received over 100,000 dollars. There was undoubtedly more which has simply not been traced.

Considering the great expenses involved, espionage is certainly less well paid than is commonly assumed. At the outset, intelligence work is limited to the reporting of gossip, research, information gleaned from naval and merchant marine men. Ruth knew how to handle men. Later the espionage is shifted among the officer class. And Ruth was clever, glamorous and desirable. Her stepfather encouraged her to meet the officers, the more the merrier, because with war drawing near more and more was demanded of the loyal espionage agent.

The Kuehns were in the service of two countries. Though General Haushofer had lent them to the Japanese, the Nazis soon discovered their value. Copies of all reports had to go to Germany. In consideration, the Kuehns thought it reasonable to ask for more money. Besides, Ruth's appetite for high life had sharpened. So had the doctor's.

Early in 1939, Dr. Kuehn decided he definitely needed a quiet place to get on with his study of the Japanese language. He moved his family from Honolulu to Pearl Harbor. Now the Japanese Secret Service plan, for which Ruth and the doctor had been sent to the islands, began rapidly to take shape. Ruth established herself as a popular favorite among the young people and the wives of the Navy men. Markedly attractive herself, she let it be known that she had a flair for the art of personal grooming. When in 1939 she announced the opening of a beauty parlor the enterprise, greeted with enthusiasm, was immediately assured the patronage of all her women friends. Despite the long planning, even Ruth was not prepared for its instantaneous success. Friedel, too, began to spend much of her time at the new *salon*. Both reported daily to the doctor what they had picked up. Couriers of the German and Japanese consulates relayed the information to the proper quarters.

Then one day the Japanese Vice-Consul at Honolulu, astute little Otojiro Okuda, sent for Ruth and her father. They met secretly. Okuda told them the time had come to get hold of some real maritime information—exact dates, locations, figures on the U.S. naval forces in the Pacific. He complimented them on their past work, but this job, he emphasized, was of another order. The Japanese would be willing to pay quite generously, and it would mean a deadly blow against the U.S. Navy.

Ruth asked 40,000 dollars but her father agreed to take fourteen thousand as an advance, the rest to be forthcoming after "success."

Father Kuehn was worried. Where could he get the information. Ruth laughed and got engaged to one of the highest U.S. naval officers stationed in Pearl Harbor. She was in the big battalion now and her stepfather had to work for her. Still, he was a good researcher. Together they made a perfect team. Ruth gave him new orders and shortly after the conversation with Okuda and Ruth's engagement Dr. Kuehn began to stroll daily along the fortified sections of Pearl Harbor. "Take Hans Joachim along," ordered Ruth.

Hans Joachim, now ten, dressed in a navy suit, was a great help. The father explained the waterfront scene to the child who was "just crazy about" every aspect of the American Navy. After a while the American sailors invited the boy on board a battleship and pointed out the wonders of this giant toy. Dr. Kuehn, an alien, would never have been permitted aboard, and he was far too clever to assume he might evade regulations. So he allowed the boy to go alone.

The same night Ruth met the officers of the same battleship and next morning reported for son, daughter and father. The report was transmitted to Tokyo and Berlin. Washington hadn't the slightest notion of this traffic.

Success incited them to greater ventures. Ruth, always ready to outdo her stepfather, sent him to inform Japanese Consul Okuda that they had worked out a signal system. It was designed to transmit information on the number and kinds of American ships in Pearl Harbor; the fleet's exact location, and on ship movements in general. The consul suggested simplifying the code but agreed it was suitable for signaling to the Japanese fleet.

The Kuehns owned a second home, a small house in Kalama, a community located in Kailu, Oahu, not too far from Pearl Harbor. Ruth now spent a lot of time at their summer place. One day she went out and bought a pair of eighteen-power Bausch and Lomb binoculars, a purchase that might have been considered unusual for a young lady.

The light signals were to be flashed from the dormer window of their Oahu home. Ruth, her father, Consul Okuda and the fourth secretary of the Japanese consulate, Tadesi Morimura, worked out a most practical code. On December 2nd, 1941, daughter and father tried out their new system for the first time. It worked. On the same day, Vice-Consul Okuda received a written tabulation of the number, types and exact location of American ships in Hawaiian waters. The previous night Ruth was not seen at home. Her fiancé admitted later she was with him all night.

Next morning Japanese Consul-General Nagoa Kita, Okuda's superior, transmitted all data via short wave to the Japanese Naval Intelligence office.

All was now in readiness for the day of infamy, the treacherous attack on Pearl Harbor. Ruth and her father knew the exact day of the attack . . . the exact hour.

Negotiations were still going on in Washington when the Japanese launched their blow against the American fleet. It was December 7th, 1941. Ruth Kuehn opened the dormer window and her father gave the promised light signals. He told the Japs what to bomb and what not to bomb. He directed them to the most strategic points. Dr. Kuehn plied the flashlight while Ruth told him the objectives. In the darkness she led the attack on Pearl Harbor from that window.

Hovering overhead the Japanese bombers spread devastation among the American fleet, one-third of which was sunk or severely damaged. Everything proceeded according to the Kita-Okuda-Kuehn plan—or almost.

Rarely is there a perfect crime. This one was no exception. In one respect their plan went awry. The Japanese consul had arranged to have a Jap submarine pick him up along with the Kuehn family and take them to Tokyo. The Kuehns had planned to move snappily. They would leave even their toothbrushes behind, concentrating only on money, crisp paper dollars of which, Ruth insisted, each should carry and keep a part. Once in Japan they would share the balance of 26,000 dollars due to them on the deal.

But amid the noise and fire and chaos of Pearl Harbor, United States intelligence officers spotted the lights coming from the window of the Kuehn house. Before the Japanese submarine arrived, Kuehn and his family were picked up by the authorities. Ruth and Friedel protested, the doctor arrogantly maintained an attitude of blank denial. But all the evidence was against them. An outline of the signal system was found. And there was far too much money in the house, some of it in Japanese currency. The women were loading themselves with the loot when the police arrived. The binoculars came to light, and copies of reports written in German. Dr. Kuehn finally admitted everything. He did his best, though, to protect Ruth and his wife. He insisted that he alone was responsible—without success. Ruth declared she was in charge, said her father only obeyed her orders. Friedel asserted she had bought the binoculars and was the leader of the gang.

156

On **February** 21st, 1942, Dr. Kuehn was sentenced to be shot. **Nazis,** once in prison, cease to be supermen. Kuehn **fought for** his life. He became frightened. Ruth's trial was **coming up.** He had to save her. He tried to bargain, to make **a deal** with Uncle Sam. For years he had been in the service **of the** Germans and Japanese and now he offered his services **to the** Americans. They told him he couldn't buy his or his **daughter's** pardon that way; the American Government **wanted** no Nazi spies in its employ. The death sentence was **signed.** Would Ruth die too? Kuehn found his lonely cell a madhouse. Ruth seemed to be stoically calm, waiting. She had always been able to find a way out.

Dr. Kuehn finally begged for mercy. He promised to tell U.S. Navy Intelligence all he knew about Axis espionage in the Pacific. He was the master spy, he had organized the network. Ruth was innocent, his wife a harmless *Hausfrau*, he claimed. United States intelligence officers made no promises but told him to confess all. He did. What he told remains unknown.

But as other spies and couriers found forgiveness by talking, as the deed of Chambers and his pumpkin spy papers found clemency, so did Dr. Kuehn. His death sentence was commuted on October 26th, 1942, to fifty years' hard labor in Alcatraz. Ruth and Friedel were interned, and are now free— in Germany. Leopold Kuehn, who had remained with Goebbels, shared the general downfall of his family in another manner—death in Russia. Friedel tried to commit suicide but was prevented. Beautiful Ruth was not present when her beauty shop was auctioned off.

Another of Friedel's daughters lives now under an assumed name in Los Angeles. She told me part of this story.

THE MAN WHO SAVED COMMUNISM

THE FRONT in the cold war is everywhere. The greatest Russian spy who ever lived, worked—like so many Soviet spies—in an embassy; but it was not the Russian Embassy.

Some called him Don Juan in hell. The official report of the Far Eastern Command of the United States, the MacArthur Report on Richard Sorge, called him the "man who saved Stalin's life."

He was the almost perfect spy—but not quite.

Everyone who ever met Dr. Richard Sorge, the Baku-born German journalist, realized he was a brilliant man. He spoke many languages, and was a deep student of history. The Japanese and Chinese felt there had been very few Westerners who came as close to understanding the oriental mentality as Dr. Sorge.

He was a tall and friendly-looking man with sparkling blue eyes; he was always smiling, a man who loved life and lived it fully.

He was the man who, thanks to his network of sixteen sub-agents, knew in advance of the secret Japanese attack against Pearl Harbor. He knew the exact day and the exact hour of the attack. He even had this message shortwaved to his Soviet superiors, but Russia never gave warning to her ally of World War II, the United States.

His greatest contribution to the cause of the Soviet Union was made during the days of the battle for Stalingrad when Russia fought for her very existence. He sent full military and political evidence to Lavrenti Beria, the MVD chief, and to Stalin personally, that Japan had decided not to attack Russia and that Japanese troops would not then endanger Siberia.

After this information was received, Stalin took practically every soldier from his Vladivostok frontier and shipped them and their equipment to the Stalingrad front. It was the turning point of the battle and also the turning point of the war.

Stalin, during this period, according to secret service reports, declared, "Sorge saved our lives. . . ."

Sorge was too intelligent not to know the Japanese would arrest him sooner or later in spite of his perfect protection as chief advisor to Nazi Ambassador Eugen Ott in Japan. He must have had premonitions, because in one of his talks with Ambassador Ott he had said:

"Do you know, Ott, how your Japanese friends execute their prisoners? Nice and slowly, piece by piece and without haste they draw the wire noose, just so you can hang alive as long as possible. They don't hang you really; they strangle you and do a good job—such gentlemen are our little Japanese."

Then he took his whiskey and said "Prost," and both he and Ambassador Ott started one of their drinking parties.

To him personally, however, the Japanese were apparently not cruel. At his execution, on October 7, 1944, his last words to the prison personnel were, "I thank you for your kindness to me."

Then he walked, proud and head high, to the prison gallows of Sugamo Prison in Tokyo. At 10:20 A.M. the trap door of the gallows was sprung and at 10:30 he was declared dead. Japanese officials said he died with his fist uplifted, saying: "Long Live the Soviet Union." Later on the same prison officials denied this story. He was the first occidental to be hanged in Japan during the war.

As Richard Sorge was doubtless the most successful spy of World War II and myths about this remarkable man have begun to spring up around the world, I have decided to publish an authentic account of his life and actions.

Here for the first time in book form is the condensed official intelligence report of General Douglas MacArthur as presented through his intelligence chief, Major General Charles Willoughby. The MacArthur report on Richard Sorge was given officially to the U.S. Cabinet, the U.S. War Department and all its intelligence branches, and the U.S. Congress. It is the most colorful espionage report given to any government after World War II.

"For nine productive years a daring and skillful band of spies worked in Japan for their spirited fatherland—Soviet Russia. Led by Dr. Richard Sorge, a German Communist posing convincingly as a loyal Nazi, this ring of spies almost succeeded in committing the perfect crime.

"Dr. Sorge, the head of the ring, and Ozaki Hozumi, his chief lieutenant, worked as spies for the Soviet Union in both China and Japan from 1929 to 1941.

"Sorge lived on intimate, trusted terms with the German Ambassador and his staff; Ozaki Hozumi, his lieutenant, had a similar close relationship to Prince Konoe, thrice premier. From these perfect sources they drew their masses of information on every subject from politics to war and transmitted their intelligence to the U.S.S.R. by concealed radio, by courier and through the Soviet Embassy. Their primary intelligence targets were Japanese plans and intentions for attack on the Soviet Union. Sorge transmitted an enormous number of carefully analyzed intelligence reports from Tokyo to the Red army's fourth bureau over the years of his work.

"The members of the Sorge ring were arrested in October 1941. Two of the most prominent leaders died in prison and lesser figures got long prison terms. On the mornings of Nov. 7, 1944, Dr. Richard Sorge, German, and Ozaki Hozumi, Japanese, were hanged for their great services to the Soviet Union.

159

"Neither the Japanese civil police, the gendarmerie (Kempeitai), the special higher police (Tokkoka) nor any other Japanese security agency ever had the remotest suspicion of Sorge or any of his gang of 16 men and women. They were betrayed by a prominent Japanese Communist, Ito Ritsu, now member of the party's central committee. He had a grudge against a minor member of the ring, never suspecting how loyally and dangerously she was working for the cause. It is ironical that this Judas is a trusted leader of the Japan Communist party in postwar Japan.

"Richard Sorge, brilliant leader of this ring of spies, was born in Baku, in southern Russia, October 4, 1895. His father was a German engineer working for a German oil firm in the Caucasus and his mother is said to have been Russian. While Richard was still an infant, his parents went to Berlin where the boy had a normal German education and grew up a patriotic son of Imperial Germany. He seems to have been impressed quite young, however, with the memory of his paternal grandfather, Adolf Sorge, secretary of Karl Marx at the time of the formation of the First International.

"At the beginning of World War I, Richard Sorge volunteered as a private, was wounded, reenlisted, and was wounded a second time. During his periods of convalescence and after the war he studied at the Universities of Berlin, Kiel and Hamburg taking the degree of doctor of political science at Hamburg in 1920. For the next two years he worked variously as a school teacher and a coal miner and then in 1922 began to write for newspapers and magazines. But even when he was teaching or digging coal he was doing his best to convert his pupils and his fellow miners to the tenets of Karl Marx.

"Immediately upon the formation of the German Communist Party in October 1919, Sorge joined the Hamburg branch. He was a natural linguist in any case, and by the time he had become established in Japan he could converse easily in French, English, Russian, Japanese, and possibly Chinese.

"Sorge began his professional Communist career in 1924. By that time he had made such an excellent reputation among German Communists and was so respected by Soviet leaders that he was summoned to Moscow. He resigned from the German Communist Party, joined the Russian and became an agent of the Comintern, at that time a body with considerable force in world Communist affairs.

"Among Sorge's sponsors to the Russian Communist Party

and the Comintern were Dimitry Zaharovich Manuilsky, still member of the Central Committee of the Russian Communist Party, and Soloman A. Lovosky, currently Deputy Commissar of Foreign Affairs under Molotov, and also a member of the Central Committee. Naturally, even after he joined Red Army Intelligence his Comintern friends maintained their personal interest in him.

"For three years Sorge was busy for the Comintern at their Moscow headquarters, presumably learning the business, but in 1927 he went abroad to begin his hazardous career of field agent. Using the cover of an obscure German magazine, he spent two years in the Scandinavian countries and Great Britain as a special representative of the intelligence and organization bureau of the Comintern.

"Three agents of the Fourth Bureau (Red Army Secret Service) went to China together in 1930: 'Alex' (not otherwise identified), Dr. Richard Sorge, and a certain Weingart, a German wireless operator. After about six months, Alex, the chief of the mission, left, presumably to return to Russia, and Sorge became head of the ring, whose headquarters were at Shanghai but which covered most of China, being especially active in Hangohow and Nanking, Canton, Hankow, Kalfeng, Hsian, Peiping, and in Manchuria. Sorge himself traveled extensively, read widely and deeply on Chinese and Japanese politics, history and culture, studied the two languages and came to be unusually well-informed on Asiatic affairs. He was a formidable agent.

"One member of the ring, Miss Agnes Smedley, has been one of the most energetic workers for the Soviet cause in China for the past twenty-odd years. She was one of the early perpetrators, if not the originator, of the hoax that the Chinese Communists were not really Communists at all but only local agrarian revolutionists, innocent of any Soviet connections.

"Sorge's most valuable single associate in Japan was to be Ozaki Hozumi, a well-known journalist and commentator on Chinese affairs. Years later Ozaki was to have the distinction of preceding Sorge in death by half an hour, the only member of the ring to share the gallows with him.

"Ozaki Hozumi came to be known as one of Japan's leading experts on China affairs and wrote widely on this subject in a variety of magazines. His articles appeared in England and contemporary Japan. He was admired for his contributions to the Institute of Pacific Relations, especially after he had attended the Yosemite conference of that body in 1936 as one of the Japanese delegates.

"In July 1938, Ozaki became unofficial adviser to the Cabinet (Naikaku Shokutaku) under Prince Konoe. With the fall of the first Konoe Cabinet, in January 1939, Ozaki resigned this post, but in June he became unofficial adviser (Shokutaku) of the Tokyo office of the South Manchuria Railway, with which he remained until his arrest in 1941.

"Ozaki originally developed his interest in the Chinese and his hostility to Japanese militarism while he was a boy in Formosa. While he was in college in Tokyo he began reading widely in Japanese leftist literature. He never became a member of any Communist party.

"A deep and genuine friendship developed between the Japanese journalist, Ozaki, and the American Communist journalist, Agnes Smedley.

"Obviously Sorge had been fully satisfied with Ozaki's loyalty through the checks and recommendations of Miss Smedley, for at their first meeting Sorge asked Ozaki to collect and supply him with information on the internal Chinese situation and on Japanese policy toward China. Ozaki consented without hesitation.

"When Sorge reached Shanghai in 1930, he found Max Gottfried Klausen, also an agent of the Fourth Bureau (Red Army Secret Service), who had the simulated rank of major in the Red Army. Klausen had come out from Moscow the year before and already had had considerable experience as an operator of secret radio stations. That was to be his role for the rest of Sorge's active life, and in Japan Klausen was to become Sorge's chief communications link with the Soviet Union."

Klausen was a heavy-set, coarse-featured German, not well educated, and the last conceivable suspect as a successful agent of the Red Army.

"Klausen must have made an excellent impression for sincerity and devotion to party principles. In 1928, a Soviet operative known to Klausen only as George, invited him to join an international espionage group as a radioman. Klausen readily accepted the invitation, and in February 1929 he went to Moscow, where he joined the Fourth Bureau of the Red Army General Staff as a radio operator.

"Klausen received only a brief indoctrination, and then was ordered to go to Shanghai to serve as radio operator for the bureau's China unit. Before leaving Klausen received a ticket to Harbin and $150 in American money. He was shown a photograph of a man called Mishin, who was to be his Shanghai contact. He was directed to go to the Palace Hotel in Shanghai, sit in the lobby with a newspaper in his left hand and a pipe in his right. When the Mishin of the photograph came up and spoke to him, he was to give the password, 'Regards from Erna."

"In due time Klausen sat in the lobby of the Palace Hotel and gave Mishin Erna's regards. He then went with Mishin to the latter's home, where he was given two rooms on the third floor, and received instructions from Mishin in radio technique. Together Constantin Mishin and Max Klausen built a shortwave radio receiving and sending set and maintained contact with another station known as Weisbaden. This was the same station which subsequently received his signals from Tokyo."

Klausen worked in various Chinese cities as directed by his chief. He put up sets in Canton and Mukden, in addition to those in Shanghai and Harbin.

"Sorge had left for Berlin in May 1933 to establish his cover. In Germany he secured assignments as special correspondent in Japan for the *Frankfurter Zeitung*, the *Bergen Kurier*, the *Technische Rundschau*, and the *Amsterdam Handelsblatt*. He applied for membership in the Nazi Party, which had just seized power under Adolf Hitler, and his credentials were accepted without question. How he secured these excellent covers remains a mystery. The key newspaper was the *Frankfurter Zeitung*, whose Shanghai correspondent was a concealed Communist and Soviet agent, Miss Agnes Smedley.

"With his Nazi loyalties established and having an excellent journalistic cover, Dr. Sorge proceeded to Japan via the United States and Canada. In America he met with some American agents of the Soviets before catching his ship at Vancouver, British Columbia.

"Dr. Richard Sorge first reached Yokohoma on September 6, 1933. There seemed nothing unusual about this German journalist and the water police quickly let him ashore. Not long afterward Sorge found a house in Tokyo, at No. 30 Nagasaka-machi, Azabu-ku, Tokyo, a good neighborhood, and settled down to covering Japan for his various newspapers. He made himself known at the German Embassy and the German Club and was readily accepted by the German community as well as by his colleagues of the press.

"Meanwhile, the Comintern, at the request of the Red

Army, began picking up unsuspected agents and moving them around the world. The Red Army needed some spies in Japan of a certain type of category. In due course the Comintern agents in France and the United States received orders. Men who were complete strangers to each other and who had never heard the name of Sorge began packing their bags for Tokyo. While others came along in due course, the two key figures were Branko de Voukelitch and Miyagi Yotoku. Voukelitch traveled from Paris, Miyagi from Los Angeles.

"The German Embassy was Sorge's major target, but he had no more immediate entree than any other German journalist. But through the man's wife he did know an assistant German military attaché, Lt. Col. Eugene Ott, then on duty in Nagoya with a Japanese artillery regiment.

"Ott was out of sympathy with the Nazi program, but he went along with the orders from his government. He had only arrived in Japan in 1933, being transferred out of Germany by higher ranking officers who feared for his safety in the Nazi purges then under way. Whatever Ott knew or thought about Germany, he knew almost nothing about Japan, and he was delighted to find in his new friend Richard an extraordinary fund of information on things Japanese, on Japanese politics and trends, as well as sage advice. When Ott made his next grade and was stationed in Tokyo, his friendship with Sorge deepened and their meetings came to be more and more frequent.

"Very early then, Sorge began his campaign for acceptance at the German Embassy. Simultaneously he developed his ring. The de Voukelitch family moved in November to a private house in Sanai-cho, Ushigome-ku. Sorge needed more privacy. Branko, an enthusiastic amateur camera fiend, had a darkroom built in his house for the furtherance of his hobby. Subsequently, documents were photographed there and microfilm was prepared for transmission to Shanghai or the Soviet Embassy.

"The Comintern continued to move their men across the world to aid their man Sorge. Miyagi Yotoku, a Japanese who had lived in the United States since 1919 and who was a member of the American Communist Party, was the Comintern's selection to meet Sorge's conditions on assistants.

"Miyagi Yotoku was a native of Okinawa, born February 10, 1903. Like many Okinawans, his father migrated, first to

Thereupon, the other would offer his packet containing the films. When de Voukelitch returned the pack after taking a cigarette, Klausen would say, 'Keep it. I've more.' It was all very natural and easy.

"In the summer of 1935 Sorge went to Europe, nominally to renew his contract with the *Frankfurter Zeitung*, but actually to attend the Comintern congress of that year in Moscow, to report to his superiors and to receive their instructions.

"He went to New York on his regular German passport, but while there a man called at his hotel room with a new passport already visaed for the U.S.S.R. Sorge went via Berlin to Moscow and then returned to Japan."

Back in Tokyo, Sorge ordered the establishment of "the firm M. Klausen Shokai (M. Klausen & Co.) with offices in the Karasumori building, Shiba-ku, Tokyo. M. Klausen Shokai made and sold printing presses for blueprints, as well as flourescent plates, and almost immediately began to make money. Among their customers were such firms as Mitsubashi, Mitsui, Nakajima, and Hitachi, as well as munition factories, the Japanese Army, and the Japanese Navy. While Klausen was manufacturing machinery from the Army's blueprints, Sorge was getting the finished blueprints of the Imperial Government. By February 1941, Klausen had done so well that he reorganized his firm as a joint stock company capitalized at Y100,000 of which he contributed Y85,000. He even established a branch at Mukden, with a working capital of Y20,000. In fact, Klausen was doing so well, and making so much money, that his earlier convictions of the perfection of Communism were almost shaken. But in the meantime his business was not only a personal cover but also a perfect cover for the financial transactions of the ring. He bought and sold abroad, and there was nothing irregular in his reception of drafts from New York or San Francisco or Shanghai for his bank account.

"In seeking to connect men now living with Dr. Sorge's activities in Japan it seems well to recall the rigidity with which he avoided all contacts with the Japanese Communist Party and its active members, the success with which he operated for years through keeping his ring small and properly covered so it would not arouse gossip even among those friendly to his cause, and his sharp avoidance of contact with other Soviet espionage agents, not assigned to duty with him.

"In addition to sending radio messages, Sorge sent a general volume of material by courier, usually in the form of microfilmed documents, chiefly of his own analyses but often actual German or Japanese texts. On occasion some shadowy Moscow man appeared to have made direct contact with Sorge or Klausen in Tokyo, and to have taken away material. But until 1939 liaison with Moscow was conducted chiefly in Shanghai and Hongkong. Most of the members of the group served as couriers at different times.

"On these trips, the men found it easy to string the film cartridges on a cord and to hide the improvised belt under their clothing. It was even easier for the women to hide them.

"By 1939, Sorge decided it was too dangerous for members of his ring to travel to China as messengers. The intensification of the war in China so increased the suspicion and scrutiny of Japanese intelligence agencies that the risks had become disproportionate. Subsequently, with the severance of economic ties between Japan and the United States, it became too difficult to secure funds through American banks. In 1939 Sorge radioed a request for establishment of liaison in Japan. Instructions soon came for Klausen. 'Two tickets with higher numbers for *Fritz*. One with a smaller number for liaison man.' Soon afterward, Klausen found two tickets for the Imperial Theatre in his mail box at the Tokyo central post office. He took his wife Anna to the show, and sat in the lower-numbered seat. In the darkness he passed to his righthand neighbor 38 film cartridges of photographs of documents from the German Embassy. In return his neighbor passed him $5,000.

"Klausen's neighbor turned out to be the Soviet Consul in Tokyo, Helge Leonidvtch Vutokevitch. The following April Klausen and Anna attended the All Girls Opera at the Takarazuka Theatre, where Max handed over another 30 rolls of film and received in return $3,000 in United States currency and Y2,500.

"The total cost of the Sorge ring was estimated at about 3,000 yen a month. This was an expenditure of considerably less than United States $1,000 a month to pay for the extremely valuable work of nearly 20 agents. Since, with one exception, they all worked for love of the cause and not for money, their monthly pay was merely to cover living and travel costs and not to compensate them for their work. Ozaki, for example, never received a penny for himself, and was actually out of pocket, since he supported some of the agents under him. Sorge, de Voukelitch and Klausen, of course, had regular incomes from their work, but still had extra expenses. Klausen was the treasurer, and about once a year he submitted a statement of income and expenses to Sorge, who had it photostated and a copy sent to Russia. During Klausen's service as treasurer from 1936 till October 1941, he received United States $24,500 and 18,300 yen through the couriers, plus about $10,000 in bank remittances, a total of about $40,000. Certainly the information which Sorge went after June 22, 1941, was worth many millions of dollars to the Soviet Union.

"Nineteen hundred and forty-one was the crucial year. After earlier general reports, on May 20, 1941, Sorge flashed the urgent warning that the Reichswehr would concentrate from 170 to 190 divisions on the Soviet border, and on June 20 would attack along the whole frontier. The main direction of the drive would be toward Moscow. It will be recalled that this attack did occur on June 22. Naturally, thereafter, the answer to the question of Japanese attack from the east became the most vital mission of the Sorge ring. All questions, whether of Japanese-American relations, the war in China or internal politics were subordinated to answering that basic question.

"Sorge was able to report on July 2, immediately after the Imperial Council of that date, that the Japanese Government had decided to push southward into French Indo-China and seize valuable bases. Meanwhile, while adhering to their neutrality treaty with the U.S.S.R., in view of the possibility of war with the Soviet Union, they would mobilize their whole forces. Late in July, Sorge reported that a few troops from the Tokyo-Osaka areas had been sent south, but that to advance into Thailand and Malaya they needed 300,000 men. So far there were only 40,000 men in Indo-China.

"Sorge's estimates of late July and early August, based on information supplied by Ozaki, Miyagi and the German Embassy, showed that 1,000,000 new men had been mobilized, that the great majority had been sent to China or further south, and that only a small proportion were being sent to Manchuria.

"By October 15 Sorge had transmitted his final sober conclusions that the Japanese had decided to move south and that there now was no serious danger of an attack by the Kwantung Army across the Siberian frontier. He felt that his mission was completed and drafted a dispatch suggesting his recall to the Soviet Union. Klausen argued that this request was premature, and the message was never sent. Three days later Sorge and Klausen were under arrest.

"Dr. Richard Sorge and his group were exposed through no errors of their own. Their operations were faultless; no one ever suspected them. The wretched Communist agent, Ito Ritsu, betrayed them in pain and in jealousy. Even he did not know what he did. Although under suspicion of Communist sympathies Ito Ritsu worked in the investigation department of the Tokyo branch of the South Manchurian Railway, the same organization which Ozaki was serving as special adviser. Then aged 29, he was arrested in June 1941 on suspicion of Communist activities. Under guidance of officers of the Tokyo Metropolitan Police Board Ito made full confession, claimed to have erred by his Communist faith, and then began to implicate others.

"Sorge's arrest was a great shock to his close friends, Ambassador Ott and the Gestapo chief, Col. Joseph Meissinger. They could only believe that the Japanese had committed another of the blunders for which they were legendary, and they worked hard to get their friend out of jail. There was also a disturbing question: if by some remote chance good Nazi Sorge actually was a Soviet Spy, where did that leave two highly placed Nazi officials who had trusted in and confided in him for so long? But the obstinate Japanese police were adamant. They insisted that they had the principals of the most dangerous spy ring ever discovered in Japan.

"The police were unhurried about their investigation, although Premier Tojo Hideki kept urging speed. So many of their prisoners talked freely that they had no problem in getting a full picture of the whole case and in separating the guilty from the innocent. Having proved their case, they became concerned with the deeper implications of the spy ring. They wanted to know more than how the spies had operated and what they had found out. They wanted to know what had motivated them, especially the Japanese traitor. Although Sorge attempted to maintain security, and was most contemptuous of Klausen's turning informant, before five months had passed, even he came to talk freely and, seemingly, willingly.

"Because of the evidence of Klausen's change of heart, and because of his free confession, the Japanese court only gave him life imprisonment. To Anna, upon whom they looked as a woman who worked against her will, they gave three years.

She was out waiting for Max when he was released from the Akita prison on October 9, 1945, by order of the U. S. Army.

"Ozaki had never really feared the consequences of treason. He had always believed that if he were discovered all he need do was die.

"Sentences were handed down by the Tokyo District Court in September 1943. Both Sorge and Ozaki appealed to the Supreme Court. Oddly, Sorge and Ozaki both made the defense that they hadn't done anything illegal. They presented the straw-man theory that they had not used force to acquire their secrets and they only passed on to Moscow information available to any intelligent man. Sorge summed up his defense thus:

" 'I obtained my information from the German Embassy, but here again I consider that little, if any, or it could be termed "State Secret." It was given to me voluntarily. I never used deceit or force. Ambassador Ott and Commander Scholl asked me to help them write reports, especially Scholl, who put much confidence in me and asked me to read all of his own reports before he sent them to Germany. As for me, I placed much trust in this information because it was compiled and evaluated by competent military and naval attachés for the use of the German General Staff. I believe that the Japanese government, in giving data to the German Embassy expected some of it to leak out.

" 'Ozaki obtained much of his news from the Breakfast Group. But the Breakfast Group was not an official organization. Such information as was exchanged within the group must have been discussed by other similar cliques, of which there were many in Tokyo in those days. Even such data as Ozaki considered important and secret was actually no longer so, because he had procured it indirectly after it had left its secret source.'

"The Supreme Court was unimpressed by this logic. Sorge's appeal was dismissed in January, and Ozaki's in April 1944.

"It is an interesting and perhaps surprising commentary on the quality of Japanese civil justice to note, however, that in the midst of a bitter war the most dangerous spies ever captured were given the benefit of every protection offered by Japanese law. It also seems surprising that of the nearly 20 guilty men and women, only two were sentenced to death, although under Japanese law every one of them subjected himself to the death penalty.

"The following is a list of the convicted prisoners, their sentences and ultimate fate:

Sorge, Richard, death; hanged, November 7, 1944

Ozaki, Hozumi, death; hanged, November 7, 1944

Voukelitch, Branko de, life; died in prison January 13, 1945

Miyagi, Yotoku, unsentenced; died during trial August 2, 1943

Klausen, Max, life; released, October 9, 1945

Koshiro, Yoshinobu, 15 years; released, October 8, 1945

Taguchi, Ugenda, 13 years; released, October 6, 1945

Mizuno, Shige, 13 years; died in prison, March 22, 1945

Yamana, Masazane, 12 years; released, October 7, 1945

Funakoshi, Hisao, 10 years; died in prison, February 27, 1945

Kawai, Teikichi, 10 years; released, October 10, 1945

Kawamura, Yoshio, unsentenced; died before trial, Dec. 15, 1942

Kuzumi, Fusako, 8 years; released, October 8, 1945

Kitabayashi, Tomo, 5 years; released, unknown date."

So ended Richard Sorge, a German, a Communist, an incredibly successful Soviet spy, and a spy who claimed the path of history.

THE AMERICAN WHO SAVED LONDON

I WOULD LIKE to tell the story of the man who saved my life back in 1940 when Hitler had taken Paris.

People everywhere went in fear and trembling, for they were terrible days and nobody knew how it would all end. I was not sure that my family or I could face the horrors of Hitler's prison camps. Death was closing in on all that men who cherished freedom held dear.

My wife, Hilda, had joined me in Sweden after she had been released from a Nazi prison and the dubious company of the aristocratic fräuleins who were finally executed as Polish spies.

I had worked as foreign correspondent in the Swedish capital, and at the outbreak of war, though I loved Sweden and her wonderful old democracy, I could not remain "neutral" in this conflict between ruthless dictators and free men.

I was deeply involved in underground activities in Sweden

and the Germans knew it. They had asked the Swedish Government either to extradite me to Nazi Germany—I had left my native Austria at the age of six—or to put me into one of the "refugee camps" in Sweden for the duration of the war.

I was arrested in Sweden and knew I was in grave peril. The gas chambers of Germany lay ahead of me. But suddenly there was a break in the clouds, and, due to the intervention of some kindly Swedish friends, I was able to meet the man who was to save my life. He was William Warwick Corcoran, the first American Consul General to be assigned to Gothenburg. Corcoran has been called America's No. 1 Master Spy.

It was this unusual man who saved the city of London by detecting the location of the V-rocket and robot bomb centre at Peenemünde on the Baltic. It was he who through a master stroke discovered the hiding-place of Nazi Foreign Secretary Joachim von Ribbentrop and was responsible for his arrest.

Like Parsifal searching for the Grail, the consul, who handled visas, marriages and inheritance cases, became a crusader for freedom and one of Uncle Sam's best agents. To me he will always be a knight, an American knight, in shinning armor.

But let's start at the beginning. Billy Corcoran, a former city editor of the *Washington Post*, had come to Sweden in 1936. He was a routine consul, a career diplomat who had served his country almost half around the globe in Calcutta, Bombay, Madras, Warsaw, Algiers, Gibraltar, Jamaica and Spain. He would violently object to being called a spy. He was never anything else but a diplomatic "reporter" and no newspaper story that made him America's most outstanding intelligence officer would ever change Consul Corcoran's opinion of himself.

Sweden, a country large in territory, at least by European standards, had only six and a half million people. All active and public figures have heard of one another, so Billy Corcoran had inside knowledge of what I had been doing in Sweden. It was highly dishonorable from the Nazi point of view. No wonder I was in trouble.

First, I had written a book on Luftwaffe Chief Herman Goering. The Air Marshal asked the Swedish Goverment to ban it because I had revealed facts in court proceedings in a family suit in which Goering had been committed to a nerve clinic on account of his drug addiction.

Then I had acquired shares in a printing works in Stockholm and we were printing leaflets to be sent by ship to Germany for underground distribution. I had also participated actively as co-editor of the pro-British, anti-Nazi paper *Trots Allt* and finally I had teamed up with Sweden's secret police in order to be protected in my work with the British Secret Service.

The Swedes knew it and the British knew it. It was perfect teamwork. The American Consul Corcoran also knew it. When I saw him he smiled and never said a word. Of course, I never saw Billy's reports either.

Suddenly overnight thousands of anti-Nazi books and pamphlets appeared in Sweden. They were mailed out every Saturday, shortly after noon. The pamphlets went to Sweden's officers, to her teachers, union members, housewives, urging a boycott of German goods. They carried a warning of Hitler's real intentions and pleaded that neutral Sweden should remain neutral and never join or lend itself to assisting the Nazis.

One Monday morning an emissary of the Nazi Embassy appeared at the Swedish Department of Justice and asked for the confiscation of the publication issued by the "Publishing House for Freedom and Democracy," which was the imprint of the pamphlets I was responsible for.

Monday at eleven in the morning, week after week, Swedish police appeared in the office, "confiscated" the previous week's pamphlets of which we had kept fifty copies for them. Of course, 20,000 had been mailed on Saturday and could not be found.

Germany was furious, and the Swedes not at all comfortable, although it was all strictly legal. Finally, the Nazis became tough and asked that drastic steps be taken against me. Naturally, I was tipped off by my friends inside the political police in Stockholm. Still the Swedes were irritated and told me that if the war continued to go bad for the Allies they might not be able to protect me much longer.

The Königsberg radio blasted day after day that I was a warmonger who wanted to bring Sweden into the war on the side of the Allies and that I must be stopped, or the Germans would find a way to stop me.

The situation became more and more critical. I was called super-spy, informer, secret agent and traitor by the Nazis and I knew my days of freedom were numbered. My Swedish Government friends advised me to go to Britain.

But how? Sweden was surrounded by occupied countries

174

Denmark and Norway. German missions were already in Finland. Russia was closed to me since I had interviewed Trotsky. What should I do?

I went to see Billy Corcoran, whom I did not then know. I certainly had no notion of what he was doing besides being a consular officer. But the late Torgeny Segerstedt, the dean of Sweden's newspapermen, sent me to Billy as the last resort.

I was anything but sanguine, because I knew that countless numbers of refugees in every part of Europe yearned for the safety of American shores without a hope of getting a visa. I wanted to get out of Sweden and reach Britain via America.

I told Billy my story. He did not betray himself, and never let on that he knew of my confiscated pamphlets or of my other activities. When I had finsihed he said to me: "I'll help you. I was in Spain and saw Franco's troops mow down dozens of innocent men, women and children. I know what Fascism is. You will get to America."

A miracle had happened. This man, with his sharp eyes, his erect figure, his grey-haired temples, who looked to me as American as the apple pie at the corner drugstore, had performed it.

As Billy Corcoran retired from active service in 1946, I think his amazing story can now be told, at least in part.

He was born in Washington, D.C., on September 5th, 1884. His mother, of German stock, was Katherine von Meyer. Perhaps through her he had learned, and never forgotten, that Prussian militarism has always meant disaster for Germany and the world.

He was a fighting editor in Washington from 1905-16. Here he showed not only integrity but an amazing zeal for righting wrongs. His heart was always with the little man and the underdog, in spite of the fact that he came from a wealthy, conservative Washington family and, at times, possessed a considerable fortune. His grandfather had owned much valuable property on the east side of the Capitol grounds. Corcoran entered the diplomatic service with the best possible background after graduating from Georgetown University Law School. He also attended the University of Lille in France and speaks French like a Frenchman—which is a rare gift for an American diplomat.

His parents died very early and Billy suddenly possessed a fortune. He spent it lavishly on such hobbies as horses, automobiles, boats and yachts. He became a gay and popular man about town.

His life was fundamentally influenced and changed later when he met a Catholic nun who became his adopted mother. Of her he says, "At the knee of my adopted mother—and remember I am not a Catholic—I learned a simple set of ethics by which I have attempted (and failed many times) to live."

Most of his inheritance had vanished when Bill Spurgeon, a fabulous *Washington Post* editor, offered him a job as reporter for fifteen dollars a week and five dollars a day expenses which he was pleased to accept. It was like entering a new world, a world, or rather an underworld, of thieves and crooked politicians. It was Billy's job to search for evidence to put the finger on them and it was thrilling and dangerous work. He came to be hated and feared by those he exposed, but elsewhere he was recognized and respected by serious statesmen and newspapermen, among them William D. Hassett, White House Secretary to both President Roosevelt and Truman, and David Lawrence, the well-known columnist. He met President Wilson and young Franklin Roosevelt when he was still Under-Secretary of the Navy.

Corcoran, too, could not remain neutral when Prussian militarism and Western democracy clashed in World War I. He quit his job in Washington and joined the French Foreign Legion. When America entered the war he became a first lieutenant in the American Expeditionary Force. In 1919 we find him in Coblenz, editor for the American service paper *Amroc News*. Later, the *Koblenzer Zeitung* was taken over and Corcoran made it a daily for American soldiers. At the end of the war, when demobilisation came along, Corcoran got his discharge papers, being declared ninety per cent incapacitated.

He had received the *Croix de Guerre* and in 1920, the French presented him with the *Medaille de Sauvetage*. He was awarded this latter honour for saving the life of a nine-year-old French boy who fell over the railing of the Channel steamer on which Corcoran was also travelling. It was an icy-cold day but in the midst of the confusion and excitement Billy Corcoran jumped, fully dressed, into the heavy seas, caught hold of the boy, and held him up until a life buoy was thrown to him. It was almost an hour before rescuer and rescued were dragged to safety.

Today, after more than thirty years, Corcoran says rather humbly about this incident:

"As I grow older I feel that the greatest satisfaction in life is not in doing brave deeds for the sake of doing them, or even for the sake of showing one's fellow men that brave deeds are intrinsically good; the supreme satisfaction comes in trying to help the other fellow, especially when he or she is in need. On that wintry morning, when I went to the aid of a drowning boy, I felt what I thought, at that time, to be the greatest thrill of my existence. But it was a selfish feeling, one of unmitigated snobbery and self-adulation, and I thrilled with it in my small way for years after. But on growing older and being in this job during the war with thousands of unfortunates coming in for aid—and in being able to help them— I experienced the greatest satisfaction which a man can possibly know. And when I retire I will carry with me solace for my conscience to offset whatever wrongs I may have inflicted."

Corcoran is retired now. Like a grandfather to his attentive grandchildren he tells about his accomplishments in the last war without even realising how heroic and important they were. He was the man who not only saved the city of London but also probably hundreds of thousands of lives. For without Corcoran's discovery of the Peenemünde robot bomb centre the invasion of Europe would have had to be postponed, or taken place elsewhere. Men such as General Eisenhower have said that Corcoran's discovery of Peenemünde saved the Allies at least six months, if not more.

Corcoran always was a lone wolf and what he had organized in Sweden was the best one-man intelligence job of the war. He was a diplomat and not a spy. How was it that he could get information so valuable?

He had many friends, especially among the Swedes. With their help, he met privately week after week the ships' captains of neutral Swedish steamers who were running the Baltic between Germany and Sweden. There in Gothenburg Consul Corcoran got a pretty clear picture of what was going on inside the Baltic Sea and its harbors. Then one day German Counter-Intelligence heard of these clandestine meetings and protested to the Swedish Government. Billy Corcoran had to be more careful, but actually the Swedes were also interested in learning the same stories of German preparations and shipping in the Baltic. They did not interfere with Corcoran in any way.

But he changed the set-up. He knew all the shipowners and all the captains, but now he wanted information from another source. So he met up with sailors, ship's mates, engineers, cooks, stevedores—the union members. Within a few months he had lifted the corner of a curtain of mystery without being able to guess what lay hidden behind it. But everyone he spoke to told the same story—which no one could analyze, not even Corcoran—the story of thousands of small boats leaving Stettin for an unknown place somewhere sixty miles to the north-east. But, pondered Corcoran, there was no place on the map to indicate any town of importance in this vicinity. But Corcoran had heard of a mystery town called Peenemünde and he asked friends to try to fix its exact location. He knew it was ringed by barbed wire and that once inside no workers were permitted to leave and no visitors were allowed. Perhaps the little boats went there to Peenemünde?

While he was still trying to discover what lay behind the curtain a bombshell exploded on his doorstep, so to speak. The Swedish papers disclosed that the German Secret Service were planning to kidnap and assassinate Corcoran. They called him America's most dangerous spy. Coincident with this startling revelation *Pravda* published an article by Madame Kollontai describing him as "Uncle Sam's No. I Master Spy." But why—what had he done? He was not yet aware of what Peenemünde really meant in the German strategy, or that Hitler believed the weapons being made there would end the war within twenty-four hours.

Corcoran had his own ideas, nevertheless. Invoice copies inside the office of the SKF Ball Bearing Companies had disappeared, invoices of those ball bearings that were shipped to Nazi Germany.

The Allies were furious. Protests came to Sweden arrangements were made to deliver ball bearings to the West, too. Stanton Griffis, the U.S. negotiator, came to Sweden to stop the ball-bearing exports to Germany.

A Norwegian and two Swedes were sentenced to three years for the theft of these invoices and the leak to the West. The Germans accused Corcoran, but he replied to interviewing reporters: "How could I do such a thing in a neutral country?" How could he? He certainly did not filch the invoices, but he saw to it that the "thieves" would have it easy. At least this is what the Soviets implied in the *Pravda* article.

* * *

But still this was only the beginning.

Escaped ships from Quisling Norway lay in the harbor of

Gothenburg behind the Nazi blockade. To leave they had to run the gauntlet of aerial and underwater attack, and it was a most costly enterprise, but Corcoran saw to it that the Allies gave air force help when the Norwegian sailors, in true Viking fashion, made their daredevil escape under the very nose of the Nazi Navy.

Corcoran was happy when so much attention was focused on the Nowegian ships and the ball-bearing affair and that he was accused of being the man behind such Allied activities. It was wonderful camouflage and allowed him to continue the investigation of the ghost town, Peenemünde.

He pleaded with the military authorities of the Allies to give him more time. They were flying now, day after day and night after night, over Peenemünde—taking photographs, always pretending they were out to bomb Berlin and Stettin, which they did. The Nazis were sure no one knew of Peenemünde or its significance.

They were clever enough to avoid the use of flak there in order not to draw attention to it; the thick forest along the Baltic was a perfect protection for Peenemünde.

More and more aerial photographs were taken and more and more seamen told of full-blast activities in Peenemünde.

Then came the night of August 17th, 1943, when 570 heavy R.A.F. night bombers headed towards Peenemünde. The Nazis again were sure the target would be either Stettin or Berlin, but they were wrong this time, for, on this occasion, the air armada did not turn towards Germany, but instead blasted the mystery town in forty minutes and Hitler's hope of totally destroying Britain was gone. Corcoran had reported fully on Peenemünde by the end of July and three weeks later the lightning bolts were released. Peenemünde was an inferno. Dante's purgatory was a garden compared with these oceans of flames. Forty assembly shops were in ashes, every laboratory destroyed and fifty buildings damaged. Of the 7,000 scientists working there, 5,000 were killed, including the chief of research and plant manager, Major-General Wolfgang von Chamier-Glisenzki, General Jeschonnek, Chief of Staff of the Luftwaffe, and General Ernst Udet, Germany's most famous flying ace. Forty-one aircraft were lost on the return flight.

It was the turning point of the war, according to Churchill. The robot bomb center was devastated, a blow that not only helped to save London but probably prevented the east coast of the United States from being bombarded by the flying missiles.

Billy Corcoran received all the decorations due to him, although after this great personal triumph he still could not reveal what had happened. His beautiful British wife, tall and slim and charming, must have been the world's proudest woman that day, though she dared not confide her joy in anyone.

While the Peenemünde victory might have satisfied most people as a great accomplishment—not so Billy Corcoran. His next achievement was something to conjure with, for, but for his intervention, the Nazi Foreign Secretary, Joachim von Ribbontrop, might still be alive today, perhaps somewhere in Argentina.

The "Consul"—with his one-man intelligence service—had worked out an amazing scheme which again showed vision and courage. The luxury-liner *Gripsholm* was in the harbor of Gothenburg. She was known at the time as a mercy ship, being used to repatriate displaced persons, diplomats, prisoners of war, in association with the Red Cross. On board the ship was Frau Jenke. No one had ever heard of her. Officially she was the wife of a routine diplomat, the Commercial Counsellor in Ankara at the Nazi Embassy. Corcoran, who had 'ist of the repatriated Nazi diplomats who had arrived on the *Gripsholm*, was sure Herr Jenke was probably one of the men who had to watch Ambassador Franz von Papen, the man who helped Hitler to power and then became somewhat "critical" of him.

Frau Jenke, it was also known, was the sister of Joachim von Ribbentrop. She was later placed under police supervision in a hotel in Gothenburg. Consul Corcoran did not need much time to make up his mind, and speaking wonderful French, visited Frau Jenke and told her he, too, was a "refugee" from France, and belonged to the Laval-Pétain sympathisers. He wanted to go to Germany or to the Argentine and explained that he had friends in Germany who would help him to go to South America, sooner or later.

Corcoran had guessed that Frau Jenke wanted to join her brother in hiding and go with him to South America, too.

"Can you help me to go to Germany?" Frau Jenke asked.

Corcoran promised.

Frau Jenke told him that in the old days when Joachim was still a champagne salesman he had a friend, a wine merchant in Hamburg. If Frau Jenke could see the wine merchant she felt sure she could find her brother. The whole world, it must be remembered, was searching for the vanished Ribbentrop at this time.

"Swedish friends" now arranged transportation to Hamburg for Frau Jenke. She was overjoyed to get permission to leave Sweden and to enter the British zone of Germany. She arrived on time and immediately made her way to the wine merchant she had spoken about. From there—where she was wined and dined—she went with beating heart to see her brother, who was staying in a nearby boarding house. Two minutes later, Allied agents had arrested Joachim von Ribbentrop. Later he was tried at Nuremberg and executed.

The Peenemünde and Ribbentrop investigations were Corcoran's outstanding achievements in the field of "reporting," but almost as vital were his reports on Nazi ships passing the Kattegat and the Skagerrak which resulted in many of them being sunk. A German consul in Norway, who was officially a Norwegian Quisling, worked for Corcoran and helped locate secret Nazi armament arsenals, ship movements, oil installations and the heavy-water experimental plant.

After Peenemünde was destroyed, Corcoran's seamen reported Nazi oil installations only thirty miles away from Peenemünde, close to the Oder port of Stettin. They too were blown to bits. Corcoran received more medals. The Swedish police guarded his offices and watched over him day and night knowing that the Nazis had ordered his assassination.

The medals Consul Corcoran received, and they are too many to be listed, were certainly welcome as a great honor, but his real monument, his real decoration, is today inside the hearts of 5,000 people—all refugees, whom Corcoran saved.

No refugee who ever came to Corcoran for aid was turned away, and practically all—where help was possible and reasonable—received permission and visas to enter the United States.

The *Gothenburg Handels och Sjöfartstidning* on February 25th, 1947, said this about a great American:

"The Consulate's achievements are numerous, one of the most important being its work on behalf of the refugees during the last few years. At present this work consists in taking care of people who have survived the prisons and terror camps of Europe and sending them across the Atlantic to relatives and friends."

It is very significant that the great North American Republic began its existence with a declaration of human rights, among which are mentioned life, liberty, and the pursuit of happiness! To thousands of people, the United States is a promised haven, and on every ship as many berths as can be commanded are occupied by refugees from the countries of Europe to whom America gives a chance of a new life and freedom.

William Corcoran has not spared himself in the service of his country and of humanity and international relations. He may rest assured that thousands are grateful to him. I was one of the many whose life he saved. I would never have been able to write this book without him. He has made history and he has done it as all great men do—with a humble heart and with courage and unselfish idealism.

THE RED ORCHESTRA

THE TROJAN horse of the twentieth century has wings. The men who infiltrated ancient Troy in a huge wooden horse have been surpassed by the passengers of the jet-propelled Kremlin "peace dove." But there always have been men and women working inside their own native governments in behalf of a foreign nation. From the harlot Rahab who betrayed ancient Jericho, to Major Vidkun Quisling who sold Adolf Hitler the Kingdom of Norway, there have always been individuals who loved power more than their country.

The autocratic nations in history always have offered handsome rewards in money and glory to the overambitious—whether it was the Imperial Austrian general staff Josef Redl, who gave away the Hapsburg military secrets to the Russian emperor during World War I; or whether it was Count Charles Esterhazy, who sent Captain Dreyfus to Devil's Island to cover up his own high treason. In our days there have been men like Pierre Laval in France, Otto Kusiinen in Finland, Richard Sorge in Japan, Alger Hiss and Whittaker Chambers in the United States, Ana Pauker in Romania, Klement Gottwald in Czechoslovakia, and Matthias Rakosi in Hungary. All of them have worked on high government levels; they have had cultured, educated, polished personalities. Some of them were greatly respected by their colleagues, who found it difficult to believe that these cultured personages could deal in the shabby game of treason. The public still thinks in moving-picture stereotypes and expects the spy to be a man with a black beard and dark glasses, speaking with a thick foreign accent, drinking vodka, eating caviar, or hanging around in waterfront saloons and union hiring halls.

The modern government which was hardest to conquer from within was the totalitarian Third Reich. It is significant that only another totalitarian country trained in the same ruthless techniques and ideologies could succeed in cracking the wall and cripple the hitherto invincible Naza secret service of Admiral Canaris.

It was 3:55 A.M. on June 26, 1941. The Eastern campaign was four days old when a monitor of the listening post at Cranz, East Prussia, intercepted a message that did not help much, at first: thirty-two groups of five figures, with sender and recipient unknown.

Day and night the monitors at Cranz listened to the polyphonic concerto issuing from their sets. Six monitors were put on the track; they spent days and nights, weeks and months, groping for the strange transmitter. Slowly they became familiar with its habits. They knew when it would change frequencies; they could make out the "handwriting" of various operators; they noticed whether the messages were acknowledged or passed unheard. They were amazed to find the lone voice shortly joined by another, and by a third and a fourth. The unknown transmitter group increased from week to week, until it broadcast messages by the dozen across every front.

Tracer teams went into action, trying to locate the transmitters by means of directional antennae. Through the directional lines traversed Brussels, Paris, and Zürich, the two strongest stations broadcast from Berlin itself.

But the most startling aspect was that messages from all the different transmitters were acknowledged in one place: in the Soviet capital. All tests pointed there. No doubt the mysterious signals were the radio communications of Soviet war espionage, with Moscow at the center.

However feverish their decoding activities, the Germans could not discover what the messages implied. They could not find the key to the code. Only two messages closed with names not in code, both obvious aliases: Kent and Coro.

But who was Kent? And who was Coro?

Señor Vincente Sierra of Uruguay was a busy man. He was chairman of the board of Simexco, a Brussels corporation with branches in Marseilles, Rome, Prague, Oslo, and Stockholm, and affiliated enterprises in the Czech protectorate, in Raudnitz on the Elbe, and in Bucharest. In Paris the firm was registered with the Chamber of Commerce under the name Simex, with offices at 24 Boulevard Haussmann and a M. Gilbert as manager.

Sierra traveled constantly between Brussels, Paris, Marseilles, and Prague. Besides, he engaged in profitable negotiations with German Wehrmacht authorities, especially with the Todt superhighway organization. After German invasion of the West, business was better than ever. And after Hitler decided to erect an impregnable Atlantic Wall on the Channel coast, the Simex firm could hardly keep up with its orders.

Not many firms collaborated with the Germans so reliably and with so little friction, and few emerged so spotless from the most careful investigation by the Sicherheitsdienst. And Sierra was Kent.

In the Mollenbeek section of Brussels, near the Place de la Duchesse de Brabant, Señor Sierra disappeared into a two-story building.

Casual nods greeted him in the small, hot workroom.

Rita Arnold, the apartment owner, was sitting by the radio, rapidly taking down a message—nothing but figures in combinations of five.

Flight Lieutenant Michael Makarov and Second Lieutenant Anton Danilov were decoding the incoming messages. Both were Soviet intelligence officers, under orders from Moscow to let themselves be trapped by the German advance and remain available for Soviet espionage in France and Belgium.

Makarov was pleased to see Kent. "Plenty of mail for you, *mon petit chef,*" he said, handing Kent a folder across the table.

KLS de RTX 1710. 1835. 101 wds. qbt. Central to Kent —Inquire concerning production capacity of German factories for chemical warfare. Prepare sabotage in plants concerned.

Central to Kent—Locate General von Rundstedt and his three corps in France.

Thoughtfully Kent pushed the folder back to Makarov. "And what did we transmit?"

From memory, Makarov rattled off a few of the messages that had gone to Central in the previous weeks:

Present production of dive bombers 9 to 10 a day. German Luftwaffe losing average of 40 planes a day.—Source Coro.

Combat units previously stationed in Crete are en route to Eastern front. Some to Crimea in a body.—Source Coro.

New Messerschmidt fighters have two cannon and two machine guns mounted laterally in the fuselage.—Source Coro.

Hundreds of reports had gone to the Moscow center, but in Berlin the Nazis were still in the dark. They had not yet found the key to the groups of figures.

The Nazi agents decided to strike hard. Their radio counter-intelligence set out to hunt down the mysterious "Coro." As yet Berlin had no inkling that the biggest Russian radio spy net had enmeshed the heart of the Nazi government and party. The secret broadcasts changed daily and the shortwave messages were brief, lasting seconds or, at most, one or two minutes. Admiral Canaris was called in; Heinrich Himmler got special instructions; all radio specialists were mobilized—but the adversary seemed to be smart, cautious, and experienced.

On November 12, 1941, the secret transmitter in Berlin abruptly stopped broadcasting. It stopped in the very middle of a message, as if someone had locked the key under the operator's finger.

Eight tracers from the OKW, Radio Control Division, looked dumbfounded. They tried all wave lengths generally used by the transmitter; they double-checked their own equipment. In vain—Coro kept silent. Mechanical trouble, maybe—or perhaps it was that Coro, at the last moment, had noticed the slow approach of the tracers from Radio Control.

Already the three blocks from which the transmitter had alternately beamed its still undecoded messages were marked with red pins on the radio defense map of the OKW. For two days and two nights the tracers lay in wait on Berlin's Bayerische Platz, on Motrizplatz, and in the Invalidenpark, hoping for Coro to make another sound. They were disguised as postal officials, in blue gold-buttoned uniforms and stiff visored caps.

At first, as supposed wire repairmen, they had set up the usual tents of the Reichspost over some manholes in the suspect areas, and installed their directional radio equipment inside. It was considered a highly ingenious camouflage.

Probably everything would have gone well if one of Coro's operators, on his way to the transmitter, had not happened to hear someone in the tent say, "Jawohl, Herr Leutnant"—plainly, distinctly, and simultaneously with the whistle of a condenser being adjusted on a receiving set.

The failure of "Operation Reichspost" upset all previous results of the investigation. At this moment Coro was farther out of reach than ever.

On the other hand, after the Berlin group fell silent, the radio control division noted a doubling of broadcasting activities by the secret transmitters in Belgium, Holland, and France.

No one suspected that Coro, during this period, broadcast three of his most important reports to Moscow over the transmitter of the Reichsministry of Aviation.

Soon Kent and the unknown Coro were to meet. Moscow had new assignments for them—rendezvous for parachute agents, facilitation of communications to Switzerland.

At 18 Wilhelmshöher Strasse, Berlin-Friedenau, Herr and Frau Kuckhoff one night were expecting a visit from a stranger whom we recognized as Kent. He would identify himself by the password "Eulenspiegel," the title of a novel by Adam Kuckhoff, who had written many novels including *The German of Bayencourt* and *Strogany*. He was a director for Prague Films, Inc., and his documentary, *Posen, A City Rebuilding*, had earned an award from Goebbels.

His wife, the economist and writer Margaret Kuckhoff, née Lorke, had made translations for the Race-Political Office of the N.S.D.A.P.—and English translations of addresses by Goebbels and large sections of *Mein Kampf*. Only later did Frau Margarete Kuckhoff reach the zenith of her career. Among other things, she is today president of the Soviet Zone Bank of Issue and an honorary member of the Soviet Zone Democratic Women's League.

At 10 P.M. on November 12, 1941, Kent arrived—the organizing genius whose radio network extended from Brussels across Western Europe. He had incessantly devised new methods which made the discovery of his transmitters all but impossible and brought the German directional operators to the edge of despair. Only Coro, if anyone, surpassed him in precision and accuracy of reporting. Kent's men were everywhere, some of them even chauffeurs for the special delegate of the Todt Organization in Paris. His official firm, Simexco, with its numerous branches all over Europe, had an annual turnover of 127,000,000 francs in Wehrmacht orders alone. Señor Vincente Sierra—as Kent was known—was *persona grata* with top military echelons in the occupied areas of the West.

The meeting of Kent and Coro arranged by the Kuckhoffs took a scant half hour. After a walk about Berlin, the following report went to Moscow:

(1) Delivery of transmitter equipment accomplished.

(2) Liaison with Prague group established; Slovak resistance group Sokol advised of wave lengths in use.

(3) Vast accumulation of material; additional transmitters urgently required.

(4) Coro has informant in the newly-formed decoding unit of Nazi Radio Defense.

Six months had passed since the operator at Cranz, East Prussia, had first intercepted the mysterious Morse signals that subsequently multiplied into the "Red Orchestra."

Wehrmacht, party, and the vast machine of the Nazi police were locked in an unequal struggle with a small group of men pursuing their plans with unparalleled audacity and unparalleled skill. On request of Canaris' counter-intelligence office, the Reichssicherheitshauptamt too had taken a hand. Special inspectors were ordered to investigate in Belgium and France. The secret military police in the respective areas were mobilized and reinforced with a staff of radio operators, tracers, and technicians. Permitted to work in civilian disguise, they made good progress.

In December, 1941, at last, the first attack was launched.

The residential section of Mollenbeek in northwestern Brussels lay deserted in the night of December 20-21. Two heavy limousines, lights dimmed, drove up through the Rue des Quatre Vents. In a side street, the house to which one of Kent's many transmitters had been traced was surrounded noiselessly. Only the old landlady, jarred out of her sleep by the clanking of the torn latch chain, stood in the hallway, petrified, a flashlight in her hand.

Before she could make a sound a policeman's hand covered her mouth. The others, pistols cocked, raced up to the third floor.

The surprise was complete. A woman sat by a radio, and

two men were busily coding messages. Two shots put them out of action before they could reach their guns. A policeman, at the last moment, tore papers out of the flames of the fireplace.

The arrested men later turned out to be the two men Señor Sierra had met in Brussels, Soviet Flight Lieutenant Michael Makarov and Second Lieutenant Danilov—both carefully trained and attached to the Soviet intelligence network in Belgium as early as 1939.

The first capture of a "Red Orchestra" transmitter had been successful. The spell was broken. Kent, the head of the organization, was still at large, but now at last the Nazis had important clues. Couriers flew the rescued documents to Berlin, to Radio Defense headquarters on Matthaikirchplatz, and the prisoners were put through the interrogation mill. "With all severity," said orders from above, and this severity, in time, loosened the tongues of Makarov and Danilov.

Now it was the German's move. Slowly and ponderously the immense organization stirred, but then it ran consistently and irresistibly, like a machine.

Kent and Coro knew the danger. Despite it, the transmitter groups in Ostend, Amsterdam, Paris, Marseilles, and on Lake Geneva got off dozens of messages daily. The preparations for the spring offensive in the East furnished innumerable subjects; troop movements, production data, new weapons, new divisions, casualty figures, transport figures—and then the vast field of diplomacy.

At the time, close to three hundred agents' transmitters were kept under supervision. The decoding section was feverishly active after the capture of the papers in Brussels; it hoped to make great strides on the basis of the documents seized there. The hardest-working and perhaps most gifted of the young men picked to work on the case was named Horst Heilmann. He had studied at the Foreign Affairs Institute before the war, had repeatedly worked as a decoder of English and Russian broadcasts, had been in the Hitler Youth since 1937, and was considered absolutely reliable—the more so as he had been recommended for the special section by First Lieutenant Harro Schulze-Boysen of the Air Ministry.

But Heilmann led a double life. He spent evening after evening with his friend the air force lieutenant, in the studio apartment at 12 Altenburger Strasse, and there a new and dangerous world of conspiracy was revealed to him. There were discussions to which he listened eagerly; these were people who, for the sake of their ideas, had discarded all values and yardsticks Heilmann had hitherto known and accepted. He was aware that he had joined a group of conspirators to whom his work in radio defense was vitally important. He understood that they had cleverly put him there, to get continuous information on the progress of the decoding efforts. But Heilmann was willing to be taken into this circle. He was obsessed with his exciting new role.

One day, the decoding section received new, important clues. A Dutch transmitter group had been rounded up, and in Paris Monsieur and Madame Sokol had been caught in the act of broadcasting from their Montmartre apartment.

Both the Dutch agents and the Sokols soon talked under questioning. They named names and addresses.

Heilmann felt the fatal net around his friend tighten. In his excitement he threw caution to the winds and called Harro Schulze-Boysen on the telephone. Finding him not in, he gave the maid his office number and insisted that Herr Schulze-Boysen call back; it was urgent.

The outstanding work in the "Red Orchestra" case had thus far been done by a corporal under whom Heilmann was working. A professional scholar, he set himself to the task with the stubborn zeal and exactitude of a scientist fascinated by an unsolved problem. He was at his desk day and night, on holidays and in lunch hours. In such a lunch hour—when all radio men, including Heilmann, were in the mess hall—he alone was studying his endless charts.

The phone rang on Heilmann's desk, and the corporal lifted the receiver and, contrary to regulations, said merely "Hello?"

"This is Harro," said a voice at the other end. Herr Schulze-Boysen was returning Heilmann's warning call. But the corporal thought he had said, "This is Coro." For weeks and months he had lived with that name on his mind—Central to Coro, Coro to Central, Coro to Kent, Coro everywhere and nowhere. The name was always in the front of his mind. "What?" he said. "Coro?"

"Are you out of your mind?" the voice said. "You can't just address me as Coro!"

The corporal sat stupefied, receiver in hand.

"Yes, Coro . . . hello, Coro . . . I mean, Herr Coro . . .," he stammered. But the other had hung up.

For some more seconds the corporal held the receiver, trying to figure out methodically whether he had been dreaming.

Then, as fast as his old legs would carry him, he ran downstairs to the officer on duty.

"Herr Major!" he reported breathlessly, "Herr Major, I've just been talking to Coro on the phone."

The rest seemed easy. The call was traced, the caller identified. Another link in the vast "Red Orchestra" spy network had been found.

In the decoding section the news of Coro's exposure spread like wildfire, in spite of all precautionary measures.

All at once everything was simple and clear. The great Coro mystery, which had occupied the police machine of a powerful nation for over a year and kept its best men chasing from Berlin to Amsterdam, Brussels, Paris and Marseilles, had solved itself.

On the morning of August 31, 1942, the phone rang in Lieutenant Schulze-Boysen's office. "This is the doorman on Gate III," said a voice. "A gentleman wants to see you urgently."

"I'm coming," Shulze-Boysen replied without hesitation.

Hatless and unarmed, he walked down the broad staircase without dreaming that these were his last steps in freedom.

Harro Schulze-Boysen's father visited his son on September 30, 1942. Here is the father's account of this tragic meeting between the old naval officer and the young air force officer charged with high treason.

Inspector Kopkow, one of Panzinger's aides, took me up to the top floor and through long corridors to a room that seemed uninhabited. An empty desk stood in a corner; along the wall there was a sofa, two plain chairs and a small table.

For about two minutes I was left alone there.

Then a side door opened to admit Harro, escorted by Kopkow and another officer.

He came with slow, rather heavy steps, as if unaccustomed to walking, but stiffly erect, with both hands behind his back, so that I first thought he was manacled—but he was not. His face was ashen and completely emaciated, with deep shadows around the eyes. Otherwise he looked almost well groomed, as if he had spruced up for our meeting. He was wearing a gray civilian suit and a blue shirt.

I took him by the hand, led him to a chair by the small table, moved the other chair next to it, for myself, and once more took both his hands which remained in mine throughout the conversation. The contact of our hands was like a silent, inner colloquy accompanying the other.

The two officials sat behind the desk, watching. One of them seemed to be taking notes.

I told Harro that I had come as his father, to help him, to stand up for him, to hear how this could best be done and why he was under arrest. At the same time I wanted to bring greetings from his mother, who was in Berlin too, and from his brother, as neither had been permitted to come along.

He answered calmly and firmly that any desire to help him was impossible and hopeless. For years, he said, he had knowingly committed "high treason"—i.e. he had fought against the present state wherever he could; he had been fully aware of the risks and was now resolved to take the consequences.

The conclusion of our talk was purely personal. In the presence of the officials we both tried to hide our feelings.

But gradually I found my grief hard to control. I got up, saying, "You have a hard road ahead of you; I do not want to make it harder. I'll go now."

Harro got up with me, straightened up, stood close before me and gave me a firm, proud look—but for the first time our eyes grew moist. I could say nothing but, "I always loved you."

"I know," he softly replied. I gave him both hands. At the door I turned around once more and nodded to him in silence.

He stood stiffly erect between the two police officers.

Both of us probably felt that we had seen each other for the last time.

The official report to Hitler said: "The detainees include regular soldiers, officials, government employees, artists, writers, journalists, professional people and students, but on the other hand just a few workers and craftsmen."

From September to November, 1942, eighty-four men and women arrested throughout Europe went to jail on suspicion of contact with the spy circle. But still the chain would not break.

From several transmitters in Berlin as well as in the occupied countries broadcasting was continued by German counter-intelligence. Messages of seeming importance were radioed to the Moscow center, as before. The so-called "radio-game" succeeded in many cases, with the result that numbers of parachuting Soviet intelligence agents walked unsuspectingly into Gestapo traps and were arrested at once.

Even though the smashing of the ring had broken the back of the Soviet intelligence organization within Nazi territory, the "Red Orchestra" was by no means silenced. With few exceptions, the arrested eighty-four kept silent.....

It was 7 P.M., two days before Holy Eve of 1942. Eight men and three women were led through the yard of the penitentiary at 7 Königsdamm, Berlin-Plötzensee, to the place of execution.

The bare hall, approximately fifty feet long, held the witnesses: Gestapo inspectors, members of the court martial, court physicians—about twenty people, all told.

The prosecutor, Chief Judge Advocate Dr. Manfred Roeder, stood on a small platform facing the entrance.

The forefront of the hall was partitioned by two black curtains reaching from ceiling to floor and concealing, on the right, the gallows and, on the left, the guillotine.

Harro Schulze-Boysen entered first.

Calm, sure, composed, he let the two hangman's aides lead him behind the curtain, to the gallows.

Seconds later, the hangman in his black frockcoat stepped before the curtain, lifted his top hat, and reported, "The sentence has been executed."

The seven other men were led in at short intervals. All of them knew how to die.

Each one was first called by name.

"Are you: Arvid Harnack . . . Rudolf von Scheliha . . . Hans Coppi . . . Johannes Graudenz . . . Horst Heilmann . . . Kurt Schulze . . . Kurt Schumacher?" Eight times the answer came, "I am," and eight times the hangman, top hat in hand, reported: executed . . . executed . . . executed . . .

Then the women, Libertas Schulze-Boysen, Elizabeth Schumacher, and Ilse Stöbe, were led behind the curtain, to the guillotine.

Later on, in January and February, 1943, nearly sixty additional death sentences were carried out in Plötzensee.

The "Red Orchestra" network had been shattered, but it was not totally destroyed. In spite of all exeuctions, short-wave broadcasting kept coming from occupied Europe to Russia. Coro was out of the way, but Kent, the other chief, was still at large. The search continued. Vast amounts of money were spent on the investigation. Hitler demanded daily reports on the case. It had taken six months to strike the first blow—back in December, 1941, in Brussels-Mollenbeek. In the summer of 1942, the Nazis gradually perceived the extent of the machinery that was still functioning with uncanny precision.

More than a hundred persons had been arrested; a dozen secret transmitters could be captured; twenty more were being watched.

For it went right on: "Kent to Central . . ."

More than five hundred intercepted short-wave messages were piling up in the Nazi Radio Defense offices, and a group of powerful Swiss transmitters had lately joined the chorus of the "Red Orchestra."

By August, 1942, the Gestapo had a report on the identity of Kent and his trail led to Marseilles in unoccupied France, where investigation was slow. But Kent did not outwit his pursuers much longer. One morning when a train left the Marseilles terminal for Paris, the man in the private compartment of the German Armistice Commission was Kent.

Kent's capture released the German secret service from its sixteen-month mightmare. A special plane took him from Paris to Berlin. The first interrogation took place on November 3; the record was brief and disappointing. The only statement he could be induced to make was this:

"I am a Russian officer. I do not deny having worked against Germany wherever I was sent. You are welcome to shoot me." The record showed that he smoked forty cigarettes in two hours of investigation. For weeks the questioning continued. Threats made no impression, and arrest restrictions were endured with stoic equanimity. He was the classic stereotype of an agent—a man who seemed able to control any emotion, any human impulse at will.

Five weeks passed, and then his sheath of resistance disappeared.

A few days after Kent's arrival on Prinz-Albrecht-Strasse, his mistress Margarete Barcza—a beautiful woman to whom he was passionately attached—was also brought to Berlin. She was questioned separately, and there were strict orders that the two should not see each other and should hear nothing about each other.

The investigating inspector was greatly dismayed when the Barcza woman was brought in, one day, while Kent was still in the interrogation room. Kent lost complete control; he swept her into his arms in the presence of the police officers. Then he walked up to the inspector and announced that he was ready to tell everything.

"Just let her go," he begged. "What do you know about Robinson, about Jim, about Rado, about Lucie, about Sissy?

I'll tell you everything—you just have to let her go. I'll work for you!"

Completely out of his senses, he dropped to his knees before the inspector, crying like a child.

Two weeks later, Kent had recovered sufficiently to begin his work for the Germans. Heinrich Himmler and Hermann Goering had accepted his offer. The master agent of Moscow "turned about" and began helping to destroy an organization so vast that the "Red Orchestra" was no more than a small cog in its machinery.

The other agents paid for their acts on the gallows. Their "Petit Chef" and his mistress, Margarete Barcza, lived in a house assigned to them in Weimar.

Two and a half years later, with the war drawing to a close, Kent was seen for the last time, in Hof. With a woman and a girl, about eight years of age, he was marching westward, toward the advancing Americans. The "Red Orchestra" had come to an end—*or had it?*

The close connections which leaders of the "Red Orchestra" had always maintained with Switzerland were finally uncovered.

U.S. Intelligence Chief Allen Dulles knew of the "Red Orchestra" when he was stationed in Switzerland. He knew that it was deeply embedded in Germany, with points of support in Asia, through Dr. Richard Sorge. It also had agents in England and America who have stolen and bought the secrets and formulas of the atomic bomb, as well as diplomats who have been arrested or have disappeared. I venture to state that the American, British, and Western European section of the "Red Orchestra" is still partly unexplored. For there is no country in the world today where the "Red Orchestra" is not active—under new names, with new faces, and, since the Russians cannot trust their own satellites and Communist quislings, even behind the iron curtain itself.

Without the network of the Red Orchestra organization, the Soviets would never have been able to change the course of history so drastically inside Eastern Germany. It was this spy group that helped Stalin to enter Berlin and to communize all Eastern Germany, with little resistance from the German people themselves. After this first step, it followed naturally to establish the early Soviet Government East of the natural boundary lines of the rivers Elbe and Oder, and inside East Berlin itself.

THE STAR WHO ORBITS THE SATELLITES

THE GERMANS, with lame humor, call him *Pfannkuchen auf Beine*—Pancake on Legs—but make no mistake, Ernst Friedrich Wollweber is anything but a figure of fun. The most dangerous revolutionary of this or any other age, he had for nearly forty years been Communisim's most ardent and bloodiest servant outside Russia. The organizer of violence, kidnap, and murder, his career as a saboteur can hardly have been equalled by anyone. His name evokes a shudder not only through Europe, but in many far flung countries where he has visited death upon ships, docks, railheads, ammunition trains and men—crimes too numerous to be recorded except in the bulkiest dossier.

The division of Germany made German-born Wollweber intelligence chief of the Eastern sector and although this is a post he had eventually to relinquish, he still remains the most formidable spymaster and Soviet executioner in Europe. There is not a police chief anywhere who would not give his right arm to get a double-lock on Wollweber.

"The Pancake" is really a charitable description. He resembles, in fact, an outsize, obese dwarf, for he is just under five feet, weighs 200 pounds and is generated by enormous energy. Wollweber's eyes frighten people—they are mere slits that glitter when he is excited. As the years have swirled about him, his receding hair-line has revealed a round, heavy skull and prominent forehead. He has thick lips and a determined mouth which he screws up in anger when he is roused. His laugh, revealing yellowed, uneven teeth, is a terrifying bellow.

Wollweber has always become excited when expressing his contempt for intellectuals and the Marxian dialectic. "I am, and have always been, a man of action," he will explain angrily. "Theories are for weaklings and if fewer books had been written about the revolution the Communist flag would be flying over more countries than it is today."

Nevertheless, despite his contempt for revolutionary theorists Wollweber possesses a massive patience. As his career advanced, and with it his record for destruction, he has known how to wait for those moments he could make his own. As imperturbable as any Oriental, he has never fallen into the error of permitting expediency a free hand. Every enterprise had to be carefully planned and allowed to mature and it is from this revolutionary tactic, often irritating to his superiors, that Wollweber has reaped his richest dividends.

Ill-educated, knowing only a smattering of French, Scandinavian and Russian, he has long fascinated women—indeed, women and drink are his greatest delights. Like Danton, he asserts that a good revolutionary requires a new mistress every night. He has been fortunate in these conquests. No woman has ever betrayed him. All have helped him in some way and many a woman agent within his espionage network has protected both his life and freedom.

There are aspects of bureaucracy that even Wollweber cannot stand. "I don't need either medals or titles," he asserts contemptuously. "They made me a colonel and then a general and even a minister under a Soviet Government. But all this meant nothing to me—it is the revolution that counts, nothing else.

He has seen many come and go, among them Zinoviev, Kamenev, Radek, Trotsky and Malenkov; the spy chiefs, too, from Yagoda to Beria—mangled in the party machine. But Wollweber has always remained aloof from the struggle for executive power and his contempt for party intrigue has been his strongest armor against the treacherous shifts of power that have brought disaster to others.

For Communist pomp and circumstance he displays an old hatred rooted in his proletarian beginnings. "You won't catch me at receptions dressed up like a dummy," he once told one of the Communist bosses. "Others may forget from where they came, but I have a long memory. My father was an underpaid, hungry miner and his only pleasure was to get drunk and then beat up my mother. There were many mouths to feed at home, so she was forced to work in a weaving factory until tuberculosis finished her off. Life was hard for all of us.

Wollweber was born in Hamburg and at fifteen found he could no longer bear the misery of his home life and ran away to sea. His first trip was to South America and others which followed not only fulfilled his natural craving for adventure but provided a sharp lesson. He began to understand how poor his education had been and how necessary books were to him in his ignorance and immaturity. He became a voracious reader and in the forecastle, among men inured to hardship and waiting for a brighter day to dawn, he listened to radical and violent espousals for a fairer deal for everybody. Young Wollweber didn't need to be persuaded that the rich had ruled the world for too long.

It was in this way that the future king of saboteurs received his Socialist indoctrination, but in 1917, when he was a stoker on the *Helgoland,* the revolution in Russia, at which most of the world stood aghast, became known and excited the radicals among Wollweber's shipmates. By then, of course, the great German dream of military conquest had faded and everybody was sick of the appalling slaughter, but the conception of a Kaiser dethroned, and a Socialist Republic replacing the rule of the Junkers, was displaced by new ideas among the older men to whom Wollweber owed his political convictions. The Socialists, he was now told, would compromise with capitalism and the masses would be sold down the river. The only hope for the workers was to emulate the Russian proletariat and seize power from the warmongers.

It was in these circumstances that Wollweber became a Communist and revolutionary and ultimately a member of *Spartakusbund,* Rosa Luxenburg's forerunner of the German Communist Party. On November 7th, 1918, four days before Germany was granted an armistice, the crew of the *Helgoland* seized the ship, pulled down the German Imperial flag and sailed into Bremen. This act was duplicated throughout a rebellious fleet and units returned to their home ports at Hamburg, Cuxhaven and Wilhelmshaven. In Bremen, as elsewhere hungry, stricken workers took their revenge. In streets, over which flew the Red flag, naval officers were stripped of their medals and epaulettes and flung into the gutter. Armed crowds sang:

> "Hoch die Hohenzollern
> Hoch die Hohenzollern
> Hoch am Laternenpfahl"

(High live the Hohenzollern, high on the lamp-post)

Wollweber, a pudgy, eighteen years old fanatic, enjoying his baptism of violence, led a crowd of ratings and rioters to the Oslebhausen prison which was stormed and the "victims" of capitalism set free. Shops, restaurants and drinking places were looted and the City Hall fell to the mob without a shot being fired.

The Socialist Democrats came out with a program of reform, but Wollweber and the other extremists had the upper hand and both Bremen and Hamburg were proclaimed Communist cities. But with the establishment of the Weimar Republic the tide of violence receded somewhat. Wollweber, ultimately, was elected Communist Deputy in the Reichstag, but in his earliest activities he was essentially a barricades fighter and at heart an anarchist. The darker side of his nature rejected parliamentary respectability and he remained absolutely true to character in becoming saboteur, spy and counter-spy for the Kremlin.

In the twenties he returned to sea and fresh notoriety. He incited the crew of his ship to mutiny against their captain. They took charge of the vessel and brought it from the North Sea to Murmansk. The young Communist rebels wished to offer it as a present to the new Communist workers' and farmers' state.

The journey was quite a feat of seamanship, for they reached port without the help of charts. In recognition of his services, embarrassing though this last one was, Lenin appointed Wollweber chairman of the International Seamen's Union.

Wollweber shipped to China and Japan, to France, Italy and the Americas. He knocked about all over the world and in the end nothing surprised him. He was repeatedly arrested for Communist activities and for his inquisitiveness about the big harbors into which he sailed. Arrests, too, came to be all in the day's work. "*Lumpenhunde*," he would say to his friends, "the dogs, they arrested me again." Promptly on being released he would return to his old ways.

By the time Hitler came to power Wollweber was the obvious person to take over espionage against hostile Germany. He headed the Western European division of the Russian counter-espionage organization. His formal title was "Secretary of the Western European Office of the Communist Internationale."

He chose Copenhagen as his headquarters and posed as an engineer for the bogus firm of A. Selo and Co. Jan Valtin worked in the same offices and describes in his book *Out of the Night* how Wollweber and his confederates operated.

"They occupied a suite of seven rooms on the third floor. The atmosphere there was that of a prosperous engineering firm. A score of typists, guards and translators, in shifts, remained continuously on duty. The guards—Scandinavians, Latvians and Poles—were armed with fountain-pens filled with tear gas. A system of warning buzers had been built into the walls. Conspicuous only was the complete absence of telephones. All messages were dispatched by courier. Aside from the front office, the home of the Westbureau was divided into six departments. . . . It was but one of nine offices which the Communist Internationale and the O.G.P.U. maintained in Copenhagen."

The Copenhagen "engineer" was only one of Wollweber's motley impersonations and he used many aliases. Police files have him listed under a great variety of names, from Anton to Spring, Summer, Winter, Schulz, Müller, Andersen and Mathieu. His ability to disappear seemed almost occult.

When the Nazis spied against Russian shipping in the Baltic, Wollweber countered with direct action. German boats which left Denmark loaded with ammunition and food shipments for the Fascists in the Spanish Civil War never reached the Iberian peninsula. Sticks of T.N.T. were mixed into the ship's coal, and explosions took place on the high seas.

After the invasion of Denmark the German troopship *Marion* left Denmark bound for invaded Norway. Four thousand Nazi soldiers were on board; not one survived. Once more the fuel had been adulterated with T.N.T. There was a gruesome sequel. For several days thereafter, fishermen's nets were laden with German corpses.

These disasters were always ascribed by the Germans to Wollweber. A year after the invasion of Denmark, the Germans in Copenhagen arraigned some aides of Wollweber. The trial was held in the *Landsretten* on July 7th, 1941. To six of Wollweber's aides the sum total of fifty-nine years' imprisonment was meted out. But the ringleader and chief saboteur, Wollweber, was conspicuously absent. The court made it known that he was wanted on charges of blowing up sixteen German, three Italian and two Japanese ships. Thus the destruction of twenty-one Axis ships can be credited to him.

The Nazis clamored for his blood. For years Admiral Walter Wilhelm Canaris and the Gestapo offered an enormous reward for the capture of Wollweber, alive or dead. But Wollweber's whereabouts were hard to discover, and once discovered, the bird invariably had flown.

The West German Deputy Herbert Wehner declared in his sensational talk in the Bundestag at Bonn that Wollweber's men had begun in 1933 to steal T.N.T. and ammunition and had transported it to Holland, where some of it was found once by the Dutch police on the ship *Westplein*. The Italian police claimed—and it was confirmed by the German deputy in 1951—that the Italian ship *Felce* was sunk in the Bay of Taranto before the war as a result of sabotage planned by Wollweber and carried out by his agents. The Japanese police have dossiers claiming that their ship *Tajima-Maru* was sent to the bottom in the same way.

International police and detectives hunted Wollweber's men following explosions on the *Cierco* and *Abrego* at Fredrikhavn in Denmark. In 1937 the Nazis became aware of an attempt against the *Claus Boege* at Hamburg and the following year one of Germany's biggest ships, the *Hapag-Reliance*, suddenly burst into flames. Similar occurrences took place at German ports on the *Phila* and *Norderney*. Wollweber's ring had been trained and equipped by the Soviets to cripple Fascist countries like Germany, Italy and Spain and this sabotage was later extended against the Soviet Union's "Imperialist" enemies.

In 1941 much more was known about Wollweber's activities and harbor strategy. After the fall of Norway and Denmark his organization in Scandinavia moved into Sweden. Report has it that Wollweber himself occupied an apartment near the Stureplan of Stockholm. He never went out of doors except late at night. No one but his closest collaborators ever saw him.

Nevertheless, in summer time, he appeared before some specially selected young Communists camped on one of the deserted islands of the Baltic. There they met a man named "Anton," who spoke Swedish rather badly, with a strong intermingling of Danish and a heavy German accent. He gave the young people a course in the ABC of espionage, the basic principles of dynamiting ships, buildings, bridges and railroads. In the course of his lectures Anton let fall the remark that on a journey to China he had learned some new tricks and had been shown how to stuff T.N.T. into a cigarette, and how such cigarettes could be used to blow up a bridge. Anton saw to it that his pupils grasped the lessons. Then he disappeared as mysteriously as he had come.

A glimpse of him was seen in occupied Norway. But that was all. The Quisling police could not find a trace of him. But Swedish iron-ore boats were attacked in the Baltic by Russian submarines and sunk. The Nazis were fairly sure Wollweber was behind the sinkings.

On one occasion a large supply of dynamite was found to have been stolen from the store-sheds of the Kiruna iron-ore mines in Lapland and the Wollweber hunt was renewed with even greater zest. He was, in fact, walking the streets of Oslo, wearing a Nazi uniform and a swastika pin, which seemed to be sufficient protection. Thus disguised, he supervised the disposal of the stolen dynamite which had been brought into Norway by skiers. There, part of it was used to disrupt the Oslo railroad terminal, and powerhouses and naval installations in the north. Points along the railroad line from Oslo to Bergen were blown up in a series of explosions.

It was for exploits such as these that Ernst Wollweber earned the appellation "The King of Saboteurs." Not that he himself did all the work. Rather, he utilized his especial talent for organization to build up a formidable coterie of saboteurs and spies. In Sweden alone, for example, he had at least fifty aides, according to the Swedish police. Now and then some of them were caught, but the entire group was never rounded up.

Wollweber had no patience with theatrical gestures that accomplished little and only hostility for Communist leaders who published underground newspapers and leaflets. They would be more usefully employed, he said, organizing sabotage and espionage. He encouraged his fellow-Communists—all those with "guts," as he phrased it—to join the Nazi Party and form a fifth column inside it.

The casualties among these agents were, of course, high. But Wollweber felt that they were well worth the results achieved. In the years before the war it had been necessary for him to visit the capitals of Europe in search of recruits. Jan Valtin relates that on such journeys he often fell into a frenzy at seeing Communist officials orating and theorizing instead of doing active work. Valtin met him one day in Paris in 1937 and found him in a fury. According to Valtin, Wollweber said:

"I've been looking around. This Paris is a treasure chest. I've learned more here in one week, I tell you, than in three years in Nazi Germany. In Germany, our comrades either starve to death or are beaten to death. And here? The boulevard cafés are lousy with deserters. . . . I'm going to round them up—one and all. I'm going to send them back to Germany, where they belong."

Few men have lived the life of a fugitive longer than has Wollweber. He had in fact been a wanted man since 1933 and it was astonishing how long he managed to survive. When a slip-up occurred at last, as it was bound to, it was not due to any carelessness on his part. He was far too wily and astute for that. It was one of his helpers who left the tell-tale footprints.

In the seaport of Gothenburg, Wollweber was forced to employ men who were well known as Communists. The espionage and sabotage league had had to be greatly expanded, and more and more men were needed. The order had come from Lavrenti Beria to let no ship through which carried iron ore or ball-bearings from Sweden, Norway or Denmark to Nazi Germany.

For many months sabotage operations ran smoothly. A telegraph operator on the Swedish *Telegrafverk*et was running a short-wave transmission set which informed Russian and Allied submarines of outward-bound ships. This agent was located in Gothenburg. Unfortunately he had to depend on a whole host of assistants. One of them was the leader of the former Aid Committee for Republican Spain, Victor Rydstedt, who was in a perfectly secure situation but was suddenly stricken by panic. On an impulse he went to take a look at the T.N.T. which was hidden in a warehouse in Gothenburg, near the harbor. It was a foolish act, for he had no reason to be worried and such inspection trips were strictly forbidden by Wollweber. The police, who had their suspicions, followed him into the warehouse that day. They found two hundred and twenty pounds of T.N.T. in sacks bearing the label of the Kiruna iron-ore mines.

Rydstedt and his collaborator, the telegraph operator, were seized, convicted of espionage and sentenced to three years in prison. The Swedish police made further investigations. The sacks of T.N.T. revealed fingerprints. A week later five workers in the Lapland iron mines were suddenly arrested.

One of them, G. Ceder, turned state's witness. He produced some dynamite shells which he had been given as samples and exhibited the method of secreting a number of such shells on a ship carrying iron ore, close to the furnaces. The explosion would occur spontaneously.

Ceder was also able to tell of his next rendezvous with "Anton," the King of Saboteurs. He was released as bait and met his boss at the home of one of the iron workers, close to the mines. The police had the situation sewn up and Wollweber, alias Anton, was arrested. Within the next few days some twenty of his operatives were also rounded up.

Wollweber remained icily calm. There was no T.N.T. in the home of the iron worker. There was, he swiftly calculated, no evidence at all. The Swedish court would have to have evidence. Wollweber contented himself with one telling reminder to Torsten Söderström, the police chief: "I am a Soviet citizen."

The Swedes instantly recognized that the situation was not quite so simple as they had at first thought. A Soviet citizen was no stateless refugee; he had powerful protection. Confirmation was sought from Madame Alexandra Kollontay, the Russian envoy in Stockholm. She attested to Wollweber's Russian citizenship. The Swedes decided it was wise to proceed slowly and carefully. They had the greatest saboteur of the century under lock and key, but were wholly without proof of his guilt. Ships had been blown up in Denmark; airfields and submarine installations damaged in Norway; and shipments of iron ore from Sweden had never reached their destination. But no crimes had been committed on Swedish soil and no real evidence of Wollweber's complicity existed.

Of course, the Nazi authorities in Denmark and Germany demanded Wollweber's extradition, as did Quisling and his police chief in Norway.

The late Lavrenti Beria bestirred himself. He rallied the entire Soviet Foreign Ministry to the rescue of Wollweber. Stalin personally intervened and asked for the release of the prisoner. He made it very clear that there were a few Swedish engineers working in Russia who might do as hostages, if things came to a really critical pass.

While waiting for a decision, the Russian Legation in Stockholm showered the imprisoned Wollweber with food and money and visitis. Finally the Swedes decided to strike an unhappy mean between offending the Russians and outraging the Nazis.

The Swedish Department of Justice laid a charge that Wollweber had been living in Sweden on a faked passport and under an assumed name. His entrance into the country was illegal. This could not, after all, be forgiven. The Nazis were advised that Wollweber would be tried accordingly and would have to serve any sentence imposed by the Swedish court before there could be any question of extraditing him to Germany. The Swedes did not even bother to reply to the demand of the Quisling puppet government in Oslo. Wollweber, whom the Axis countries would have hanged, received a sentence of eighteen months, to be served in a relatively comfortable prison of a democratic country.

The Soviets in an official reply now alleged that Wollweber was wanted by them for embezzling government funds and insisted on his immediate deportation to Russia. Sweden, a small and neutral nation, decided to ship Wollweber out of the country as quickly as possible.

Wollweber shook hands warmly with his friends from the Soviet Legation. "I'll be out in time to meet our Soviet troops in Berlin," he said.

The Swedish court judged it wise to declare that the proceedings of the trial should be kept secret for fifty years.

As he had promised, six weeks before the Russians stormed into Berlin, Wollweber and a dozen of his agents had infiltrated the German capital as an advanced Soviet espionage unit. On May 1st, 1945, the Red army officials were presented on their entry into the city with a detailed military map showing every concrete defence bunker.

This strategic map had been smuggled out of Berlin in a most ingenious manner. An engraver and old friend of Wollweber had drawn maps of twelve sectors of the city on the surface of a dozen eggs. A Communist agent, an elderly woman by the name of Frieda Schueler, had casually walked through the lines, ostensibly selling the eggs from her farm, and handed them over to Wollweber's contact man.

Four days before the Soviet capture of Berlin, Frieda Schueler again strolled through the lines with yet a further supply of eggs, thus completing the famous battle map which enabled the Soviet army to take the city with far fewer casualties and more quickly than had at first been thought possible.

Within three months Wollweber was appointed Minister of State Security for Eastern Germany and thus became the founder of the Secret Service there. The organization, whose headquarters are now located in Normannen Strasse, employs, it is estimated, no fewer than 9,000 agents. Its informers number over 100,000.

As a Soviet citizen by adoption, Wollweber exercised jurisdiction over Russian army personnel as well as that of East German nationals, and the Soviet Secret Service trusted him completely.

Irmgard Schmidt, one of his women agents who had wormed her way into the confidence of the American staff, tipped Wollweber off that a certain Soviet Major-General Igor Tropanov was fraternizing with the Allies and was supplying them with information from the Soviet zone.

Wollweber selected one of his more beautiful women

agents, Grete Bernau, to check on the dubious Russian Major-General. At a briefing session at his villa which he had "requisitioned" in Lehnitz for just such an occasion, Wollweber instructed Grete to use her charm to get to know the truth.

The plot moved rapidly and three days later Grete Bernau was sipping her first cocktails with Tropanov at Kempinski's. In five days she was installed in his house as a "guest."

In her report to Wollweber, Grete admitted she had been unable to get any information from her lover, but added, "Tropanov is very careless."

"How do you mean, careless?" he asked the spy chief.

"He leaves important documents lying around. Only this morning while he was bathing, I went through his desk and came across a book with a green-black cover entitled *Soviet Army Order of Battle*. It must be highly confidential. I could have stolen it, and so could any of the servants there."

Wollweber frowned, for he was aware that the book was a top secret publication. Only two hundred and fifty copies had been printed for distribution among the General Staff and top members of the Politburo. It would be a plum for the Allied Intelligence service.

Grete returned to Tropanov's home to continue her spy work, little realizing that she, in turn, was being watched by one of Wollweber's other agents. Secure in her niche in the Soviet espionage scheme, she had not the least suspicion that she was being shadowed now by him ... even when she had an intimate conversation with an American officer over cocktails at Schloss Marquart.

The list of Grete's suspicious meetings with the Allied personnel lengthened. Wollweber finally gave the fateful order. A "Totschlaeger" (assassination squad) Kommando was sent from Wollweber's offices to the hotel room where Grete and Tropanov were relaxing during an evening of talk, lovemaking and vodka. The Major-General, comfortable in his shirt sleeves, wheeled to face his killers. Before he could cry out, the leader fired three bullets into his chest from a 9 mm. automatic muffled with a silencer. Grete screamed, but her cries were never heard, for she too was cut down. Wollweber's men melted into the darkness, later sending the brief message: Mission accomplished.

The following day a special courier left for Moscow with a report on Tropanov's eliminiaition and the reasons for it. His copy of *Soviet Army Order of Battle,* taken by the assassins from the hotel room, was produced as evidence of his unfitness.

By 1953 Wollweber operated on the huge budget of 40,000,000 dollars, considerably higher than that of General Ivan Serov's Committee for State Security in Moscow. He was responsible, not only for East Germany, but for Communist Poland, spying against the United States, Britain and France as well as maintaining his old spy rings in Norway (where he had been briefly married to a Norwegian girl), Sweden, Denmark, Finland, and other countries. He seldom forgot his faithful friends and many old cronies were appointed as captains and majors in the new East German police and army.

Another great feather in Wollweber's war-bonnet came in postwar days when he succeeded in obtaining one of the U.S. codes by the familiar technique of planting a lovely lady in the direct path of an American code clerk.

Although the American, British and French counter-intelligence agencies were deeply concerned about the many assassinations instigated by Wollweber, they realized that he struck his most telling blows by various kidnap plots. German scientists from the old V-rocket centers in Peenemunde, biochemists, metallurgic engineers, designers, specialists in many technical fields have been taken over the border into East Germany and Russia and plied for information which has helped Soviet missile research.

Perhaps the best known case concerned the disappearance of Dr. Linse, a great opponent of Wollweber, who was snatched on his way to his office, taken to East Berlin from the Western sector and has never since been heard of.

Today Wollweber hovers around sixty. He has lost his hair, his attraction for women, and worst of all his powerful position as spy head in East Germany. When the frantic East Germans began their purge in 1958, it was assumed that Wollweber could not possibly survive. True, he lost his membership of parliament, his East German army rank, his post as intelligence chief, but the million-dollar head did not roll, for Moscow decreed that Wollweber must not be touched. A Soviet plane was sent to Pankow to take him home to Moscow where he was received with acclaim. Khrushchev awarded him the Lenin Medal and the Order of the Revolution plus a brand new assignment.

East Germany was a problem even to the Russians, and Wollweber was needed elsewhere. China with its 600 million people, the fifteen restless satellite countries plaguing the

206

Soviet Empire with their rebellions in Poland and Hungary all need to be watched carefully, as well as ruled with a strong Bolshevik fist. Wollweber, contrary to the hopes of his East German rivals, was not pensioned and sent into oblivion. Instead Khrushchev promoted him to the important position of chief of all satellite intelligence officers, the commander-in-chief and inspector-general of the spy services of every Soviet-controlled country. Perhaps more impressive than anything else in the career of Ernst Friedrich Wollweber is that he is the only Soviet spy boss since 1918 who is still alive. That in itself is a remarkable achievement.

THE MAN WHO DID BUSINESS WITH HIMMLER

by Edwin Mueller

EARLY IN THE war Mr. Eric Erickson of Stockholm was posted on the Allied Black list, accused of trading with the enemy and aiding the German war effort. Allied Intelligence had reported that Erickson was dealing in German oil, making regular trips to Germany, and that he was on intimate terms with high-ranking Gestapo officials.

The disclosure was a stunning shock to Erickson's family. His old friends, all of whom were strongly pro-Ally, now crossed the street when they saw him coming. His wife was ostracised. Although he was a Swedish citizen, Erickson had been born and brought up in Brooklyn, graduated from Cornell. Now he got scathing letters from his family in the United States. But nothing stopped him.

"Red" Erickson was the American salesman type, the sort whose career is in making "contacts" in selling his genial self along with his line of goods. He had gone into the oil business because it was exciting and got you places. He spent years in the Orient and later in Europe, working for Standard, then for the Texas Company.

The "oil crowd" in the '20's and '30's was an international clan. You'd see a man in Shanghai one year, in London or Teheran the next. One year you might be competing ruthlessly with him, the next you'd both be on the same side of the fence. American, English, Dutch, German, they lived in an atmosphere of adventurous gambles and deals whose strings were drawn across national frontiers. Erickson became manager for Texas in Sweden. Then he became a Swedish citizen, and started his own company, to import and sell American oil products.

Soon after the war began, he saw an opportunity to do business with the Nazis. Germany then had oil to export, and it was absurd to suppose that the Allies could ever affect the supply materially by bombing. So Erickson began to play around with German businessmen. He joined the German Chamber of Commerce in Stockholm. He drew away from most of his old friends, but kept on good terms with Prince Carl Bernadotte, nephew of the King of Sweden. The Prince, too, was playing with the Nazis—to the disgust of the great majority of Swedes.

Erickson knew that Gestapo Chief Heinrich Himmler would make the final decision on the oil deals. So the prospect on whom Erickson did his heavy work was Herr Finke, Himmler's chief representative in Sweden and a fanatical Nazi. Finke's weak point was a snobbish susceptibility to royalty. Prince Carl helped make the contract and Erickson did the cultivating. Soon he was entertaining Herr Finke at his place in the country.

Other prospects, however, didn't come along—notably Herr Ludwig, commercial attaché of the German Legation. He didn't like Erickson at all. But despite Ludwig's aloofness, Erickson got permission to visit Germany in the spring of 1941, with letters of introduction from Finke and others.

At Bromma Field, outside Stockholm, the plane to Berlin was held up, while Erickson was ordered off by the Swedish police. They made a brusque and thorough search of him and his baggage. But nothing incriminating was found, and he was allowed to proceed.

In Berlin, next morning, an official car took him to Gestapo headquarters. There he met two men who had been on the plane with him—Gestapo agents. They agreed that the incident at Bromma had been the work of Allied representatives.

Erickson made his contacts with German oil men, especially in Hamburg. He visited refineries there, talked with the managers, discussed the terms of the contracts he wanted. He also looked around for some of the oil crowd he used to know. First he found Captain von Wunsch, a Junker who had had part of his education in England, and had at one time been associated with Shell Oil. Since Erickson hoped to keep his deals secret, his talks with von Wunsch were very hush-hush. One day Erickson gave von Wunsch a certain mysterious document which von Wunsch put in a tin box and buried in his back yard. Another contact was Herr von Stürker, an oil banker, of an old Hamburg family. Von Sturker also got a paper. Erickson took pains to let neither of the men see him with the other.

Soon after Erickson went back to Sweden, the first deliveries of German oil began. It was then that the Allies put him on the black list. His alienation from his old friends was complete. Some of them would get up and leave a restaurant if he entered it. His Swedish wife suffered intensely. She was still anti-Nazi, yet she had to entertain her husband's new friends.

In the months that followed, Erickson made other trips to Germany and continued to cultivate his friends in the Gestapo. He was invited to their homes, and he'd bring wives butter and leather coats and other presents from Sweden. And he continued to make deals with other men like von Wunsch and von Stürker, though it became harder to get oil from Germany as the Allied bombings were stepped up. Once, after he had inspected a big refinery, the managing director asked him to stay for dinner. He hesitated but found it hard to decline. The meal was served in the director's office. It was nearly midnight when the party broke up, and just after midnight when Allied bombers arrived. There wasn't any plant left. The Allies then and there almost put an end to Erickson's trading with the enemy.

The Allied attack on German oil was increasingly effective, yet in the latter part of 1944 a substantial portion of the industry was still functioning. Repairs were made more rapidly than the Allies had thought possible. Moreover, many refineries had been so well concealed that they were still untouched.

In the autumn of 1944 the Allied war effort was moving towards the climatic battle of the Rhine. Erickson had to work fast if he wanted to make more deals. He had long wanted to make an inclusive tour of the German oil industry. Now was the time for it. He figured that it was one of those cases in which a salesman had to get to the man at the top, in this case Heinrich Himmler.

Erickson worked out a grandiose "big deal," the kind of thing any high-pressure salesman would love. He proposed to construct a huge synthetic oil refinery in Sweden, to cost $5,000,000. It would be finanaced by both Swedish and German capital.

This proposal was calculated to appeal to the Germans for

two reasons. First, it would put a source of oil for Germany in a neutral country, outside the reach of Allied bombers. Second, it offered a way of planting Nazi funds in a neutral country if Germany should be defeated.

Erickson prepared a prospectus and took it to Finke, who was delighted. The Nazi big shots in Germany expressed keen interest. There was one dissident voice—that of Herr Ludwig. He maintained that Mr. Erickson was a phony. Ludwig was a Foreign Office man, one of Ribbentrop's faction. More and more as the war went on that faction had come into collision with the Gestapo—in other words, with Heinrich Himmler. Himmler usually won. And so in this case Ludwig was overruled. Erickson was acceptable to the Gestapo, and the way was cleared for him to see Himmler.

It was October, 1944. Once more Erickson took the plane from Bromma Field and flew over the grey waters of the Baltic and the dreary plains of northern Germany to Tempelhof Aerodrome. He was given a suite at the best hotel in Berlin not yet smashed by Allied bombs, and in the morning the big black car with its Gestapo guards called for him.

At Himmler's headquarters, the Gestapo chief greeted him cordially: "We have heard great things about you from Herr Finke." They talked at length of the refining plant, and of the need for Erickson to see, first hand, the operation of German plants. Then they went on to discuss other matters.

"What would happen," Himmler asked suddenly, "if the Wehrmacht were to invade Sweden?"

"The Swedes would fight like hell," Erickson replied.

He figured that the way to impress Himmler was not to kowtow. He was right. The result of the interview was that he was given a unique document which certified that he should be allowed to go anywhere and see anything in the oil industry. He was given a car and a generous allotment of petrol.

Erickson covered Central Europe from Cologne to Prague. He inspected Leuna, Annendorf, Halle—all the big plants. He talked with managers, found out what they were doing, and proposed to do. Like a salesman covering a new territory, he got the whole picture.

And took it back to Sweden.

When the war was over, the American Legation in Stockholm gave "Red" Erickson a big luncheon. All his old friends were invited. With innumerable toasts and congratulations he was put right with his world.

It was told how a representative of Allied Intelligence had called on him soon after the beginning of the war. How Erickson had agreed to act as a spy but had refused any pay for his services. How at his own suggestion he was put on the black list. How Prince Carl Benadotte, with whom he had worked, was also an agent for the Allies. How the oil which had been delivered to him from Germany was turned over to Vacuum Oil and British Petroleum and was eventually used against the Germans. How he had had to give von Wunsch, von Stürker and his other contacts signed letters acknowledging their services as secret Allied collaborators, for use after Allied victory. How each such paper was another sword hanging over his head, so that he could hardly sleep in Germany, waiting tensely through the long nights for the knock that would mean the Gestapo and death.

His information—and that of others in his hazardous line of work—paid off. In those months before the Battle of the Rhine the offensive against German oil rose to its climax. Our pilots knew the exact location of the refineries, big and little. The day a new plant was completed they had it down on the map and could fly directly to it, no matter how well it was camouflaged. They knew the location of the fighter-strips, the ack-ack batteries and the smoke-screen installations that defended it. After they had put a refinery out of commission they knew how long it would take to repair it. On the days it was scheduled to resume production they'd be back again.

The supply of fuel to the Wehrmacht and the Luftwaffe was cut to a trickle. When our last great assault began, many German tanks stood helpless in the fields, and many German planes were grounded because of lack of petrol.

The Allies have made good on Erickson's promises to von Wunsch, von Stürker and the others. Herr Ludwig however is a prisoner, with leisure to reflect on the soundness of his judgment concerning Erickson. Herr Finke was finally caught, after months of masquerading in Denmark under a false name.

And now salesman Erickson is reverting to his old love—the oil business. Consorting with the oil crowd from Teheran to London. The heady atmosphere of big business. Real adventure.

MOKUSATSU

THE DAY Nazi Germany surrendered to the Allies in the second World War an emergency meeting was called at the Kremlin. It was attended by the late Lavrenti Beria, Khrushchev, Bulganin, Molotov, Vishinsky, Stalin, and a group of four military staff officers who were the experts on Japan and the Far East.

The Western secret services who knew of the meeting would have given a million dollars to have known what was decided that day inside the Kremlin. The analysts surmised that the topic of discussion must have been more than just the future of defeated Germany, and that the future role of Soviet infiltration and conquest of Manchuria, China, Japan and Asia in general was high on the agenda.

Ten years later, the Western intelligence offices finally knew what was discussed that day. It was perhaps the greatest spy plot in the last war—greater than Sorge's operation inside Japan, greater than the Red Orchestra operation where dozens of Soviet spies worked as high-ranking Nazis inside the Göring air force ministry.

Decisions were made at the meeting for secret service operations to delay peace and surrender of Japan in order to prepare Soviet power to swallow Manchuria, China and, if possible, even Korea.

Failure to realize this secret plot in time was probably the deadliest mistake the American intelligence services committed. They, as everyone else inside the American government, at that time naively hoped the Soviet Union was an honest Ally of the United States.

The unawareness of the plans of the Soviet secret services during this critical period led to the ultimate downfall of Western strength in Asia.

The first person to speak up was Admiral Zacharias, naval intelligence chief of the U.S.A., who declared: "America did not have to use the atom bomb to knock Japan out of the war. Japan had sued for peace long before and had only asked to keep their Emperor."

The second man to speak up was Fleet Admiral Chester W. Nimitz who told the American Congress: "The Japanese, in fact, had already looked for peace before the atomic age was announced to the world with the destruction of Hiroshima and before the Russian entry into the Japanese war."

If two American admirals claim Japan was ready with surrender to avoid atomic warfare and to salvage as much of her country as possible, why then was no peace granted? Why did not Japan make this peace and get it? Why did Russia instead enter the war for such a short period, and why was the atom bomb used at all?

Diplomatic espionage is as old as the Bible. While the diplomats toasted each other at the Potsdam conference, the Soviet spy mills worked day and night—and inside Japan.

It was after the surrender of Germany, in July 1945. American troops had advanced in the Pacific from island to island and occupied Okinawa.

At the same time, on the 26th of July, the Big Three issued the Potsdam Declaration declaring that Japan must surrender immediately or be totally crushed. The Potsdam Declaration was signed by the United States, Britain, and China.

The Allies, while still enjoying their victories, waited patiently for an answer from Japan. President Truman played the piano at Potsdam; Clement Attlee was briefed for future political tasks; Truman and Stalin quarrelled and Communists slowly took all of Eastern Germany, Poland—and there was still no answer from Japan.

Two days later an indirect answer came over the Japanese news wires. The Domei agency mentioned a flash from Tokyo saying, "Premier Kantaro Suzuki and his Imperial Cabinet have decided to 'ignore' the Potsdam Declaration of the Big Three."

Three weeks later Japan asked for surrender terms. During these three weeks the most violent history of the first part of the 20th Century was written. The atom bombs were dropped over Hiroshima and Nagasaki and the Soviet Union officially declared her entry into the war against Japan. Thus started the Communist attack against Asia.

During these three weeks of Soviet-Japanese war the Soviet troops conquered, without Japanese resistance, all Manchuria and Sakhalin, disarmed the Japanese troops and handed the arms over to the Communist Chinese to continue the war of Communism after Japan's final surrender.

How was this possible? Only through the shrewdest espionage plot ever engineered by a modern government.

What actually had happened was that the Japanese government had accepted the Potsdam Declaration and was willing to negotiate with the Allies on terms of surrender. Through a deliberate "mistake" organized by the Soviet secret service —this news did not reach the Big Three in time and the atomic war was started.

The first person to break this story in Japan was Kazuo Kawaii, former editor of the Nippon *Times*—and no Japanese statesman has ever denied the truth of the "mokusatsu" mistake.

Premier Suzuki's cabinet had accepted the surrender and informed the Allies through the Domei News Agency that his cabinet "was holding to an attitude of mokusatsu."

Mokusatsu is a difficult word to translate into English.

Mokusatsu, as meant by the Japanese cabinet, informed the West that "a decision was not yet to be given."

While the Domei Agency, which had been infiltrated by a most clever translator on the payroll of the Soviet Secret Service, blared to the world the deliberate falsification that Japan's government had decided on "mokusatsu"—to *ignore* the Potsdam Declaration of surrender.

After Japan had "ignored" the Potsdam Declaration, there was nothing to stop President Truman's decision to use atom bombs over Hiroshima and Nagasaki—and nothing to stop Stalin from beginning his conquest of all Asia.

World history today would look different if the word mokusatsu had been translated correctly.

This is no wild fantasy. British and American secret service have today full evidence of the mokusatsu affair engineered by the successors of Sorge's spy ring in Japan.

As early as Spring of 1945 Japan was ready to sue for a separate peace. She did not want to be annihilated and destroyed as the German cities were. Her production was gravely crippled. Steel production was down 75 percent; airplane production down 60 percent. A severe shortage of aluminum, metals and coal was felt daily. The American attacks had destroyed bridges, factories, railroads, airfields, harbors; the Australian-New Zealand attacks had crippled Japanese manpower. Britain's navy had played her traditional part. Millions had died for Japan. Half of the homes in Tokyo were leveled. Tokyo looked worse than London. The Japanese fleet had been sunk or scattered.

When Suzuki took over the government, he declared frankly: "We must stop the war at the earliest opportunity." Actually he had already advised the emperor in February 1945 to surrender on all conditions in order to save Japan.

A peace party had been appointed to ask the Soviets to

214

intervene with the rest of the Allies for a separate peace. In the peace party were Prince Takamatsu, Prince Konoye, and Marquis Kiochi Kido. The emperor was behind the peace party and so was Suzaki, who, after some hesitation wanted first to move cautiously but later tried to speed up the peace negotiations.

In the meantime the Soviet Union knew of these peace feelers but was not at all interested because her war in Asia was slated to come first.

Finally, on June 3, 1945, the former Prime Minister Hirota, who had once been ambassador in Moscow, visited the Soviet Ambassador Jacob Malik at the hot springs of Hakone.

Malik learned nothing that the Soviet secret service had not known before: Japan was ready to surrender.

Malik played the suave, disinterested diplomat. It was a cool and short discussion. When Hirota tried to meet Malik again, the Soviet ambassador refused to talk to the emissary and pleaded a severe cold.

After this failure, Kido, a member of the peace party, visited the emperor and asked for stronger and more direct methods, perhaps coming from the emperor in a declaration to obtain peace.

This was on June 9. The same night the Soviet secret service obtained from the palace a copy of the "peace memorandum."

Kido tells of his visit:

"I reported fully to His Majesty on my tentative peace plan and obtained Imperial sanction to counsel the prime minister and the three ministers of war, navy, and foreign affairs.

"His Majesty, who was more deeply concerned than anybody over the adverse developments of the war situation, was satisfied with my report, especially since His Majesty grieved that many medium and small towns, one after another in quick succession, had been reduced to ashes by bombings and attacks. A large number of innocent people were homeless. His Majesty commanded me to set my hand to the tentative peace plan immediately."

On June 18, 1945, the Japanese Supreme War Council met secretly and finally decided to make proper arrangements "to ascertain the Soviet attitude by the beginning of July with a view to terminating the war if possible by September."

The next day, the peace offer was made to Moscow.

Why did Japan make the offer to Russia instead of Sweden,

Switzerland, or any other country? Mainly because Russia was the strongest and most powerful of all neutral countries as far as Japan was concerned.

This was the deadliest error Japan could make. The Nipponese had failed to discover that Stalin had promised the Yalta powers to enter the war against Japan after the defeat of Germany.

At this point of the war, when Allied victory was assured, Russia was not interested in any peace in Asia because Russia's ambitions were boundless and greedy.

Hirota met Malik twice. The Soviet ambassador remained aloof and cold and promised nothing.

Malik was quite cynical. His Soviet secret service kept him informed of Japan's desperate position. Russia would only gain by waiting. At one point Malik said frankly to Hirota:

"If we help you to get peace, what will there be in it for the Soviet Union?"

By July 7 the emperor was annoyed with the Russian *laissez-faire* attitude. He called on Prime Minister Suzuki and asked permission to hasten up the peace negotiation and to look for other vistas of negotiations. Said the emperor:

"We may miss a precious opportunity while we are trying to ascertain the attitude of the Soviet Union."

Still it did not occur to the emperor and premier to make contacts with any other country to seek peace. At that time the Russians had not informed the other Allies of these peace feelers.

On July 12 Prince Konoye was ordered to Moscow to obtain the Kremlin's help to get an armistice. Prince Konoye had instructions to sue for peace on any terms—even total surrender and, if necessary, to promise the abdication of the emperor.

But nothing happened. Prince Konoye was to fly into Manchuria where a Soviet plane was to take him to Moscow.

In the last minute the prince was told that Stalin and Molotov were busy preparing for the Potsdam conference and could not see the envoy.

At the Potsdam conference the Soviets were not exposing the Japanese peace move. All Stalin said to President Truman in Potsdam was "The Japanese sent some peace feelers out—but we laughed them off. They were insincere."

The American delegation accepted Stalin's interpretation, for the U.S.A. expected peace overtures to come through the usual neutral sources of Switzerland or Sweden.

Secretary of State James F. Byrnes recounts that President Truman did not give a second thought to Prince Konoye's mission. At Potsdam, a politically naive America still trusted the Russians and had not seen through the scheme of delaying the peace in Japan for ulterior motives.

Secretary of State Byrnes said later—with hindsight instead of foresight: "Why did Russia refuse to mediate? Why did Russia smother all our efforts for many months to make peace? It was a dark plan to keep the war going until they were ready to get into it at the last minute—with the results we can now see only too well."

The Potsdam Declaration was signed on July 26, 1945. It was a declaration showing leniency toward Japan. The Allies did not ask for total surrender of the country, only total surrender of the armed forces. Japan was not asked to dethrone the emperor and was offered the right to choose her own government.

The Japanese cabinet deliberated for many hours. The opposition against acceptance was small but vehement; the majority was ready to agree to the terms. But what about the peace negotiations with Moscow? Were they stalling? Even Japan knew by then that Russia had not helped to secure surrender terms.

The Japanese cabinet decided to start negotiations with the Allies on the basis of the Potsdam Declaration, still hoping that the Russians at Potsdam would discuss further details with the United States and China. Japan was confused at this moment and still did not know whether Russia was helping or stalling the armistice terms.

On July 28, the next day, Premier Suzuki spoke of "mokusatsu" which he meant as "to wait" and which was translated, thanks to Soviet help, as "ignore."

William J. Coughlin, a Far East expert and former United Press foreign correspondent, said in *Harper's Magazine*: "The word *mokusatsu* has two characters in Japanese. Moku means silence and satsu means *kill*, thus implying in an absolutely literal sense 'to kill with silence.' This can mean—to a Japanese—either 'to ignore' or 'to refrain from comment.'"

Ignorant of the fact that Soviet agents inside the Domei News Agency gave copies of special bulletins to the Soviet embassy at the time of release, the Japanese government was victimized—and hundreds of thousands died in the additional and unnecessary three weeks of war—because a Communist deliberately translated "mokusatsu" as "ignore."

Tokyo radio repeated the Domei News. America knew that Japan had "ignored" the Potsdam Declaration, and the punishment came fast. The first atom bomb was dropped over Hiroshima on August 6. The Japanese government, at first, could not believe that the Allies had misunderstood Japan's peace feelers. Nobuya Uchida, a former war time cabinet minister who heard the word mokusatsu on the radio, wondered why it had been used in the first place.

"I was surprised to hear this news," he said. "Why did we send Prince Konoye to Russia? The result was utilized by the Allies; the atomic bomb was dropped and Soviet Russia entered the war."

This fatal blunder was all that Russia needed to enter the war and get her fat share out of Asia. The moment that Oswald Spengler called "the decline of the West," had come.

The tragic error produced anger in the West and even the moderate New York *Times* wrote on July 28th an excited six column story: FLEET STRIKES AS TOKYO IGNORES TERMS.

The late Henry L. Stimson, United States secretary of war during 1940-45, wrote in his memoirs about Japan's decision to "ignore" the Potsdam declaration: "On July 28, the premier of Japan, Suzuki, rejected the Potsdam ultimatum by announcing that it was 'unworthy of public notice.' In the face of this rejection we could only proceed to demonstrate that the ultimatum had meant exactly what it said. . . . For such a purpose the atomic bomb was an eminently suitable weapon."

President Truman, who only hesitantly had ordered the use of the atom bomb, mentioned the Suzuki "rejection" and the "ignoring" of the Potsdam declaration in a statement on August 6, 1945: "It was to spare the Japanese people from utter destruction that the ultimatum of July was issued at Potsdam. Their leaders promptly rejected that ultimatum."

The Russians knew this was not the truth—and they still kept silent.

In the meantime, while Russia's diplomats pretended they knew nothing of Japan's wishes to get peace, their secret service agents prepared for the invasion of the Red armies. The atomic attacks had made Japan helpless. Meanwhile Soviet troops were shipped from the European theater to the Manchurian borders.

Japan, frantically hoping to end the slaughter, was paralyzed and pleaded in Moscow for help or an armistice. Stalin refused to see any Japanese emissary. He was out for victory in Asia. His armies overran the steppes of Manchuria much as a toy train runs through a nursery.

Molotov remained in icy silence. No audiences were granted while Russia scored victory after victory and occupied port after port.

The mokusatsu translation error gave the Soviets all the time they needed for their conquest. The Japanese were frantic, watching their empire crumble in a two-front war.

"We had asked for an olive branch and received a Soviet dagger thrust," said the prime minister.

Russia had double-crossed Japan in its most diplomatic way with finesse, gusto, and intrigue.

Nothing could stop the onrush of the Soviet armies. They overran the Kwantung army in Manchuria. They invaded the island of Sakhalin. They went over the Hingan range and swept swiftly down to Manchuria's capital Harbin, the key city in the country.

Then, with the speed of a racing car, they ran through the Gobi desert into Southern Manchuria. Their plan was to separate Manchuria and to separate Korea from the Western sphere of influence. Even after the Japanese had finally surrendered, the Russian armies were still engulfing more and more territory in the best Red imperialistic style—befitting the new masters of Red colonialism in Asia.

The Japanese finally begged General Douglas MacArthur to stop the Russians. Ten days after the final Japanese surrender the Soviets temporarily halted their steamrolling conquest of Asia.

The Soviet secret service, due to the effectiveness of the Sorge spy ring and the mokusatsu error, scored the greatest victory any spy brigade had ever delivered. Russia's secret service in Japan outdid all known spy rings in the war.

Still many a question was unsolved. Why did not the emperor simply broadcast his peace offer and peace message? The Soviet secret service was prepared for this too. A surrender proclamation had been recorded by the emperor. The Military War Party, which opposed the peace move and was informed by the Soviets, broke into the palace and stole the record. They issued threats of reprisal if the emperor's message was read on the radio.

Russia's secret service had their men inside the palace, inside the cabinet and inside the oppositionist War Party. The money the Soviets invested in its spy ring in Japan paid enormous dividends. Without the Russian victory in Manchuria and the mokusatsu error—there might never have been a Soviet China, a Soviet Manchuria, a Soviet Northern Korea and Soviet Indochina.

Russian Spies have made history—and British and American Spies lost this battle of the wits—all because of one word:

Mokusatsu.

BRACHA—HEROINE OF ISRAEL

THIS IS the story of a tiny, nineteen-year-old-girl, who played an amazing role in helping to defeat Britain's policy in the Middle East. Her story was never told before. It was suppressed when she was killed on March 26th, 1946.

The girl's name was Bracha Fuld. She possessed a strange beauty; her very dark hair was neatly put together on the back of her head. Her searching blue eyes were as charming as they could be hard; her erect figure, her feminine domination and her tailored clothes betrayed the college girl.

Why did this woman help to undermine British power, she who loved everything British? What could a nineteen-year-old girl do in this eternal struggle of political intrigue in an unstable world of power conflicts?

Was she a spy? Was she a heroine? Why did she wear the uniform? She loved the British, but her uniform was not British.

I, who have written the history of the last three thousand years of espionage, still believe that this is the strangest story I have ever heard.

Bracha was born in Berlin on December 26th, 1926. Her father was one of the great industrialists of Germany. Bracha and her older sister Petra were reared and educated in economic security. In a magnificent surburban Berlin home there were a nurse, a governess and four servants. There was a father who loved his children very much, though he was busy with large business projects and political friendships. There was General Karl Haushofer, the father of Nazi geopolitics, who belonged to the group of intimate friends. Another friend of the family was Rudolf Hess, deputy Führer until he escaped to Britain with his infamous peace offer, only to become a prisoner of war.

220

Bracha's mother, a cosmopolitan, was not happy in this German home. Yes, she was German, too. They were all good Germans but somehow these marching Prussian, Nazi military and Junker circles gave her the chills. She knew she was not wanted, as every member in her family was Jewish. She often pleaded, "Let's leave Germany; Hitler means war."

"This is our country," her husband replied. "I fought in the first war on the Kaiser's side. I am a veteran. I was decorated. Nothing will happen to us. We, the Fuld family, have lived in Germany for four hundred years; we are an old and respected family."

However, a drastic and barbaric Nazi order went into effect on November 9th, 1938. Fire was to be set to all synagogues in Germany, and all male Jews were to be rounded up, sentenced, deported and liquidated.

Here starts the eternal story of a fearless mother escaping danger, combing the globe for sanctuary for her two children: Petra, fifteen, and Bracha, eleven. It was an odyssey for Petra, who landed in the United States. It was an exciting escape to London for the child Bracha.

When Bracha landed in London, her father committed suicide in Berlin; his world had come to an end.

Britain, to Bracha, was a new world. It meant real freedom, understanding, decency. The people were friendly, good, tolerant, and there were no storm-troopers, no "heiling," no fears.

The new school was difficult for her—a boarding school—but beautiful and peaceful. At the same time Bracha's mother was stranded in London, without means, without a plan for the future.

Petra, now in America, had received a scholarship to a Mid-Western university. These Anglo-Saxon countries were good to the German refugees.

Then in March 1939 Mrs. Lotte Fuld and her daughter Bracha landed in Palestine to join some of their relatives.

"Why couldn't we stay in Britain?" Bracha asked her mother.

"We were only visitors, with temporary permits, no chance to work. We were guests only. We have to find a country, a homeland," the mother answered.

Bracha repeated what her beloved father once had told her: "In Palestine! Only HOTTENTOTS live there!"

Bracha was only twelve and loved the mature British way of living. Of course, it was an unhappy first year in Palestine:

of resettlement, adjustment and new life. Bracha cried at home. She was displaced in Palestine. It was so different from Britain. She did not speak Hebrew as all the other children did. She knew nothing about Zionism. She was confused, irritated in a primitive country, in a home without a room of her own, no servants. Here everyone was sloppily dressed. And above all, everyone was a crusader; no one seemed normal. No one had time. Her mother sent her to school, hoping that the children of her own age, facing similar problems, would calm her down. But Bracha grew more impatient and unhappy. To her this school was so different from Britain. It was filled with immigrants, displaced persons and refugees. They spoke many languages. To Bracha this school and its analytical teachers was a preparatory school only, and the students seemed to her second-rate citizens, not wanted by other countries, not yet a part of the *Yishuv*, the Israel community.

She remained lonely. The world of the *sabras* was closed to her. The *sabras* are Jewish children born in Palestine; they learn Hebrew first and are taught English and Arabic in their schools. *Sabra* children are very different from Europeans. *Sabra* means fruit of the cactus, because the cactus fruits are tough and prickly on the outside and soft and bittersweet on the inside. The word describes perfectly the new generation born in the Holy Land. The European children wanted to be accepted by the *sabras*.

As Bracha failed, her teacher said: "She is arrogant, conceited, isolated and just plain difficult."

Any mother would have been unhappy and worried about this state of affairs. Finally she and one of Bracha's teachers solved the problem. Both had watched Bracha for months. They saw her conflicts and gave her the one thing she needed: time and understanding. The educator taught her the new language, Ivrith. He asked her to join Habonim, "The Coming," a youth organization. He made her a part of Young Israel. Suddenly Bracha spoke Ivrith and, when war started on September 1st, 1939, she refused to speak German at home.

The Jews of Palestine knew that the second world war could mean independence for them. Would the Jews mobilize against Hitler, as a Jewish Army? Or would the British be hesitant to put arms into the hands of Jews and Arabs? History has its own laws.

The British were hesitant. But as the war went from bad to worse, and the British Isles were in mortal danger, Churchill was finally willing to accept any Palestine Jew in defence of democracy. It was here that Britain co-operated with the "illegal" Haganah, the Jewish defence organization, and its own commando raiders, the Palmach. Haganah, a Hebrew word meaning defence, was the name of the new underground Jewish army. Its birth goes as far back as 1870, when Jews armed themselves to safeguard their Jewish settlements. Then an organization called Hashomer (Jewish watchmen) was formed back in 1907. The father of the modern Haganah became Colonel Orde Wingate, of His Majesty's armies. When the Germans were coming towards El Alamein, Jewish assault companies were created. It was the birth of Palmach. Boys and girls came from the towns and settlements. They trained with sticks and stones, because there were no guns. Then they left for their posts in the hills and on the borders to wait for the Nazis. They were trained to live among Hitler's soldiers as Arabs.

Then Rommel was beaten and the Palmach returned to Palestine. They continued their military training.

Bracha Fuld, seventeen by now, went to school, never dreaming that one day she would be the heroine of this very same Palmach.

A few months later, Bracha, shortly before her high school graduation, came to her mother and declared: "I have participated in secret training—I want to join Palmach, but I need your permission."

Mother Fuld knew the fate of the death brigades. Dozens of young Jewish boys and girls were dropped by parachutes into Yugoslavia, Hungary, Rumania and Italy. Almost none of them returned. On the Jewish gold star list were Enzo Sereni, Haviva Reik and Hannah Senesh.

Mrs. Fuld knew that her daughter's request meant a meeting with destiny.

"Let's discuss it at a later date," the mother advised, stalling for time. But Bracha was untamed, young and impatient.

Back in 1945, it seemed that Labor Britain would give independence to Palestine, Britain would fulfil her promise to create a Jewish State.

Lotte Fuld, like many a mother in many a country, knew she could not keep a radiant idealistic daughter from serving her people. She could warn, but she could not prevent. Perhaps she did not even want to stop her. The mother has to accept the girl's wishes or lose her. These young women of Palestine, who were willing to parachute over Europe, who had been trained in the art of war and defence, they would run away and continue their work—without parental permission.

By now the British Labor Government, finally, decided against an independent Jewish State; and former allies started to fight each other. Two democratic peoples met in open warfare. Bracha Fuld, age nineteen, became an instructor for Jewish women soldiers. She was made an officer, and finally advanced to the responsibilities of an underground leader.

In the meantime Britain had closed the doors of Palestine to Jewish immigration. The boys and girls of Palmach helped Hitler's and Stalin's refugees organize the illegal immigration. The Palmach created a naval branch, the Palyam, for assisting these immigrant ships. The new comers to the Holy Land were secretly taken to settlements, they were fed and clothed and then scattered all over the country.

Bracha Fuld gave her life to protect this illegal wave of immigration. The ships were filled with victims of Nazi concentration camps and Soviet slave labor brigades.

Bracha led her own platoons, commanded several secret military detachments. She participated in the battle of Sarona.

The immigrant battles turned into open war. British police stations were blown up, underground armament arsenals had to be protected—sabotage—mine clearance—all to get homeless, displaced Jews to Palestine. Bracha was only one of many, but she too knew that the British had declared the death penalty for any Haganah or Palmach member found with weapons in their possession. One day in 1945 Bracha met the one man who actually gave her her first political and intellectual training. Gideon was twenty, tall and handsome. He was an idealist who hated war, who had started out as a pacifist, but now was ready to defend the rights of Palestine. He told her with all the sensitiveness of a native Israeli: "Bracha, we do not want to kill. We do not want to kill British soldiers, who were with us in the same foxhole. We want to build Israel, we must have independence. We want to have a state of our own."

It was a strange love affair that started between the two. He probably never possessed her, but he, the *sabra*, was drawn to her, the Western woman. To her he was heart and brain, ideal and idol, all in one. He was the new Palestine, young Israel. Bracha was attracted to him, but there was no time for love in the hills of Judea.

The sand of Galilee, where the greatest Jew of all—Jesus of Nazareth—had walked, was now soaked with blood, sweat and tears. As Jesus was crucified by those who did not understand Him, the Jews were crucified again by those who believed. Two thousand years of Galuth, of exile, of wandering, of torture, and pogrom and gas chambers, created a new nation of warriors. Those Westerners who believed the age of colonialism could continue suddenly woke up and saw out of the ruins of Europe's death chambers the birth of new Maccabi fighters. They saw rising, Phoenix-like, out of the concentration camps, the pogroms of Russia, men; women and children fighting under the star of King David for freedom, their own land, their own soil, their own dignity, their own pride, their own nation.

War and hatred faced the British and the Jews. Jewish attacks were organized against the British authorities. The British answered with martial law, shooting, execution. All the Holy Land had become a military camp. No Briton dared to move alone. Secret Haganah ammunition depots were raided, spies and traitors worked on both sides. Curfew was over Jersulem and Tel-Aviv, blackout over Jaffa and Nazareth. No one was safe. David fought Goliath. The whole world and the United Nations watched. Thousands died.

The Mandatory Authority was out to crush this revolt of one more colonial country. Many members of the Labor Party condemned their Government's action. Churchill came out in defence of the Israelis. President Truman openly favored independence for the Jews in Palestine. The United Nations begged for peace.

Jerusalem was the beloved mistress everyone wanted to possess: Protestants, Catholics, Jews, Mohammedans. While blood was spilled daily, while emotions ran high, one of the greatest spy stories of all time took shape.

Until her friends gave me all the papers and documents of Bracha Fuld, it was not known that the young girl who was attached to Gideon, was also, at the same time, involved in a sincere and deep friendship with one of the officers in the British army.

Was Bracha a spy? She might be called an officer of combat intelligence. If Gideon had not been arrested by the British and sentenced to death, she perhaps would never have accepted the love of this officer—the man who finally became one of Israel's most valuable helpers in her war of independence.

It was in July 1945 that secret maneuvers of the Palmach held somewhere in Israel, near the Dead Sea. The location was a secret spot, far away from the nearest settlement. The wilderness of the territory was ideal for war. But the war games were betrayed to the British. Troops arrived and arrested everyone they could round up. Death sentence seemed sure for all. Gideon, the leader, was brought to the Government prison in Jerusalem. His sentence was commuted to fifteen years. That Bracha was not among the arrested seemed to be pure accident. Gideon had sent her to Tel-Aviv with an important message. Bracha was mad with anger and fury; her friend, her leader, in British hands! Mother Fuld tried to stop Bracha from further underground activities. With Gideon arrested, she might be next. In the small apartment at Rechov Pinsker, near Mograbi, a desperate mother was fighting for her child.

It was an emotional showdown, but a hopeless attempt. Bracha declared she had to take Gideon's place. If her mother tried to stop her, she would run away and live underground with the rest. She would never come home again. She, Bracha Fuld, was not a deserter. This was open war between Jews and Britain.

The result of the showdown was that Mother Fuld finally asked: "What can I do? Let me help, too."

Mrs. Fuld, who had opened a confectionary shop, agreed to send packages into the prison of Jerusalem. Messages were concealed in her excellent pies, cakes and candies. Bracha visited Gideon once every two months; she could not see him more often because of prison regulations.

In the meantime the disturbances spread. The underground war was more violent. Britain mobilized against a handful of Jews. The United Nations was concerned with the war in Palestine. America seemed to be unhappy about this unfortunate conflict between two democratic nations, while the Soviet dictators planned to overrun all of South-Eastern Europe, Berlin, Korea, and China. Surrounded by a hostile Arab world, the Israelis, without knowing it, had many millions of friends beyond their own land.

The British officer (let's call him Shelby) now entered Bracha's life. She met him in front of the Jerusalem prison. He was tall, slim, handsome. He had been often decorated. He was inspecting the Jerusalem prison when he saw

Bracha visiting Gideon. He stopped and asked Bracha if she thought that the Jerusalem prison was a fair one; if she could confirm that no brutalities were committed.

Bracha challenged the man. No, there were no slave labor camps in Palestine, no gas chambers, but the British Government had no moral right to jail the Jews; they were behaving like traditional colonizers, and in the spirit of Socialism.

One of the most wonderful love affairs started that day. A young Jewish woman challenged an idealistic Anglo-Saxon. Many nights they sat together and talked. She told him about her people, their ideals, their will to freedom. He told her of Gandhi, whom he had met, and Socialism, and that he was not a professional soldier. He ran risks in taking Bracha to the concerts in Tel-Aviv, and she, as a Jewess, took chances in being seen with him in public. Shelby was jealous of Gideon and she told him bluntly there had never been a real affair between them. She also said she was terribly mixed up. She was fond of Shelby, but she could not marry him. He was an enemy officer and she was an underground officer of the Palmach.

Bracha made him see the plight of the Jewish people. The rest was natural. Bracha was not a spy, but Shelby finally gave help to Haganah.

At the same time Bracha was still visiting and writing to Gideon in prison. Shelby asked her again to marry him. They spent much time together, but Bracha, feeling guilty about Gideon, asked Shelby to wait until the war was over.

Bracha was training 300 recruits at a Kibbutz (community settlement) in the blooming valley of Sharon. There was also a Jewish arms depot here. The British arrived, surprisingly, in large forces. They searched the dormitorites, the mess hall, the farm. They spent five hours, but could not find a thing. They saw Bracha, leading the group in gymnastics on the dining-hall floor. No one spoke one word to the British. It was the same silence the Nazis encountered in Norway when they searched among the Norwegians; the Russians encountered it when they searched the Finns.

The British left, never to know that Shelby had warned Bracha the night before the raid. The recruits had put all arms under the dining-hall floor, cemented it during the night and saved all their equipment.

The disturbances continued. Jews were beaten and arrested, Britishers were kidnapped, and two days later a police station near by was blown up. Communities were isolated. Bracha did not come home for a week. Shelby had disappeared. Bracha's mother was distracted until a message came from Shelby, telling her: "I saw Bracha, she is fine; she will be home soon."

A few weeks later an illegal immigrant ship landed under the noses of the British. Bracha knew the British maritime positions. The landing was successful and hundreds of displaced persons found a new home.

At two-thirty in the morning Bracha and a Jewish soldier came running home. She gave a gun to her mother and said, "Don't let them find it." Three minutes later, a well-educated British officer and two soldiers searched the Fuld apartment, finding neither a revolver nor the Haganah fighter who was hiding in a laundry hamper on the terrace! That night Lotte Fuld had saved the life of her daughter and an unknown Israeli soldier.

Now more than ever the mother felt that if Bracha did not quit the underground war she was heading for tragedy and disaster.

The mother pleaded with her. She could save her daughter's life once or twice, but not all the time. "Let's go to America for a visit. Your sister is there. Every soldier deserves a furlough." And Bracha finally agreed to leave Palestine. Six weeks was all Bracha asked. Six weeks to wind up her business, to visit Gideon and to get her successor installed.

The illegal landing of the immigrant ships were scheduled a long time in advance. Bracha promised by April 15th, 1946, to take a vacation and she would be ready to go to America.

But all these plans were never realized. She still visited Gideon in Jerusalem. Shelby still asked her to marry him. During this period the two came probably closer than they had ever been.

That Bracha died on March 26th, 1946, was more a coincidence of unhappy circumstances than fate. The day that made Bracha Fuld the heroine of all Israel was an unforgettable one in its history. Around noon, one thousand Palmach avant-gardists were called to special duty. The secret radio gave warning, blackout was to be expected. Illegal ships were to land, with the displaced persons or, as they should be called, delayed pilgrims. Bracha went out in the darkness to meet her fellow-fighters and to plot the next move.

Author Thomas Sugrue, in his impartial *Watch for the Morning*, gives a perfect description of that night:

"Everyone was a conspirator. The power company turned off the electric current. The transportation companies used their buses to block the streets. The taxi drivers carried ammunition. It was dark and quiet ,and the people waited on the beach. The *Wingate* did not come. . . ."

Bracha was stationed on the cross-road from Sarona to Tel-Aviv. Sarona was the headquarters of the British. Bracha was in charge of eight male soldiers armed with machine guns, rifles, and hand grenades.

One young woman and eight boys, all still children, were trying to protect the road so that Jewish immigrants could find refuge. They fought against British tanks.

Bracha fought in ignorance of the fact that the entire plan of British attack that might have saved her life was at home on her living-room table. In the total darkness she discovered a light on Marmorek road. She could not make out what it was. The searchlights of a British tank had discovered her platoon. Not knowing the strength of the Israelis, the Britons turned back to Sarona to get help and reinforcements. Then came a messenger by bicycle, bringing the bad news. The British had caught the *Wingate*. "Give up," said the messenger, "all is lost, save yourselves, all action is over."

But Bracha, the nineteen-year-old woman officer, answered: "I have no official orders, no official radio communiqué. I must stay, but you men are free to leave if you want. The tank will return any minute." Four boys departed. They knew they had five minutes, perhaps, before the British would return. When the troops came back they shot everything to pieces, including the machine-gun nest held by Bracha Fuld on the terrace of an old, ramshackle house.

A bullet hit her in the breast. "I'm hit. Run fast," she said to the remaining boys. "I'll hold the post and shoot as long as I can."

Mortally wounded, she was captured along with the four boys who had remained.

The tank brought her to the police station in Jaffa. They asked questions . . . "How many are you? How did you know where we were? Who gives you the arms? Where are you hiding them?" Not one word came from her lips. Finally, she fell into a coma. Brought to hospital, she died a few minutes later.

Bracha's mother arrived home next morning at eleven. At noon was to be her daughter's funeral. She still knew nothing of the incident, but seeing two letters from Shelby on the table, she put them into her bag. At that moment British police arrived. They searched the house without explanation.

The city was closed. Driving to the cemetery, her mother saw on the walls posters:

BRACHA
NAFLAH CHALEL BEAMDAH AL MISHMAR
HAFALAH LAAREZ.

BRACHA FELL ON THE RAMPARTS.
SHE WATCHED FOR HER COUNTRY.

The funeral was conducted hastily behind barbed wire. There were no speeches; only a few friends of the family. Thousands of paraders were refused entry to the cemetery.

After the funeral, the British searched the house again, though the soldiers, touched by this tragedy, almost had tears in their eyes.

In Bracha's room they found Gideon's picture. There was nothing that ever pointed towards Shelby. Bracha's mother has destroyed his last letters.

More immigrants were carried to the free republic of Israel on a ship named *Bracha Fuld* and after they landed in Tel-Aviv they were shown the remnants of an old ramshackle house at the corner of Bracha Fuld Street.

HOW RUSSIA STOLE THE SECRET OF THE ATOM BOMB

THE SCIENTIST spy is a relatively new and reversed figure in Soviet espionage. The reason for his eminent position is not difficult to determine. Since he is the creator of new and terrifying weapons of war on earth and the possible conqueror of outer space, he virtually holds the future of mankind in his hands.

The roster of scientist-spies who stole the atomic secrets for the Soviet Union include:

Dr. Alan Nunn May
Dr. Klaus Fuchs
Harry Gold
Julius and Ethel Rosenberg
Morton Sobel
David Greenglass, and others.

This is their story.

"An atom bomb in Russian hands will force America *not* to use it" was the stated belief of Dr. Alan Nunn May. It was also his motive for stealing uranium samples which he gave to officials in the Soviet Embassy in Canada. At the conclusion of his trial, Dr. May received a prison sentence of ten years. Then followed Dr. Klaus Fuchs.

I: KLAUS FUCHS

DR. FUCHS was tremendously ambitious, but had to take hurdle after hurdle. He was never fully recognized. He was always struggling. Psychologists know very little about the history of this man Fuchs. He pleaded guilty at his trial and therefore the question never arose.

J. Edgar Hoover, the chief of the F.B.I., has given a good psychological description of why some intellectuals fall for Communist espionage when he said:

"How did (this man) get started as a traitor? He considered himself an idealist, which made him feel above the law, justifying means by ends. . . . He became a Soviet agent through association with Red friends, through misguided idealism for the 'underdog.'"

This also fits Klaus Fuchs or any of our technical and scientific spies of the last decade.

Klaus Fuchs' youth can tell us why he revolted against society, why he, the frustrated pastor's son, wanted to do something really big. When it is considered that Fuchs was the son of a father who always had tried to make him different, a father he had often revered and often hated, a father who even today advocates union with Communist Germany—his conduct becomes understandable.

The British never thought of his background. The Soviet psychologist, however, knew these details and utilized their knowledge.

Klaus Fuchs' father was a minister and pacifist in war and revolution-loving Germany. His son was only little Klaus in Germany, while the big Klauses went marching to conquest. They were prussians. He hated Prussia, They were Nazis, he became a refugee. They were "Aryans," and Fuchs was a Jewish name in Germany though his father was a Protestant. Perhaps there were always two Klauses inside him.

The courts did not consider heredity. But the fact remains that one of the family committed suicide.

Dr. Fuchs' fanaticism was fostered by the conditions of his political persecution, exile and his internment by the British in Canada. He was stateless for years, and his friends were killed in the Nazi concentration camps. His father also was a victim of the Nazis.

Unstable, persecuted, unhappy, confused and afraid of his own future, he needed a violent outward allegiance, understanding, and the love of a real country. In those critical years he was often close to a complete breakdown. It is here that the secret Soviet machine moved in. It was at this point he listened to the agent sent by one Lavrenti Beria, the incredible head of all Soviet espionage. Fuchs, though underpaid, was not interested in the $500 thrust upon him by the agent. It was a twisted "humanitarianism" that motivated him.

Indeed, most of the scientific spies in the Soviet fold were actually willing to work without fee. But the Soviet Secret Service insisted on paying and demanded receipts in order to have proof of collaboration. Any receipt for moneys, even if signed with a fictitious name, hung like the sword of Damocles over the head of the victims.

Klaus Fuchs' price was not payable in money but in his own hope of avenging a miserable childhood in Germany and the Prussian militarism that he believed had ruined his life. He wanted to get even with those Nazis who had murdered his friends and he wanted to show up the British, who had been kind to him personally but who, as a nation, had appeased Hitler. He ran berserk in his hatred. He wanted love which he had never received in Germany or Britain. Russia held out a promise.

Klaus Fuchs' field was science and, like so many brilliant mathematicians and physicists, the experimental and analytical techniques he used so scrupulously in research, he abandoned completely when confronted with emotional arguments. He accepted every naïve cliché of Communist propaganda. Russia was the workers' fatherland; all weapons were permissible in the global class struggle; the Communists were fighting for a final classless society; there was no such thing as absolute freedom or real truth, or objective science; art and science were class weapons, the artist and scientist who believed in Communism were "men in uniform" and the pioneers of a new society.

Fuchs had gone to Edinburgh University, where he took his degree as Doctor of Science. His original research in atomic and nuclear physics lifted him among brilliant company. The stateless refugee was indeed making a name for himself.

On September 1, 1939, Hitler invaded Poland. Klaus Fuchs suddenly found that the British regarded him as a German —as an enemy alien. A few months later, despite his hatred of Hitler, his antipathy to pan-German nationalism, his successful research at British universities, he was told to pack a bag and get ready for internment. To him, British tolerance was a joke, as his Communist friends had told him; in the final political showdown, the British "capitalists" were ruthless, heartless, vicious and "Fascist."

The effect of war internment on Klaus, the trip as a prisoner over the ocean to Canada, through waters infested by submarines, was to revive the Communist dream which had become quiescent. It also added the self-pity of martyrdom to a nature that was still immature.

In this internment camp for German citizens a traitor was born. The Soviet spy Klaus Fuchs was created from feelings that were sensitive and irretrievably embittered.

His father was in a Nazi camp. He, Klaus, had fought the Nazis long before the British did—and now the British had interned him along with thousands of his enemies.

He, the anti-Nazi, received the same treatment as the Nazis. It was ridiculous, unfair and brutal. But he was powerless, as powerless as he had been when the Nazis had marched through the streets of Kiel and he, a student, had to dive underground.

But was he really powerless? Letters had come from his old friends. The Communists had not forgotten him. His old girl-friend, Hilda, who had worked with him in the party, had even sent him packages from the United States.

Solidarity, understanding and love came only from the Communists. His mind was made up. He would rejoin them as soon as he could leave the barbed wire of this cold internment camp in the wilderness of Canada.

Finally, the British reviewed his case. Bureaucracy admitted its error. Fuchs was an anti-Nazi refugee and not to be confused with his fellow inmates who were confessed Nazis.

In 1941 he was released from internment to his work, research, which was to help in the development of the atom bomb. A year later Fuchs became a naturalized Briton.

His work with Professor Peierls, one of the outstanding atomic research scientists, showed that he was clearly a genius in his field, perhaps a candidate for a Nobel prize or for a membership of the Royal Society. He was sent now to America to work on the U.S. atomic installations.

In the months that followed Fuchs was to be found at many an international atomic conference. But he always returned to Britain.

Finally the hour struck, Scotland Yard called for Fuchs and he believed he had been unmasked. His confession was complete.

Ironic was the fact that M.I.5 had really no evidence against him and had called him to secure information concerning other men under suspicion.

Was he a typical Soviet spy?

He was weak, lonely and lost in this world of chaos. He did not fit the requirements of a Soviet spy as defined in Soviet Intelligence Order 185796:

"Agents must be of the intelligentsia; they must not shrink from the last sacrifice at the crucial moment."

Fuchs was not capable of this last sacrifice. He betrayed his co-workers, many of whom were new Soviet atom spies.

Klaus Fuchs served his fourteen-year sentence in the Wakefield Prison. After his release, he returned to Eastern Germany, married, and has now become one of the outstanding physicists of the Soviet Empire.

II: HARRY GOLD

To THE SHORT, chubby man huddled in a corner out of the wind on a bleak January afternoon sixteen years ago, there was nothing incongruous about the tennis ball clutched in the hand of the approaching stranger. Chubby had been waiting at an appointed spot in New York's lower East Side for just such a stranger; the tennis ball would be his sign of recognition. To identify himself, Chubby carried a pair of gloves and a green book.

They made an unprepossessing pair. Chubby, ordinary looking, mild-mannered, and diffident, the other a thin, sallow-faced, stoop-shouldered young man whose weak brown eyes peered anxiously through thick lenses.

They were, in fact, two of the most dangerous spies who ever met on American soil and between them they did the United States incalculable harm. The shorter of the two was Harry Gold, a Philadelphia chemist who, on that January day in 1944, had been selling his country to Soviet Russia for several years.

The man with the tennis ball was Dr. Klaus Fuchs, the brilliant German-born physicist who, as a naturalized British subject, was assigned to the Manhattan Engineer District, the secret code name for the atomic bomb project.

The offence of these two men, described without exaggeration by J. Edgar Hoover, Director of the Federal Bureau of Investigation, as "the crime of the century," was to steal for Russia the secret of the A-bomb.

But let's get on with their meeting—their first. Exchanging nods of recognition, they took a cab to a Third Avenue restaurant where Gold identified himself as "Raymond." Fuchs gave his right name and briefed Gold on the Manhattan Project. This was a year and a half before the first successful atomic bomb test, but Gold was enough of a scientist to appreciate the potential of such a weapon.

Today Gold is in a Federal penitentiary serving a sentence of thirty years. Fuchs, sentenced to fourteen years, was released from Wakefield Prison after earning full remission. The evil they did persists and if their two countries face the peril of obliteration by the ambitious men of Moscow, Harry Gold and Klaus Fuchs can claim much of the credit.

Springing from widely different backgrounds, both became eager pawns of the Communist conspiracy. In Dr. Fuchs' motivation, a repudiation of the religious teachings and stern discipline of his father, the Rev. Emil Fuchs, played a part. So did the arrogance and brutality of Hitler's Nazis, which impelled him to join the Young Communist League in Germany.

Gold lived quietly at the home of his parents at 6823 Kindred Street, Philadelphia, to which he immediately returned after his introduction to Fuchs. A son of Russian parents who fled their homeland in 1907, he had been born Heinrich Godolnitsky in Berne, Switzerland, and was brought at the age of three to Philadelphia, where the family anglicized his name to Harry Gold.

His, by choice, was a lonely life. A bookish introvert in whose mild manner there seemed a touch of insolence, he graduated from South Philadelphia High School and attended classes at the University of Pennsylvania and at Drexel Institute without acquiring any close friends of either sex. He drove himself at work, substituting for normal human contacts a life of fantasy, peopled by relatives and friends that existed only in his imagination.

The devious trail of his treachery over a period of more than a decade can be traced quickly. He described it many times, both in his own confessions and in court proceedings involving other defendants. What is less well known is the story of the F.B.I. investigations that nailed Gold, Fuchs, and fellow traitors.

Gold was no bemused puppet of Moscow who hadn't realized the enormity of his crime. As he told the F.B.I. at the end:

"I began the work of industrial spying for the Soviet Union in 1936 with the full realization of what I was doing. I felt that as an ally I was only helping the Soviet Union obtain information that I thought it was entitled to."

A character referred to by the F.B.I. as "Troy Niles" steered Gold into Communism and introduced him to his first contact in the Soviet espionage apparatus, a "Paul Smith," an agent of the N.K.V.D. secret police masquerading as an employee of the Amtorg Trading Corp., a Russian business agency in the United States. He was the first of Gold's Soviet superiors in a series that ended with Anatoli Antonovich Yakovlev, a graduate of the Moscow Engineering Economic Institute.

Gold was working at the time for the Pennsylvania Sugar Co. and "Smith," in his domineering manner, demanded that he obtain the secrets of a new process for manufacturing ethyl alcohol. He was never able to deliver that information, but he did pass along valuable data on lanolin, the manufacture of soap, a carbon-dioxide recovery process, and a number of processes involving commercial solvents.

To improve his qualifications, Moscow helped pay for Gold's belated training in chemistry at Xavier University in Cincinnati. He made an excellent record there in all but one course: his lowest grade was in "Principles of Ethics."

Having demonstrated his dependability and trustworthiness, Gold received his supremely important assignment. He was to drop all other work and make contact with the pale stranger with the tennis ball.

Fuchs at the time was attached to a British scientific mission, his loyalty certified by British authorities, and during the next six months he met Gold half a dozen times or so, passing along various technical data on atomic research. Gold, in turn, passed them into the pipeline to Moscow. Their meetings were strictly business, allowing no time for small talk, with one exception. Fuchs did mention that he planned to entertain his sister, Mrs. Kristel Heinemann, of Cambridge, Mass., at his New York apartment.

Suddenly, without warning, Fuchs dropped out of Gold's world. He had been assigned to the A-bomb project at Los Alamos, North Mexico, and it was almost a year before Gold met him again, by prearrangement, on the Castillo Street Bridge in Santa Fe, on the first Sunday in June 1945.

Gold had traveled by train from Chicago to Albuquerque, thence by bus to Santa Fe. To avoid asking directions of passers-by, he obtained a city map from the chamber of commerce and on it marked the route to the Castillo Street Bridge. Fuchs, at the wheel of a dilapidated car, showed up on the dot of four o'clock.

The Los Alamos project, Fuchs reported, was proceeding nicely but he gave his personal estimate that the bomb would never be finished in time for use against Japan. He and Gold arranged to meet three months later and just before parting —a standard practice for spies—Fuchs handed Gold a package containing highly secret information. Within a matter of days it was en route to Russia.

They met again, as planned, on September 19th, 1945. The scientist had proved a poor prophet: by then the test A-bomb had been exploded successfully and two more had eliminated Japanese cities. The war was over.

Fuchs was feeling talkative. He rambled on about his father, who had never approved his Communist associations. He speculated at length on the vast new force for good or evil that man had at his disposal in the controlled atom. As he took leave of Gold, he handed him another envelope. His car disappeared down a dark street. Gold never saw him again.

Russia, it was learned many years later, hoped to explode its first atomic bomb by October 1952, more than seven years behind America. Actually, President Truman was forced to announce, in August 1949, that Russia had achieved the "impossible," ending America's monopoly of the weapon.

Long before that, the American government learned that its basic secrets of nuclear fission had been stolen, just when the sickening discovery was made is a closely guarded F.B.I. secret.

Eventually, however, the F.B.I. learned that there had been a serious leak in America during and after the war. Fuchs, by this time, was conducting atomic research in

England and the British counter-intelligence service, M.I.5, took up the hunt because of his earlier Communist record.

By January 1950 his guilt was established beyond doubt and on January 24th he made his first confession. His conscience, he insisted, was clear; his only concern was what close friends in England might think of him.

Whether Fuchs ever made a complete confession is still doubtful. Certainly he was vague enough in his first description of his American contact—a man he described as about forty, five feet ten inches tall; stocky build with a round face. It might fit millions of men but it was all the F.B.I. had to start with.

No case in F.B.I. history, according to Director Hoover, has been more important and none has subjected its agents to greater pressure. It may never be possible to tell the entire story but some facts can be told.

Agents started with Fuch's sister in Cambridge, Mrs. Heinemann. She knew of no spies in her brother's background but did recall a visitor—a stocky man who was a chemist and had mentioned a wife and children in Philadelphia.

In Washington and in fifty-two field offices, G-men tracked down chemists meeting the unknown's specifications. Some 1,500 photograps were shown the Heinemanns and were flown to Fuchs in England. In some, the Heinemanns noted familiar details; in others Fuchs did the same. But there was no positive identification.

Agents questioned persons who lived near Fuchs' New York apartment on West 77th Street. They questioned his British and American associates, examined hotel records in Santa Fe, checked bus, air, and train ticket offices and New York chemical laboratories.

The 1,500 suspects boiled down to about a score and one man was beginning to stand out—Harry Gold. He fitted some of the clues but not others. For one thing, he wasn't married. But agents concentrated on him because his name was already in their files, in connection with an inconclusive investigation of another Communist matter in 1947.

Gold's photograph was flown to England, where Fuchs examined it at Wormwood Scrubbs prison and shook his head. His American contact, he declared, was not Gold. The F.B.I. hung on. It first had learned of Gold through Elizabeth T. Bentley, a confessed ex-Communist courier, and, in questioning her associates, encountered a man who identified Gold as Frank Kessler. The suggestion of an alias intensified their suspicions.

On May 15th, 1950, two F.B.I. agents entered Philadelphia General Hospital and asked for Gold, who was in charge of the hospital's biological laboratory for heart research. He was "busy" but agreed to talk with the agents later. He did so that evening, adopting the pose of a citizen who was anxious to help but who was honestly puzzled by the G-men's questions.

He recognized Fuchs' photo—but only because it had appeared in the papers after the man's arrest in England. He didn't know Fuchs, didn't know his sister, Mrs. Heinemann. Asked about his travels, he said he had never been west of the Mississippi.

In a series of interviews over several days, Gold pictured his life as depressingly normal—hard work, small salary and little fun. To prove his innocence, he readily gave his written consent to a search of his home.

For every item the searchers turned up—books, papers, scientific journals—he produced a reasonable explanation. An agent fished from a bookcase a map of Santa Fe. On it was traced the route to the Castillo Street Bridge.

"How about this?" Gold was asked. "You said you hadn't been west of the Mississippi."

Silence.

"Would you like to tell us the whole truth, Mr. Gold?"

The answer, suppressed for years, blurted out.

"I—I'm the man Klaus Fuchs gave his information to."

Then, for days, Harry Gold made his confession. At first, as if by force of habit, he embroidered it with lies. Eventually, however, as Hoover disclosed, "he poured out the whole story," not only of his spy career but the fantastic imaginary background he had painted for himself.

Arrested May 23rd, he pleaded guilty July 20th. The Government he betrayed obtained for him the services of an eminent attorney, John D. M. Hamilton, former chairman of the Republican National Committee. On December 9th, 1950, Gold was sentenced to thirty years' imprisonment by United States District Judge James P. McGranery.

Gold's case did not mark an end but a beginning. Making belated restitution, he ransacked his memory for names, dates, and incidents. Gradually the rotten structure of which he had been a part began to collapse trapping in its wreckage some of the most vicious Americans who had ever betrayed their country.

III: JULIUS AND ETHEL ROSENBERG

NEWS OF Klaus Fuch's arrest struck like a knell in a fifty-one dollars a month apartment in Knickerbocker Village, a low-rent housing development on Manhattan's lower East Side. Far more than most Americans, Julius and Ethel Rosenberg, who lived there with their two young sons, appreciated the significance of Fuch's downfall. They were key figures in the Soviet spy apparatus that included Fuchs and Harry Gold, a network that had enjoyed incredible success, thanks to professional skill, American carelessness, and sheer good luck.

Then all the good luck ran out at once. Fuchs was trapped; so was Gold. A pliant brother-in-law developed a stubborn streak. The Rosenbergs were arrested and, worst of all, the Communists invaded South Korea.

Earlier, the Rosenbergs' treason might have been regarded as the work of misguided dupes. The Communist resort to force in Korea placed it in its proper perspective. Rosenberg and his wife, who regarded themselves as destined by fate for the glorification of Communism, found their destiny in the electric chair.

"Plain deliberate murder," a judge told them sternly, "is dwarfed in magnitude by comparison with the crime you have committed."

The arrest of the Rosenbergs with the underlings climaxed one of the finest achievements of the F.B.I. And the international Communist conspiracy, in trying to make capital of their case, betrayed itself for all America to see it as the enemy of truth, freedom, and decency.

Like Fuchs himself, Rosenberg was the product of a religious household dominated by a devout father who glorified in the freedom and the modest living he had found in the New World. He entered the College of the City of New York to study electrical engineering, became known as a campus radical and a convert to Communism. He was a man who gravitated naturally to the sources of power in the party.

Ethel Greenglass was three years his senior, a small, dark-haired girl of literary and artistic pretensions. She had joined the party in the 1930s and met Rosenberg at its affairs. Between them, they sandbagged her younger brother, David Greenglass, with lectures on Communist idealogy to such good effect that, when they married in 1939, David joined the Young Communist League. It was his wedding present to the happy pair.

More than a year before Pearl Harbor, Rosenberg became a civilian junior engineer in the Brooklyn supply office of the Army Signal Corps. By May 1943, he had advanced to associate engineering inspector and by the spring of 1944 began spying for the Soviet Union as the world-wide conspiracy rounded up its fellow-traveling scientists and technological experts in an emergency effort to keep pace with the solution of atomic and other scientific mysteries.

His Communist associations brought about Rosenberg's suspension in February 1945, but he promptly went to work for Emerson Radio Company, one of the concerns whose war production he had inspected for the Signal Corps.

Greenglass, meanwhile, had married and entered the Army. A machinist in civilian life, he was transferred to the bleak mesa of Los Alamos, North Mexico, where he made up gadgets to the specifications of scientists. He knew his project was top secret but, aside from his immediate job, had no inkling of its true significance. Nor did he much care.

His wife, Ruth, who had remained home in New York, mentioned her husband's assignment to the Rosenbergs. Julius was well aware, through his espionage contacts, that Los Alamos was working on the A-bomb and to have an "insider" on the premises, in the person of his brother-in-law, came as a stupendous stroke of good luck. Greenglass, he informed Ruth flatly, would have to get him secret information.

When the sergeant's wife demurred, Rosenberg parroted the familiar Communist arguments, claiming that Russia was an ally with whom the United States and Britain churlishly refused to share secrets. Ethel Rosenberg chimed in as the sergeant's "older sister." Their clincher, though, was more concrete.

They offered Ruth Greenglass 150 dollars to visit her husband in New Mexico and, separated from him for months, she accepted. Their instructions to the sergeant were specific: they wanted a physical description of the project, approximate number of employees, names of scientists, security measures, and distances from Los Alamos to nearby cities.

Learning from his wife for the first time, that he was working on an A-bomb, Greenglass began by refusing to spy for his brother-in-law. Before his wife returned to New York, however, he gave her some of the desired information. Just one item, the fact that Dr. Niels Bohr, the famous Danish nuclear scientist, was at Los Alamos, was in itself invaluable to the Russians. Bohr had been using the name Nicholas Baker to conceal his real identity.

In January 1945, Greenglass himself visited New York and, in Rosenberg's apartment, drew from memory a rough design of a lens mold used in atomic experiments.

Rosenberg then made new arrangements. He gave the Greenglasses money with which to rent an apartment in Albuquerque and told the sergeant that thereafter he would pass his information to a courier who would call on them, identifying himself with a carefully cut half of a panel from a Jell-O box. The Greenglasses kept the other half, even though Ruth objected that they were getting "mixed up in things that are too big for us."

On a Sunday morning in the following June, at the Greenglass apartment at 209 North High Street, Albuquerque, a plump young man appeared with the greeting: "Julius sent me." He presented his half of the Jell-O box, which matched that half by the Greenglasses. The stranger, who identified himself as "Dave from Pittsburg," was Harry Gold. He gave Greenglass 500 dollars, receiving in return drawings and a written description of A-bomb components.

On August 6, the first atomic bomb used against an enemy wiped out Hiroshima. Three days later a second bomb of a different type devastated Nagasaki. The following month, Greenglass—back home in New York—drew detailed drawings explaining how the second bomb differed from the first. Ethel Rosenberg retyped his reports, correcting his English, and Rosenberg passed the information to his superiors.

That just about concluded Greenglass' spy work. He left the Army, returned to New York, and saw the Rosenbergs occasionally although relations, for personal reasons, were severely strained. Then Fuchs was arrested.

Greenglass had not known the Briton personally but realized from newspaper stories that he and Fuchs had been part of the same spy network. He was not, therefore, unprepared for the F.B.I. phone call that came to his flat a few days later. He invited the caller to drop in.

After polite preliminaries, the agent asked whether Greenglass had known Dr. Fuchs. Only as the name of one of the British scientists, the sergeant replied. There was a brief discussion of other scientists and of security rules and the agent withdrew, complimenting Ruth Greenglass on the cup of coffee she had poured for him.

"I was almost on the verge of telling him something," Greenglass confessed as the agent left.

"I wish you had," she replied wearily.

Within a week they had another caller—Rosenberg. He hustled Greenglass to Hamilton Fish Park, where they could talk safely.

"Remember the man who came to see you in Albuquerque?" he asked. "Well, Fuchs was one of his contacts. Now Fuchs is talking. He'll lead to the man you knew. Then that man will be arrested and he'll lead to you. You've got to leave the country."

He outlined the standard escape route for suspected Soviet agents in America: Mexico, to Switzerland, to Czechoslovakia, to Russia. Whether the Greenglasses might ever have started that dreary journey will never be known because the next morning Ruth suffered painful burns when her flannel nightgown caught fire from a gas heater.

She remained in a hospital until mid-April and soon entered another to have her second baby. She had been home only two days on May 18th, when Rosenberg burst into the apartment, clutching a newspaper. On its front page appeared the picture of Harry Gold, arrested as a spy suspect.

Rosenberg had the Greenglasses' future all arranged. He handed them 1,000 dollars in cash. They were to obtain five sets of passport photographs and inoculation certificates, give them to him, and head for the Mexican border.

When Greenglass reached Mexico City he was to write to the secretary of the Russian Ambassador. Three days later he was to go to the Plaza de Colon with his fingers stuck in a guide book and stand in front of the statue of Christopher Columbus.

There, with the proper passwords, he would meet a contact who would produce passports and money for the next stage of the trip.

Greenglass did get the passport pictures and gave them to Rosenberg, who handed him another 4,000 dollars and confided that he and his wife would soon be following them to Mexico.

"We've all got to leave sooner than we expected," Rosenberg confessed shakily. "They're closing in on us."

Ruth Greenglass looked at her husband.

"We're not going," she said quietly.

"No," her husband agreed. "We're staying here."

"Be sensible," Rosenberg shouted as he stalked out angrily.

The Greenglasses didn't see Julius and Ethel again until they faced each other in court. When four F.B.I. men walked into the Greenglass flat on June 15th, the sergeant greeted them quietly.

"Have a seat," he invited. "I'll talk to you as soon as I finish the baby's formula."

The following day, three agents called at the Knickerbocker Village apartment of Julius Rosenberg. He invited them in, excused himself, and drew his wife into the bathroom.

"Shall I talk to them?" he said desperately.

"You'd better," she shrugged. "It might look funny if you didn't."

The interview shifted to the Federal Building at Foley Square. The conversation was restricted to the affairs of Greenglass until one agent remarked:

"Do you know your brother-in-law said you told him to supply information for Russia?"

"Will you bring him here and let him say that to my face?" Rosenberg demanded.

"What would you do if we did?"

"I'll call him a liar to his face," Rosenberg shouted righteously. "You ask me to give you information on Greenglass, now you're trying to pin something on me. I want to see a lawyer."

With the agents' permission, Rosenberg telephoned his attorney. The lawyer, told that Rosenberg was not actually under arrest, advised his client to come to his office. Rosenberg turned to the agents.

"Good day, gentlemen," he smiled blandly, as he walked out.

Within a day or two, Rosenberg, his wife, and their two sons appeared at the photographic studio of Ben Schneider at 99 Park Row. They ordered 36 passport photographs in a variety of poses. Obviously, they were about to embark on the Mexico-Switzerland-Czechoslovakia-Russia escape tour. But from then on they were uncomfortably aware of F.B.I. surveillance.

On July 17th, a little more than a month after Greenglass' arrest, two agents called again at Knickerbocker Village. This time there was no sparring. Rosenberg was arrested. His wife, after refusing to answer a Federal grand jury's questions in three truculent sessions, was taken into custody three weeks later and on August 17th both were indicted.

They were charged with violation of the General Espionage Law of 1917 in having conspired, in time of war, to transmit information concerning the national defence to a foreign power. The act does not specify that the foreign power must be an enemy.

Brought to trial with the Rosenbergs was their friend, Morton Sobell, another New York electrical engineer and radar expert. He had fled to Mexico to escape prosecution but was picked up by Mexican undercover police and escorted to the border, where he was seized by waiting F.B.I. men. He was charged with joining the Rosenbergs in conspiracy to persuade Greenglass to work for Russia.

At the trial, which opened in New York on March 6th, 1951, before Judge Irving R. Kaufman, the Rosenbergs' defence was simple. They denied everything: denied any connection with Communism and attributed their arrests to a frame-up.

But the evidence documented by the F.B.I. and confirmed in large part by Harry Gold and David Greenglass and his wife, convinced the jury of eleven men and one woman. On March 29th, after nineteen hours of deliberation, they brought in verdicts of guilty against the three accused.

Greenglass, who had pleaded guilty, received fifteen years' imprisonment—a reward, so to speak, for his co-operation in nailing the Rosenbergs. Sobell was given a thirty-year sentence. Judge Kaufman reserved his verdict on the Rosenbergs until April 5th, on which day they were sentenced to death.

"Only the Lord can find mercy for what you have done," he said. "I believe your conduct, in putting into the hands of the Russians the A-bomb years before our best scientists predicted Russia would perfect the bomb, already has caused the Communist aggression in Korea, with resultant casualties exceeding 50,000 Americans. Millions of innocent people may pay the price for your treason. Indeed, by your betrayal, you undoubtedly have altered the course of the history to the disadvantage of your country."

Over two and a half years were to elapse, however, before the Rosenbergs died in the electric chair at Sing Sing, on June 19th, 1953. In the interval, having received the full protection of the law. Eminent attorneys carried their cases seven times to the United States Court of Appeals, which upheld the death sentence each time.

Another seven times their cases came before the United States Supreme Court, which refused a review. Three appeals for clemency were presented to two Presidents of the United States. These, too, were denied.

There was a way out for the condemned couple—if they would reveal the identity of their fellow-conspirators, and any plans being prepared for further Soviet spy coups in America, clemency would be granted and they would be saved from the chair. On six occasions this proposal was put to Julius and Ethel Rosenberg, but they refused to talk. In the letters they wrote to each other they showed no wavering in their determintaion to continue to refuse the terms which would have led them out of the death cell.

They were the first Americans ever to be sentenced to death for treason by a civil court and on the day they died Presidnt Eisenhower ordered that a telephone line should be kept open between the White House and Sing Sing so that the execution could be stayed if they repented.

Coincident with the Sing Sing executions, a German house painter named Willi Goettling was shot to death by a Russian firing squad near his home. He was accused of having taken part in the East Berlin revolt against the Kremlin and he had been arrested only twenty-four hours earlier.

For Willi Goettling there was no trial, no prominent legal defenders, no appeals to higher courts. And Communists around the world coldly ignored the fate of the German house painter if, indeed, they ever heard of him.

But in the two years preceding the deaths of the American traitors, there emerged a gigantic propaganda campaign designed to hide their crime behind a smokescreen and to exploit Julius and Ethel Rosenberg for the purposes of international Communism.

Fraud was its hallmark—fraud with a sinister purpose and a spectacular profit. It sought to blacken the name of America throughout the world—with Americans paying the bill to the tune of about half a million dollars.

Millions of helpless and innocent persons have perished behind the Iron Curtain through execution, wholesale butchery, planned starvation, and the deliberate extermination of minorities. Together, they exemplify the real methods of Soviet justice—a bullet in the neck without benefit of trial. Communists and their confederates have uttered no protests.

But for the Rosenbergs—duly tried and convicted of a shameless betrayal of their country—Communists brazenly demanded "justice." For sentencing the convicted traitors to death, the United States was assailed in fifty languages from pole to pole as savage, barbaric, and inhuman.

The campaign was, of course, never intended to benefit the spies. As individuals, the Rosenbergs were of no concern to Communism. Had they lived—and perhaps talked—they might have endangered the movement. Dead, they were martyrs. A study of the activities and records of the campaign points clearly to the fact that its objectives were these:

To vilify the United States and to spread the lie that Government persecutes minorities and political dissenters.

To raise funds for overall Communist activities.

To recruit new members and sympathizers.

To restore the badly tarnished reputation of the party.

To bolster the campaign to infiltrate American churches.

To discredit American courts and to cast doubt on the investigation and conviction of all Communists.

The trial established the guilt of the Rosenbergs beyond doubt. The separate threads of testimony wove themselves into a solid fabric of guilt. Against all the facts elicited from the prosecution witnesses, the Rosenbergs presented only bare unsupported denials. They could not refute a single point. The prosecution, ready to call more than one hundred and twenty witnesses, needed to call only twenty-two. The Rosenbergs did not call a single witness for themselves. They testified on their own behalf. Morton Sobell did not even take the stand.

And, during the course of the trial, the Communist press published not a single word on the trial. Nowhere was there the slightest whisper of "frame-up" that was to be roared so loudly in the campaign to come.

Neither was there so much as a hint of duress, prejudice, or intimidation from counsel for the defence. Emanuel Bloch, chief of the defence, was skilled in Communist legal strategy; he had represented more than one party leader. Yet not once did he or his colleagues challenge the conduct of the trial. On the contrary, all the defence lawyers—especially Bloch—were effusive in their praise of the trial procedure.

He thanked the court, Judge Irving Kaufman, for having

reated the defence with "utmost courtesy." He paid tribute to the courtesies extended by the F.B.I. and conceded that 'the trial has been conducted . . . with the dignity and decorum that befits an American trial."

This is the same Bloch who, when the Rosenbergs' bodies ay in a Brooklyn funeral chapel, screamed:

"I place their murder at the door of President Eisenhower, Attorney General Brownell, and J. Edgar Hoover. This is not American justice. America today is living under the hell of a military dictator garbed in civilian attire."

He said the Rosenbergs were convicted only because they were Communists. At the trial, he congratulated the court for "keeping politics out of the case." He claimed the jury was packed with jurors intent on sending the defendants to the chair. At the trial, he did not even use all his challenges to eliminate "prejudiced" jurors.

After the "Save the Rosenbergs" campaign began, Bloch denounced Harry Gold as a "pathological liar." At the trial he didn't even bother to cross-examine Gold—his chance to expose his so-called lies.

Throughout the campaign, Communists shrieked of "new evidence" found in defence of the Rosenbergs, long after the so-called evidence had been considered by the courts and thrown out.

The Rosenbergs' service to the Soviet Union began with espionage and ended with their silence. They betrayed their native land and maintained their allegiance to Moscow. Beyond this, they provided a rallying point for great numbers of Americans who displayed a shocking readiness to join hands with treason.

The first hints of a Communist campaign on behalf of the spies came with the announcement that the newspspaer *National Guardian* would "expose the evidence" on which the pair had been convicted. In a series of seven articles in August 1951, William A. Reuben characterized the trial as a "frame-up" resulting from the collusion of the F.B.I. and a "self-confessed spy and stool pigeon" (Greenglass), designed to convince the public that all Communists are a danger to the nation's existence.

As a next step, shown by the records of the Chase National Bank, the Communists set up a bank account for the "National Committee to Secure Justice in the Rosenberg Case." on November 8th, 1951. It was not until two months later however, that the *Daily Worker* formally announced the creation of a committee.

The reason for the delay was obvious: Moscow first had to make sure the Rosenbergs wouldn't talk. They could not afford the risk that the imprisoned husband and wife might confess in the midst of a campaign on their behalf.

By January of 1952, the party could be sure not only that the Rosenbergs were "safe" but that they could be counted on for a steady flow of propaganda material from their cells. The confidence was not misplaced. Until the night of their deaths, the writings and statements of the prisoners never deviated from the party line.

After the rejection of the first Rosenberg appeal by the Circuit Court of Appeals, in February 1952, the campaign gathered momentum. This started a pattern which was to be followed without change until the execution. Each reversal in the courts brought proportionately louder screams of injustice and persecution, at mass meetings across the nation.

The committee suffered two reverses. One lay in its effort to introduce a "civil liberties" note; the other in attempts to link legitimate Jewish organizations to the campaign.

On May 2nd, 1952, the American Civil Liberties Union, through its counsel, Herbert M. Levy, issued a memorandum repudiating every one of the Communist arguments and summarily denying there was any violation of civil rights in the Rosenbergs' trial and sentence.

The next phase began late in November 1952, after the Supreme Court refused, for the first time, to review the case. At this point there began an avalanche of Rosenberg activity throughout Europe. Although there had been no Rosenberg committees in England and France for the previous two and a half years, committees suddenly sprang up in London and Paris.

As the Rosenbergs' last hours approached, Communists whipped their followers and their dupes into a last great effort. In Washington, the White House was picketed. Chanting sympathizers jammed Union Square in New York. Thousands of demonstrators groaned in London's Hyde Park, in Paris, in Rome, Genoa, and Vienna, flogging themselves into a fury of anti-Americanism.

Viewed in its entirety, the Communist Rosenberg campaign stands forth as a design of monumental cruelty and deceit. There is no way to measure the damage it inflicted upon American prestige but it was extensive and lasting.

The campaign deserves notice because of the insight it offers into the operations and techniques of the Communist front. One of the greatest propaganda advantages of the Communist Party is the widespread belief that its front organizations pose less danger than the party itself.

Actually, it is through its front organizations that the party seeks to effect its subversive aims. They represent a major source of financial support and of new recruits and draw in great numbers of persons who would recoil from any overt association with Communism.

The Rosenberg campaign had every feature of an effective front organization: the broad base of non-Communists; the rigid, behind-the-scenes domination by Communists; the camouflage of party rule and objective by humanitarian appeals, and willing dupes calculated to entrap the unwary into partnership with conspiracy.

The Rosenbergs left behind them two children. They were of school age and it was not possible to withhold the truth from them. Both were young, too young to be much more than bewildered by the onset of disaster. One of the ugliest aspects of the whole Rosenberg affair was the manner in which the two orphans were pilloried because their parents had died the death of felons.

When the children were enrolled once again in a school in New Jersey they had to face tauts, threats and abuses both from parents and schoolmates. It was an intolerable situation and, seemingly, beyond the control of the school authorities. The removal of the Rosenberg children was therefore requested "in order to maintain harmony in our educatonal system." It would be superfluous to speculate on what education was taught there and it could not have been otherwise than to the advantage of the little Rosenbergs that they were taken away. They were sent to Canada and received into a civilized and compassionate home. To save them from further cruelties they began life anew under an assumed name.

THEY KILLED A SAINT

THE FANATICS of the Mohammedan and Hindu worlds might not be fundamentally different from those of the Occident but they seem to have fewer scruples when it comes to the techniques of assassination, violence, and terror.

Death for their religious and political opponents seem often the most natural approach and religious laws are set aside to justify the fanatic's misdeeds. "Thou shalt not kill" is still the essence of any religion, East or West; but despite this commandment the twentieth century has produced political murder in the name of religion.

In 1947 tragedy struck India—free India—the India that despised violence, which in spite of all the theories on revolutions won her freedom without fighting on the barricades or the battlefield.

The saint prayed, then he rose and spoke lovingly to his flock of five hundred who had assembled at the prayer ground.

"I, the Hindu, can see no difficulty in my daughter regarding every Mohammedan as a brother, and vice versa. I have asked you, each one of you, to bring a Mohammedan friend to our prayer meetings."

There was silence in the prayer room; the door stood open to the great park; not a voice was to be heard. The people looked up to him, the Hindu saint.

Mahatma Gandhi was silent, too, for a moment. At seventy-eight, speaking was now an effort for him. Then his soft, penetrating, warm voice continued, "How can we achieve this Hindu-Mohammedan unity? How can it be best promoted? The answer is simple. It consists in our having a common purpose, common goal and common sorrows. It is best promoted by co-operating to reach the common goal, by sharing one another's sorrows and mutual toleration. A common goal we have. . . . We have enough sorrows to share. . . . *Mutual toleration is a necessity for all time and all races.* We cannot live in peace if the Hindu will not tolerate the Mohammedan form of worship of God and his manners and customs."

Gandhi had no fear of death, and had ordered that none of his many unknown visitors should be searched for arms by the guards. He believed in man's essential goodness. This belief finally cost him his life.

The first attempt to kill Gandhi was made as early as June 25, 1934. The plan was originated then in Poona by the Hindu Mahassabha (Grand Society). At that time a bomb was thrown into Gandi's car, but no one was hurt.

The second attempt to kill Gandhi was made on January 20, 1948.

Two weeks earlier Nathuram Godse, a tall Hindu, editor of *Agroni,* and a proud Brahman, visited his bank in Pangoon and made arrangements that in case of his death his life insurance benefits would be paid to the wife of his co-worker, Apte, and to the wife of his younger brother, Gopal.

The great success and the results of Gandhi's last fast had infuriated all members of the chauvinistic Mahassabha Society. To them the only good Mohammedan was a dead one. As Hitler had to get rid of all the Jews in Germany, these Hindu fanatics had to destroy the Mohammedan world inside India and conquer her "greater" frontiers. Gandhi had been in their way for years. They were maniacs, hypnotized by their own mad dreams of a Greater Hindustan. With Godse as leader, the macabre tragedy unfolded in the conspirators' den. His audience had come to Poona to hear Godse, their uncrowned leader.

What he felt at this meeting with nine other underground leaders of the super-nationalistic Grand Society he expressed himself when he testified at his own long trial:

"I sat brooding intensely on the atrocities perpetrated on Hinduism and the dark and deadly future if left to face Islam outside and Gandhi inside . . . and I decided all of a sudden to take the extreme step against Gandhi."

With Godse was his younger brother, the twenty-seven-year-old Gopal V. Godse, who was an employee of the Indian government arsenal at Kirkes. The third conspirator was the general manager of Godse's newspaper, *Agroni*, a certain Narayan D. Apte. He was thirty-four, a former teacher who had worked at one of the colleges administered by an American religious mission.

The fourth plotter was Vishnu R. Karkare, an extremist who was organizing, at the age of thirty-seven, special refugee camps from areas where Moslems and Hindus clashed or still lived in great tension. The fifth accomplice was a youngster of twenty, Madanlal K. Pahwa, a refugee who escaped from the Moslem riots in the Punjab and who had been recruited in the refugee camps by Karkare. He was to throw the first bomb. The sixth accomplice was Shankar, a twenty-year-old servant boy.

The seventh seditionist was Digambar Badge, who dealt in small weapons and daggers. He was later pardoned after he had turned state's evidence. Other plotters were the sixty-five-year-old Vinayak D. Savarkar, the oldest of the conspirators, who gave his blessing to this "youthful" assassination enterprise, and Dattartaya S. Parchure, a public figure in the state of Gwalior. It was he who procured the death pistol.

Madanlal and Nathuram Godse were to spy on the Gandhi household, and learn its habits and customs. They had to be fully familiar with Gandhi's living quarters, the park, the prayer ground, the visitors, and the location of the government guards, their shifts, watch periods, and other routine. The rest of the gang would assist in procuring the bomb which was to be placed in Birla House. With Gandhi out of the way, the conspirators believed they could make India really "free."

The nationalist spies began to scout immediately. Their observations were carried out in the most minute details. While the plotters were praying and fasting with Gandhi, observing and scrutinizing the visitors and the police guards, the final plot took shape in the brain of the elder Godse.

All nine men were in Delhi at the same time. It was a most unorthodox plot, since assassination is usually planned and executed by as few as possible. Gandhi's assassination was planned for January 18. But when Goodse and Badge went to Birla House on the eighteenth they were stopped at the gate. They said they wanted to see the secretary. They were asked politely to write their names in the book of visitors. They signed their aliases but decided to postpone the assassination for a day or two, when they could enter with a whole group of pilgrims.

The original plan called for the use of a bomb made out of a slab of guncotton. Deciding to use more than one weapon, they went to the woods and tested out a new .38 calibre pistol.

Finally the new weapons were distributed as follows:
Madanlal: one guncotton slab and one hand grenade.
Gopal Godse: one hand grenade.
Karkare: one hand grenade.
Shankar: one pistol.
Badge: one hand grenade and one pistol.
N. Godse and Apte were to be unarmed in order to give signals undetected.

The group changed their clothes, putting on the pilgrims' garb—dark blue coats and trousers, Gandhi caps, English jackets, and khaki shorts. Karkare even put a red caste mark on his forehead.

But the plot did not go according to plan. There were too many pilgrims inside the prayer house. Last-minute changes were hastily made, and the bomb was thrown from the outside instead of inside the prayer house. It exploded on a garden wall, 150 feet from Gandhi, who was sitting and praying.

The pilgrims were stunned, and Gandhi said only:

"What is it? I don't know, but don't bother about it. Listen to me"—and they continued their prayers. The bomb which was intended to kill the man who wanted to bring unity between Hindu and Mohammedan had not touched anyone. The crowd continued to pray, the Hindu for his Mohammedan brother and the Mohammedan for his Hindu neighbor.

Without knowing that it was a Hindu co-religionist who had just tried to assassinate him, Gandhi said in his calm and searching way, "So long as there are different religions, every one of them may need some outward distinctive symbol. But when the symbol is made into a fetish and an instrument of proving the superiority of one's religion over others, it is fit only to be discarded."

Madanlal was caught and arrested. Witnesses had seen three men escaping in a jeep, and others in a taxi.

After this the Birla House guards were tripled. All India was shocked. The conspirators did not dare to leave their hotels. They were sure Madanlal would not give them away, for they had taken an oath not to betray one another.

Gandhi continued to remain calm and said to his twenty new police guards, "If I have to die, no precautions can save me. I am seventy-eight. My only protection is God."

His end came only ten days later, on the unforgettable day of January 20, 1948.

This twentieth-century saint, who, though not a follower of Christ, was probably the greatest Christian of our time, went into the empire of silence by an assassin's bullet.

The conspirators had had a last meeting; they had sworn again to destroy the enemy of Hindu greatness, the appeaser of Mohammedan power.

It was a meeting of fanatics who were filled with hatred and lust for power. One cannot catalogue these Hindu assassins, but fundamentally they were touched by the same blind megalomania that made Hitler send the Jews to gas chambers and made Stalin purge his opposition.

Now the day dawned for them to strike. They spent about three hours in Gandhi's peaceful house before the fatal shots were fired.

It was about 4:30 in the afternoon. Gandhi's two granddaughters, Abha and Manu, were with him. They brought him what was to be his last meal, in a basket. It included goat's milk, raw and boiled vegetables, fruits, ginger, and hot butter with the juice of aloe.

Gandhi sat on the cold floor of his room deep inside Birla House in New Delhi. He ate and talked with his guest, S. V. Patel, the deputy prime minister. Patel's daughter, Maniben, and his secretary were also present.

There had been a rift between Prime Minister Nehru and Patel, and it was now up to Gandhi to bring about a reconciliation. He did his best, with the sincere humor that was so typical of him. He had the wisdom of the saint who never lost the sight of the really great and important things in life.

Abha, Gandhi's granddaughter, seemed restless. She hated to interrupt the two men. She knew their talk was important. But she also knew her grandfather's desire for punctuality. The prayer meeting had begun; it was time for him to go. She picked up Mahatma's archaic nickel watch and showed it to him.

"I must tear myself away," Gandhi said. He put his arms around the shoulders of his granddaughters and said to Patel:

"They are my walking-sticks."

He joked with the two girls while going toward the park. Abha had given him carrot juice that morning. "So you are treating me like grazing cattle," he said smilingly.

"Ba used to call it the horse menu," answered Abha. Ba had been Gandhi's late wife.

"Isn't it nice of me," Gandhi continued to joke, "to eat what no one else wants?"

"Bapu (father)," interrupted Abha, "your watch must be very lonely; you would not look at it today."

"Why should I, since the two of you are my timekeepers?"

By now they had reached the grass near the prayer grounds. "Yes, I know, Abha," continued Gandhi, "I'm ten minutes late. I hate being late. I should be here at the stroke of five."

This was his last recorded conversation.

Gandhi had just reached the top of a short flight of brick steps. Abha, who was twenty, and Manu, who was seventeen, were helping him up the steps when someone greeted the saint. He turned away from his granddaughters and gave the traditional Hindu salute—palms together and the points of the fingers touching as in a Christian gesture of prayer.

At this moment, a man broke through the crowd and came

close to them. Manu, knowing they were late, tried to catch his arm. He pushed her away violently. Then, standing two feet in front of Gandhi, he fired three shots from a small European pistol.

The first bullet hit the Mahatma in the chest and went through his heart. The two following shots went through the right side of the stomach.

He fell forward, his hands still in the attitude of prayer. After the second shot he murmured, "Hey, Rama" (Oh, God). These were his last words.

The crowd was paralyzed as the two grandchildren lifted the frail Gandhi and carried him into his room in Birla House.

Tom Reiner, the United States vice-consul, a newcomer to India, who had attended the prayer meeting, seized the assassin—Nathuram V. Godse. Godse shouted as loud as he could to the police and the foreign correspondents, "I'm not sorry at all." These, too, were his last words on the day he was hanged, a year later.

But the fanatics had not really destroyed Gandhi. They had taken his life, but his soul lived on. He had said, just a few days before he was assassinated, "Death is no fiend. He is the truest of friends. He delivers us from agony. He helps us against ourselves. He even gives us new chances, new hopes. He is like sleep a sweet restorer."

Godse, the assassin, was brought to the Tughlak Road police station and later to the Red Fort, a seventeenth-century prison. He was unshaken, and he knew that all his accomplices had escaped during the confusion and panic following the shooting.

Gandhi received the burial of a saint. He died because he believed there was only *one God*: that Moslem, Hindu, Catholic, Protestant, Jew—all men and women of all creeds, races, and religions—were brothers and sisters.

Men and women chanted Hindu scriptures, and knelt down to pray. Gandhi's head was half covered and he was illuminated by five lights, representing the five elements: air, light, water, earth, and fire.

All that Nehru, Gandhi's greatest disciple, could say was: "Godse—the murderer, I can only call him a madman." He was.

It was obvious to all that the fanatic Hindu Mahassabha

was behind the assassination. Godse had been an active member, as had Madanlal. Arrest warrants were issued for all their leaders. Badge was seized in Poona, after the embittered crowd had burned down his house. Parchure was seized in Gwalior, and Inspector Pinto caught Godse's brother, Gopal, on the road to the village Uksan where he had hoped to hide. Savarkar and Shankar were apprehended the same day. Apte and Karkare went underground in Bombay. They switched their place of hiding three times a day, but finally a phone call of theirs was traced to one of the bigger hotels and they were arrested and brought to New Delhi.

The entire law machinery and investigation apparatus of India was put into action. Thousands of agents and informers produced witnesses, handwriting experts, hotel clerks, rail and plane clerks who identified and testified against the Gandhi assassins.

Godse complained about his treatment in prison, and asked no other favor than better prison treatment. He admitted he had killed Gandhi and expected to be hanged. "I do not desire that any mercy be shown me or that anyone beg for mercy in my behalf."

Godse never understood the meaning of mercy nor the teachings of Gandhi, who believed mercy and forgiveness were the godly attributes of man.

"Truthfully speaking, my life came to an end simultaneously with the shots fired by me at Gandhi. Since then I have been passing my days as if in a trance and in meditation."

The United States intelligence officer, Colonel Richard Hirsch, gives an account of Godse's own testimony in his book *Crimes That Shook the Worlds*.

I stepped in front of him. My idea was to shoot at point-blank range so that no one else might get injured. I bowed to him with my pistol in my hand. I think I fired twice, but however I learned later that I fired three times. After I had fired the shots there was a lull for about half a minute. Then I also got excited and shouted, "Police, police, come."

Soon after a constable came and caught me. At the same time some members of the public removed the pistol from my hand. A large number of persons thereafter caught me. A gentleman struck me on the back of the head with his stick. After two or three blows, blood began to come from my head. I told him that I would not oppose him even if he happened to break my skull. I told him that I had already done what I wanted to do, for which I did not repent.

The police then tried to take me away from the crowd. I saw a person with my pistol in his hand and I told him to put the safety catch on otherwise he might injure someone in the crowd.

He then told me that he was going to shoot me. I told him that I did not mind if he shot me, but what I told him about the safety catch was in his own interest. After two hours of the incident, I asked a doctor to examine me in order to find out whether my pulse and heart were normal. They were.

At the trail, Godse seemed bored; he was not concerned about himself. He thought he had helped to make history—and that history would remember him as a great man.

As the trial progressed the defendants became propagandists. Led by Godse, they elaborated on Moslem atrocities, and on the dangers of the "British satellite" Pakistan which would "swallow" India.

India was divided during this trial. Because Gandhi had opposed violence and death sentences, his disciples prayed for Godse and his gang. They said Gandhi would have asked forgiveness and would have opposed a death sentence for Godse.

Nobel prize winner Pearl Buck, the famous author and lover of Asia, wrote in the United Nations World: "If we are to take Gandhi literally, that man Godse should not die by violence." Then Pearl Buck concluded her editorial with the words: "Oh, India, dare to be worthy of your Gandhi."

But Godse was sentenced to be hanged, and all the other defendants of the spy and murder ring were sentenced to life imprisonment. After the sentence was pronounced, they shouted arrogantly: "We will conquer. Long live Hindustan."

Since the murder of Gandhi the world has realized that no fanatics will be able to destroy the ideas of Gandhi. His philosophy has become the beacon light for modern India and it may well be that his great beliefs in democracy and brotherhood will prove to be the stronger idea in Asia's struggle against Communist dictarship.

THE DAUGHTER OF MATA HARI

WHEN Margarida Gertrude Zelle-MacLeod, better known to the world as the infamous Mata Hari, was shot as a spy, her daughter Banda was only seventeen. The child knew little about her mother and less about her father. She grew up with relatives in Batavia. Her father had "disappeared," she was told by her aunt. He was "a good for nothing," a drinker, a gambler, whose brutality forced his wife to leave him to go to Holland. She was told her mother was a dancer, and sooner or later she would return to Java to see her. But the First World War had interrupted plans and travel was difficult. The child had to wait.

Banda was a beautiful girl, a Eurasian type not at all like the Dutch. She had Mongolain-slanted eyes, was tiny, about five feet one, and was aware of her beauty and distinction.

One November day in 1917 Banda received the last letter her mother ever wrote. It came from Vincennes, France, where she was executed. This was the letter:

My dear child:

There is much I would like to tell you and so little I can say. My time is getting short. Fading out. It is four in the morning and within an hour or so, I will be among the dead without ever having had the chance of seeing you again. You were a baby when I left you. Believe me, I did nothing that was wrong, but the war has its own brutal laws. I do not believe in mercy for me, not even political friends can help me this time.

I had a good and full life. Perhaps it was not a happy one. Oh, we know so little of each other, but Aunt Rose always sent me your report card, always told me what a fine and beautiful young woman you are. I had your picture.

I was young when I came to Bali and Java, too young to know. I fell in love with your father, who started out as a fine man, but the tropics and the liquor, the death of our son, made him what he was. He almost killed me, once. It was then I left him. Now others will kill me. I know. I should have never deserted you. But perhaps a better life is ahead for you without me. I will die courageously, thinking of you. Money alone was not enough. Will you pray for me, will you remember me as a woman

259

who wanted to do right? Life and circumstances were stronger than I.

Goodbye my child, find your happiness in life and find it without hating me.

Your mother,
Margarida Gertrud Zelle-MacLeod.

There were no tears in Banda's eyes. She remained unshaken, stone-like, paralyzed. She read the letter a second time, left the house and went to church, to say the last prayer for a mother who had written world history in blood, a mother who became the greatest spy since Delilah—Mata Hari.

Banda's reaction was astonishing. She never spoke about the incident. She told her aunt that she was now old enough to make her own way. She wanted to be a teacher, she wanted to form her own life apart from relatives. Few people know the tragedy that befell to her.

Banda ran away that night and went to live with a middle-aged Dutch civil service official who became her father, lover and educator. He was forty years older than she. She loved this man of fifty-seven, and told him a few happy years with him were better than a whole life without love.

It was a strange, but honest love between the young girl and the older man. They never married, as he always said: "I do not want you to care for me when I'm seventy and sick." She begged him to marry her, but he refused.

This high Government official sent her to college, a teacher's college where the children of Dutch administrators and diplomats went and where Banda received an excellent cosmopolitan, broadminded education.

Banda became a teacher. She opened one-room school houses on many of the islands of this Dutch colony. It was a happy, constructive and normal life until her protector, who was one of the three men closest to the Governor, died.

This was in 1935, and Banda was a beautiful woman of thirty-five. She did not have to be alone. But she was content with her work with the children. She was teaching them to read and write, in a country where the Dutch had not been able successfully to combat illiteracy.

Banda, in her behavior and sympathies, was Dutch, though being a Eurasian she often wondered why she was fully accepted. But her culture, her manners, and her intelligence were outstanding. She became popular in Batavian society.

She gave gay parties and literary teas attended by all nationalities. Race or creed made no difference to her. At forty years she was still a charming and beautiful woman. She was a rich woman too, as her protector had left her quite a fortune.

So she drifted for years, happy and content. Then reality came also to her life. War had been declared in 1939, though Java was not yet involved. Her tea parties now became the focal point for diplomats, spies, journalists and those who wanted to find out the news behind the news.

Then came Pearl Harbor. The Japanese struck. The British Empire seemed to crumble. Holland was occupied by the Nazis. The Dutch colonies were all that was left to this democracy ruled by a wonderful and great queen. The natives of former days became the backbone of a defeated empire. Spurred on by the Axis success, the Japanese took one Pacific island after another, not asking who was the owner, the Dutch, British, French or Americans. They came like a tornado. They landed in three places in Indonesia: Rembang, Pasirputik and Tangerang. As they advanced the whites fled. The Eurasians were scared, and the natives were promised heaven on earth—money, independence, freedom, food, self-rule. The Javanese wanted to trust the Japanese.

It was in 1942 that Banda again remembered that her own mother had been caught in the intrigue of politics, and secret service. Banda would do better, she would survive this storm. To her way of thinking, and she was much of an Asiatic, tyrants come and go but the people remain; poverty remains. During this period when confusion and anger, fear and danger came to Indonesia she told the children in school, "the world is like a big rotating wheel. On top are the oppressors having all the power, under the wheel are the oppressed. As time goes on, the wheel turns, the oppressors get under the wheel and the former slaves are then on top and become the oppressors."

The Japanese did not approve this kind of teaching and she was told to stop. At the same time one of her uncles came to visit her. Though he was a Dutchman, he wore a Japanese uniform. Banda knew that he had been an advisor to the Japanese Navy for ten years, long before the war had started. He was one of the few who knew of her mother. Banda was scared. What was he up to? She had not seen him for ten years.

She knew he had high prestige with the Japanese and that

he would ask her to collaborate. He did. It was not a request. It was an order—and a threat. The daughter of Mata Hari might be exposed and branded. If Banda wanted to have her secret maintained she must reopen her cultural teas, her cocktail parties, invite all the people she knew, as well as people selected by the new Japanese rulers.

Japanese and Indonesian had to mix. There were also the neutrals who had to be pumped; the Swiss, the Portugese and the Swedes. It was pure blackmail and Banda knew it.

From now on Plato and Schopenhauer, Dante and Tagore were discussed at her parties. There was no more home life, no quietness. Her Batavia house became overcrowded. Her many servants had their hands full. All kinds of people came: the Japanese officers, the Indonesians who trusted the Japanese and wanted their aid to get National independence and the foreign diplomats in town. It went on for many months and the Japanese were highly pleased. Banda was very cooperative. Japanese and Indonesians were mixing and meeting socially.

The Sons of the Rising Sun had decided to create an Indonesian Home Guard, but they must ensure that this military unit would not revolt against Japan. Leaders were picked, and often picked in Banda's house—the social way.

It was here that Banda began a new chapter in her life.

She wanted to love and be wanted. At one of her parties she saw the man whom she knew would change her life. He at first played ball with the Japanese, organized the desired Home Guard of Indonesians for them. But, in reality, he was one of the first and most prominent leaders of the underground. He wanted this new Indonesian Home Guard to fight Japan, to team up with the Dutch and the other Allies to defeat Japan and, afterwards, to get full independence for the new United States of Indonesia. He was a wise man, a courageous man, and he was younger than Banda. He was beloved by the youth of his country and the Japanese seemed to be happy to have him in their ranks.

There was a wild and passionate affair between this man and Banda. Let's call him Abdul. Abdul loved her, saw her often, but his one and only love was his country. He was fascinated by her beauty, intelligence and esprit, but he knew she was too old. It was only an affair to him, a beautiful and happy one. But it was deep love for Banda.

Abdul had complete confidence in Banda. He told her of his underground movement. She joined, thousands of Indonesians joined. The Japanese had come as liberators but wound up worse oppressors than the Dutch. They had promised prosperity, but their victories in Singapore, Indo-China, Burma, the Phillipines made them megalomaniacs. They promised independence but it was never given. They took out of the country all the rice, oil, rubber, quinine, copra, ore they could find. They drafted Indonesian labor gangs to build railroads in Malaya, Siam, New Guinea and Sumatra. They used the Indonesians as slaves. There was starvation in the land.

Banda worked now for both sides, the Japanese and the underground. Abdul, who later was to be one of the leaders of a free Indonesia, secretly planned to make the Indonesian Home Guard into the nucleus of a new Indonesia army. His next step was to offer his movements to the Dutch and to the Allies fighting the Axis.

Abdul became the spiritual leader of this new movement to rid parts of Asia from Jap dictatorship. He had secret contacts with Gandhi and Nehru, the great Indian leaders. He wanted victory for the West and an independent Indonesia.

Banda became his best agent. The daughter of Mata Hari outdid her own mother. It was she who found out the Japanese plans for the battle of Guadalcanal, and what supplies were in Japanese hands. She knew of troop concentrations, airforce re-inforcements and ship movements. At the same time she helped Abdul to send couriers to all the islands to recruit more and more Indonesian youth for the new nationalist movement.

The British and the United States Intelligence services had heard of Banda. They did not know at this time that she was the daughter of Mata Hari, but they knew that Abdul gave the Dutch the best information in the Pacific and Banda was his girl.

Not until the end did the Japanese suspect Banda. They suspected Abdul, but thought it was better to keep his friendship than have him in open revolt. Finally the British landed. They liberated nine cities in Java and the Japanese left one island after the other, as fast as they had come. The year was 1945. The end of the terrible war was in sight. Abdul and his friends were now in command of the Indonesian Home Guard, the new army, but would the British liberators give the country independence or would the Dutch rulers return? The fall of the colonial regime was near. The Japanese had given the decisive blow to the old standards and norms. The

Japanese had behaved like barbarians. Indonesia had enough of foreign rulers. At this moment the formation of the Ashrama Indonesian Merdeka, the Association for a Free Indonesia, was publicly proclaimed.

Indonesia was ready. The people seized the radio station. Thousands of young men and women of the underground were ready to tell Japan, the British, the Dutch, the world, that Indonesia was to be free. The new republic of the United States of Indonesia was proclaimed.

But all this was not according to Dutch plans. The British liberators had never figured on such a turn of events. They wanted to fight the Japanese and not the Indonesians. On the other hand, the Dutch expected to take over Indonesia again as their colony.

The Dutch returned and skirmishes started.

Banda's cocktail and tea parties continued. Her secret service set-up seemed to be more effective than ever. There was no time for love now. She did not see Abdul for days and weeks but always had his orders. She had to find out what the British or Dutch boundary ideas were for Indonesia, about the Dutch occupation policy, the phone services had to be watched and tapped. Abdul wanted to know a thousand things.

Banda found all the answers and they were right. Never a mistake. And still the cocktail parties continued. A new favorite at her parties was one of the political advisers to the Dutch. She knew almost every plan.

Then Banda outdid herself and surpassed any spy who had ever worked in Asia. She gave the exact plan of attack, the blue print of the Dutch offensive, the zero hour when the Dutch would strike.

One of her informants was a Korean by the name of Mato, employed in the Dutch Governor's office.

On December 19, 1948, the Dutch army struck, declaring the Indonesians could not rule themselves nor keep law and order.

That night one of the bloodiest conflicts started in Asia, a colonial war, in defiance of the United Nations. The Dutch called it a "police action." This fine, democratic nation was not yet ready to give democracy to Indonesia.

Abdul, now thirty-five could not keep the secret that he was about to marry a girl who also had worked in the underground. She was twenty. Banda was now almost fifty.

And so the fourth chapter started in Banda's life.

She had been close to a breakdown during the war years. The emotional upheaval, the underground dangers and now, above all, the realization that her love for Abdul had to come to and end, put her to the test. But she told herself, she had duties in America. Perhaps, if she made good, she would atone for her mother. The guilt complex of being the daughter of Mata Hari had never left her and was to remain with her for the rest of her life.

So to America on a special mission went Banda. Her tiny but elegant figure, her faultless English and her flawless complexion created an impression wherever she went. She lectured on Indonesia, gave interviews, and radio talks, traveled right across the country and finally settled in Los Angeles. It was there that she actively began to develop the plan which Abdul had instructed her to carry out. The Inodnesian republicans needed money and arms and it was Banda's task to get them. She obtained the sympathetic interest of a freedom-loving industrialist and he was so impressed by Banda's pleading that he promised to help. It was not without hope of reward, however, for Banda told him that there remained hidden in Indonesia 750,000 dollars worth of gold which neither the Dutch nor the Japs could find. He was finally won over to the cause by his wife-to-be, a noted film star, who threatened to jilt him if he did not help. He made available a huge supply of dollars. Second-hand planes were bought and were flown to Indonesia by American pilots. One plane was specially adapted to carry the gold out of Indonesia.

But the Government of the territory got wind of the plan and there began an amazing hue and cry. From one place to another the republicans moved the hoard of gold, always just one jump ahead of the official pursuers. Over roads, mountains and lakes the gold was carried before it was at last put aboard a plane and later landed in the Phillipines, where it was transferred to neutral ownership. It was used to buy more arms and equipment for the Indonesians fighting their war of independence.

Banda, her mission completed, returned to Djakarta, as Batavia is now renamed. She had helped, with the aid of her industrialist friend and his wife, to create the new Republic.

But her career was by no means over. The fifth and last great episode in her life was about to begin. From America came an emissary who wanted Banda for a special mission. So many men in her life had missions for Banda. Washingotn had found out all about Banda's activities in America. The Intelligence service knew what she had done and they even knew the secret of her parentage.

So the daughter of Mata Hari went out on her final adventure. In the service of the United States she set out for China. Working with the Chinese Communists she obtained valuable information.

She informed America that there was no hope that Chiang Kai Shek could win and remain in his country. She reported on Soviet supplies to Communist China. She remained in the camp of dictator Mao Tse Tung until she was given instructions to proceed to Korea. That was in March, 1950. She reported then, that North Koreans, with Soviet and Chinese help, were to attack the Republic of Southern Korea. The reports seemed to be true, but the will to believe them was lacking. "They would not dare," said the politicians. So Banda's warning was discarded. A few months later war started in Korea.

And it was not long after this that the daughter of Mata Hari was caught—by accident. The long arm of fate reached out. One of the many Communist Commissars appointed in Korea was none other than Mato, the employee of the Dutch Governor in Batavia, who was once on her pay-roll. It was he who had helped the Indonesian freedom movements, while a servant at the Governor's palace. When the battle was won in Indonesia and the Communists realized only the national and not the Communist revolution was the victor, Mato's orders were to go back to his native Korea. The ex-spy became a Commissar with the Red troops. And it was this very Mato who recognized Banda in Korea and brought about her doom.

Banda was arrested. She was shot without trial. The time was 5:45 A.M.: the same hour her mother, Mata Hari, had been executed.

A CRAZY, CRAZY COUPLE

SHE WAS NOT born to be a spy. Though she received great public attention and publicity, she was not the type of spy one can really hate. Posterity is not angry with Mata Hari, neither does it hate Delilah, who betrayed Samson. What, however, will be history's verdict on this woman, Judy Coplon, who became a victim of love. She was oversexed. She carried on affairs with two men at the same time. Ever her lawyers fell for her. One feels sorry for her. It was sex that threw her into the field of espionage, aided by her inexperience, stupidity and foolishness.

It was shortly before Christmas, 1948, that a bombshell exploded at the F.B.I. headquarters in Washington. A report reached them telling that top-secret F.B.I. and Department of Justice documents were now in the hands of the Soviet Embassy in Washington.

J. Edgar Hoover, F.B.I. chief, called a staff meeting. He informed Attorney General Tom Clark, and one of the most tragic cases in the history of espionage began to take its course.

The information came from an F.B.I. agent operating in the Soviet spy network in the United States. His name is still a secret. This man had never given wrong information. But in this case his information was incomplete. All he knew was that two types of report were now in Soviet hands. They contained secret information about American Communists, as well as data on foreign agents and foreign diplomats.

This informer thought the reports had been transmitted by a woman who had formerly worked at the Department of Justice in New York and who was now probably in the Foreign Registration office of the same department in Washington.

One of the most thorough F.B.I. investigations began that winter's day. Every woman in the Foreign Registration office was screened and checked. There were three women who might have been able to spirit away or copy secret documents, but there was only one of them who had worked with the department in New York. She was a bright twenty-seven-year-old analyst, a Barnard graduate named Judith Coplon.

Attractive, small, dark-haired, Judith loved music and the arts. New York's magnificent Museum of Modern Art was one of her favorite haunts. She also frequently visited the National Art Gallery in Washington. Of keen and lively mind, she had a comprehensive grasp of foreign affairs. Back at Barnard she had written editorials for the college paper. They were rather on the radical side. But young people are always radical, so no one took this too seriously.

She had started out as an idealist, eager to serve the people. She wanted to be wanted, too, and to love. She also wanted to be a success.

Judy was a conscientious worker. Her desk was in Room 2220 in the Department of Justice Building, where she dealt with foreign and internal security matters. It was a friendly, large-sized room which she shared with a Government attorney, Nathan Lenvin. The two got along fine. There were file cabinets in the room, with most of the pending and current cases; there was a library-type table in the middle, where records and dossiers were placed before they were put into the files.

In May 1948, Judy had been promoted to a 4,100-dollar-a-year job. She even received a personal letter from Tom Clark, the Attorney General:

"Dear Miss Judith,
"P-3 is really an accomplishment and I congratulate you on it. I did not know we had political analysts in the Criminal Division, but on checking I find that you are in the Foreign Agents Registration Section. Keep up the good work.
"(Signed) Tom Clark."

Today Tom Clark is Supreme Court Justice, and Judith Coplon has twice been sentenced for stealing Government documents and for conspiracy against the United States Government.

Why? How? Psychologists rather than criminologists might find the answer. Judith Coplon perhaps never wanted to harm her country. But blinded by sex, love and inexperience she fell into one of the nets spread by a shrewd man, Lavrenti Beria, then head of the Soviet intelligence service.

An equally shrewd F.B.I. special agent, Kenneth T. Delavigne, was put in charge of investigations. He was to organize total surveillance. So far the F.B.I. had only accusations, no proof, no facts. As a matter of fact they did not know all of Judy's old addresses.

It was not hard to discover she had lived in a two-story apartment house at 2634 Tunlaw Road, N.W., in Washington. She was the quiet, intellectual type, said the landlord and neighbors. She did a lot of reading and typing, even on Sundays. She was always coming home with newspapers and magazines instead of young men. "Long-haired intellectual," was the verdict.

F.B.I. men, however, discovered she had moved from that place a few months earlier and had rented a one-room apartment in Jefferson Hall, McLean Gardens, as it was closer to her work.

From then on, for many weeks, Judy Coplon was watched

and followed. Not a single move she made was unknown to the F.B.I. The shadowing was discreet and efficient. Not once did Judy Coplon suspect she was being watched.

For the first month the investigation was rather disappointing. Judy came of good family. Her father was a well-to-do manufacturer known as a great humanitarian. Samuel Coplon believed in helping the poor. His wife was a quiet type of good mother. All the F.B.I. could pin on Judy was that she had men in her life. The neighbors were young. She saw many men, but never at home.

On January 7th, 1949, the F.B.I. saw her drive off in a car with a young man. They went to the Southern Hotel in Baltimore. They registered as Mr. and Mrs. H. P. Shapiro, 122 Burnside Avenue, Hartford, Conn. They were given Room 412.

Armed with microphones and X-ray machines capable of taking pictures through the hotel room walls, the F.B.I. moved into the neighboring room.

Neither politics nor espionage were discussed that night. There were emotions, soul-searching, sex. The next morning the F.B.I. found that Mr. Shapiro was an able, loyal Government attorney working in the same department as Judith.

The couple in Room 412 did not leave until the next afternoon and then they headed for Philadelphia. The F.B.I. caravan followed them. This time they registered at the Bellevue Stratford Hotel, under the same names with the same Connecticut address. They were in Room 1523. The F.B.I. again moved into a neighboring room with the same standard equipment. All that happened was a repetition of the previous night. There was no sign of espionage. The F.B.I. agents were rather angry with their department head who had spoiled their week-end in a hunt for spies who were just a pair of lovebirds.

The F.B.I. were baffled. Samuel Coplon was an honorable man. Mr. Shapiro was a fine lawyer. Judy's record was perfect. Was the information they had received wrong? Was it one of those accusations against innocent people, so frequent in a cold war?

But next week Judy Coplon made a somewhat irregular move. She went to her department chief, who had been informed of her surveillance and investigation. "I was promised," she said, "the top-secret report on the Soviet agents in America. When can I see it? I need it in my work."

William E. Foley, her boss, stalled for time. "Later," he

said. It was restricted, and he pretended that he himself had not yet seen it.

A few hours later J. Edgar Hoover visited Foley, who told him about the Coplon visit. Mr. Hoover had a plan. He admitted his men had been unable to find any evidence against Judy. In fact, they wanted to close the case. But he knew, he said, where there is smoke there is fire. His informant had never been wrong. He wanted to try something else. One more test, perhaps a spectacular one, but it might work if she were really connected with a foreign Power.

Mr. Hoover insisted that this letter should be given to Ju- and marked "Top secret." This letter named three top-ranking officials in the Washington Soviet set-up, their Amtorg Trade Division. According to the letter, these three Soviet agents were secret F.B.I. men and a new loyalty test had been ordered to make sure they were still on our side.

Mr. Hoover instructed that this letter should be given to Judith Coplon. "Let her work on the case," said Hoover. "If she is an agent she must warn her friends. It should be information for them to have."

Mr. Foley called Judy. He gave her the letter and asked her to study it and to bring him all the files and dossiers on these three people. What he did not tell her, however, was that the letter had been faked by Hoover's department.

On Friday, January 4th, 1949, Judy Coplon asked her boss for a personal favor. She wanted to take the afternoon off for a long week-end in New York. Permission was granted and she took the I P.M. train from Union Station. Four F.B.I. men were on the same train. Four hours later they arrived in New York's Pennsylvania Station. A dozen more F.B.I. men were waiting there with cars and radio. Judy went upstairs to the ladies' room. She returned after forty-five minutes, checked her bags in a locker, went to a bookstore, a drugstore, sat down at the counter and ate a sandwich. Then she took the I.R.T. subway to Manhattan's 191st Street station.

Once in the street she walked for almost ten minutes. It was already dark and the lights were on. She looked from time to time over her shoulder as if afraid someone was following her. Finally, she stopped, remained looking in the window of a jewelry store so she could see what happened on the street.

She stood in front of that store for almost seven minutes, until a dark-haired, stocky, well-dressed man appeared. He passed by. He had high cheekbones and looked Slavonic, but New York has plenty of Slavs.

He walked around the block for several minutes, often looking over his shoulder. He was followed by Judy. Not a word was said, no greeting exchanged.

Both entered a small restaurant, the De Luxe, and sat down in an alcove. The F.B.I. men sat near by, but they could not hear their conversation as both were putting nickels in the jukebox and the loud noise drowned their voices.

They were in the restaurant almost an hour. Judy talked and gestured a lot. She seemed quite excited when they left and took the Eighth Avenue Subway downtown. And F.B.I. men were also on the train. When the train was just about to leave 125th Street station the dark-haired unknown man jumped from his seat, squeezed through the doors, and was out on the platform. All but one of the F.B.I. men were left behind.

For half an hour this unknown man took taxis, street cars, buses and subways until he had lost his pursuer. The F.B.I. agent was furious when he returned to headquarters, but all his colleagues were as sure as he that this man was a Russian.

Who was this mysterious Russian? Was he in the country legally? They decided he might be a Soviet official, attached to the New York Diplomatic Corps.

Next morning G-men took up posts at the Soviet headquarters at 68th Street and Park Avenue. Shortly before ten o'clock the man appeared. They recognized him right away. He did not seem to suspect anything. They waited. An hour later he came out. He went by bus and subway to 110th Street and then to his apartment at 64 West 108th Street.

Questioned by the F.B.I. men, the janitor gave them information they needed. The mystery man was a Russian engineer attached to the United Nations Architectural Department. His name was Valentin A. Gubitchev.

This was the first lead to victory. Hoover had been right not to give up the case.

By the end of January 1949, Foley was advised to prevent Miss Coplon having access to top-secret matters. She was much disturbed over the change. "Why?" she asked. She objected. She thought this was a criticism of her work. She was angry. She had tears in her eyes.

Foley only said that her new assignment was important and someone had to take care of it. Her salary was to remain the same.

But Judy had her own ways and means. She visited her old office daily. She made friends with her successor, Mrs. R., who was new and needed her help. In this way Judy saw all the top-secret F.B.I. files on Mrs. R.'s desk. She even saw the one report that Mr. Foley had denied her previously, the highly confidential document on Soviet agents in America. Mrs. R. later testified she had given Judy about sixty documents to read.

The F.B.I. knew of these visits. Still, Judy had to make the next move. The G-men had no real evidence yet. In the meantime she saw Shapiro again. When would she see Gubitshcev? The F.B.I. were waiting patiently. Then it happened. Again Judy asked for an afternoon off, and left Washington on February 18th, 1949, at 2 p.m. The F.B.I. men again were on the train. Others again met the train in New York. This time a woman agent, Miss Sappho Manos, chief clerk of the New York office of the F.B.I. was there too.

Miss Manos followed Judy and watched her check her bags in a locker. She followed her to the subway where Judy again took the train to upper Manhattan. Miss Manos looks pleasant, has long hair, and could pass for a salesgirl at Woolworth's, but she is probably one of the best Government woman agents.

The subway was crowded. Judy was surrounded by agents, and when she opened her handbag to rearrange it one of them saw typewritten papers in it.

Judy left the same 191st Street station. She was the last one to take the elevator to the street. Miss Manos and another agent rode with her. Upstairs they walked again for several blocks. Judy led them into a dead-end street and finally turned and noticed the two again. Cornered, the two agents giggled like sweethearts and spoke: "We're lost, too. Where is Broadway?" "Oh, God," was all Judy answered. Had she guessed who they were?

Judy went to a shoe repair store to have a broken shoe-strap fixed. Then she continued to walk, covering several blocks. She seemed to be impatient. She had just left Broadway to turn into one of the side streets when Gubitchev finally appeared.

They met this time for only a few seconds. It was too dark to see whether any papers were exchanged. The two parted, Gubitchev taking a taxi downtown and Judy going back to Pennsylvania Station.

The agents were certain that papers had been passed, but

they had no proof as Gubitchev again made one of his sudden dashes and shook off his pursuers.

Then, on February 28th, 1949, a teletype message came from New York informing the F.B.I. in Washington that Judy had phoned her mother in New York and would spend the week-end with her family.

On March 3rd, Judy again asked for a half-day off. Permission was granted. That week Judy again asked her boss to see some of the top-secret files. He asked her if she remembered the three men under investigation, the ones who worked for the Soviet Amtorg Trade Division. He had some more papers on the case now.

One of them was a "hot" letter. As this letter became so important at the trial, I reproduce it here:

"Date: March 3rd, 1949

"To: Mr. Peyton Ford
The Assistant to the Attorney General
From: Director, F.B.I.

STRICTLY CONFIDENTIAL
"Subject: AMTORG TRADING CORPORATION
INTERNAL SECURITY—R

"As supplementary to my memorandum to you dated January 27th, 1949, regarding the Amtorg Trading Corporation, I want to call your attention to a recent development in this investigation which may be of potential significance in any prosecutive steps contemplated.

"In the referenced memorandum, I mentioned that we are presently using on a confidential basis, informants, two highly placed officials of the Amtorg Trading Corporation. One of these is Isadore Gibby Needleman, the Amtorg legal representative, with whom we have been maintaining a rather indirect contact through an intermediary. We have not been entirely satisfied with this arrangement, or the extent of the information being supplied by Needleman, and for that reason, in order to check his sincerity, we desire to obtain from him more complete information on a variety of matters including his knowledge of the activities of the Amtorg Trading Corporation which would be in possible violation of the Foreign Agents Registration Act.

"We would therefore appreciate your making available to us a memorandum outlining your views on what you think would constitute a violation on the part of this Corporation and any questions you think should be asked of this individual. We would also like to know if Needleman is registered as an agent of a foreign principal.

"I have previously furnished you with information concerning the efforts of the Amtorg Trading Corporation to obtain equipment relative to atomic research developments. In this connection, the Bureau has recently learned through an informant that Amtorg Trading Corporation has been in contact with the Geo-Physical Research Corporation concerning geophones to measure blast pressures which this company has manufactured in small quantities for the original bomb test at Alamagordo. The fact that these geophones are used for the purpose of making blast measurements at Alamagordo and other testing points is highly restricted but apparently the Amtorg Trading Corporation must have some knowledge of the use of these instruments.

"The above represents another example of the security risk present in the activities of this Corporation. We are continuing our investigation of this Corporation in an effort to determine whether Amtorg is sending out of the United States information and equipment relative to our atomic research."

The trap was set for Judy—would she run into it?

This was Judy's third and last trip to New York to see Gubitchev. The F.B.I. were mobilized again. They watched the same performance, which meant neither Judy nor Gubitchev suspected a thing. Again Pennsylvania Station; again the subway to 191st Street; again the street walking; again the darkness of small streets. Again a restaurant, a candy store, a jewelry store. Always looking over the shoulder to see if they were followed, they avoided direct contact. Again subway and buses, running and stopping, finally speaking.

But now they realized they were being trailed. The F.B.I. came out into the open. Gubitchev again tried his tricks. Judy also tried to escape, using taxis and subways. But the F.B.I. stuck close. It was a mad hunt. Three times they almost shook off the F.B.I. But at 9:35 P.M. they were finally cornered at 16th Street and Third Avenue, and arrested. Gubitchev said: "This is ridiculous." Judy cried.

They were taken to Foley Square, to Headquarters. They were searched. Judy complained about being stripped by the matron. But the Government was not taking any chances.

Not a scrap of evidence could be found on Judy's person. Then they opened her handbag. It contained all a woman needs to be beautiful, even an advertising circular for stockings. It was folded in half, sealed with Scotch tape. The tape was removed. Inside the folder were thirty-four copies or digests of copies of top-secret Government documents. Here too was the fake letter Hoover had given her boss and the one previously reproduced concerning Amtorg.

One copy was typed before she left Washington. It read:

"3-3-49.

"I have not been able (and I don't think I will) to get the top-secret F.B.I. report which I described to Michael on Soviet and Communist intelligence activities in the U. S. When the moment was favorable I asked Foley where the report was (he'd previously remarked that he'd had such a report); he said that some departmental official had it and he didn't expect to get it back. Foley remarked there was nothing 'new' in it. When I saw the report, for a minute, I breezed through it rapidly, remember very little. It was about 115 pages in length; summarized first Soviet 'intelligence' activities, including Martens, Lore, Poyntz, Altschuler, Silvermaster, et al. It had heading on Soviet U.N. delegation but that was all I could remember. The rest of the report I think was on Polish, Yugo, etc., activities and possibly some info on the C.P., U.S.A.

"Beginning with spring semester of 1946, I attended the American University, Washington, D.C., until the time I completed my class credits for an M.A. in International Organizations and International Relations. All I need for my degree is the completion of a thesis. While I'm not enthusiastic about it, I think I should complete this thesis by summer. My subject will deal with certain aspects of international propaganda and its control."

Not all documents found on Judy can be reproduced here, but according to Lieutenant-Colonel Richard Hirsch, one of the leading espionage experts, they contained:

1. C-279 who is familiar with the activities of the Russian Embassy personnel, advised that he has received no info indicating that any person in the Swiss Legation might be connected with Soviet intelligence activities. . . .
2. Bureau letter 3/26/48 authorized investigation of Stojan Krstic employed by Yugo Consulate at Chicago in or-

der to verify and implement info that subject is engaged in intelligence activities.

3. Dept. of State Source advised that individual who filed passport application in name of Charles Francis Chase was believed to be Soviet agent who also used name of John Sherman.

4. Subject reported by Informant as suspected of working for Bulgarian or Russian intelligence services, believed to have obtained U.N. position so that he might have freedom of movement in U.S. Subject at present in Immigration Section, Dept. of Social Affairs at U.N.

5. According to T-5, First Sec'y Bulgarian Legation is the party whip in the Legation and has taken on administrative functions so far as security is concerned.

6. Stuart Legg—possible Russian espionage agent.

Gubitchev was deported. Judy broke down. She cried, she fainted, she yelled. She said she was innocent. She lost both cases in the lower courts. What did most damage to her was her story about Shapiro. The jurors did not believe that she had loved both Gubitchev and Shapiro. She said she was never undressed in either hotel room with Shapiro, but no one believed her—certainly not the F.B.I. men who were in the neighboring room with their X-ray machine and microphones.

She confessed nothing, denied everything. She met Gubitchev in the Museum of Modern Art. They enjoyed looking at the modernistic art. She met him in Central Park, where he confessed he was married. She still hoped he would get a divorce.

At the trial the two did not greet each other. He was silent. She giggled and enjoyed the court procedure. But the jurors took it more seriously. They did not believe she was only in love with Gubitchev. They saw only the thirty-four stolen Government documents. She, who had never written a book, said these were notes for a novel. Gubitchev had 125 dollars in an envelope on him when arrested. He said it was household money, but the jury did not believe him.

Archibald Palmer, Judy's first attorney, presented her case in a burlesque fashion. While she was giggling he told the jury: "When you are in love with a person, you don't care whether he is red or green. Love knows no bounds."

She liked the performance, but the jury always asked: "And what about Shapiro and her love for him?"

"I spent the night with him, during which time I did not sleep nor make any attempt to sleep."

"Both nights?" asked the prosecutor.

"Both nights."

The jurors were convinced this tiny little woman could not have stayed awake for two nights without sleep and that she was not telling the truth.

She was not convincing when she stated in her Brooklyn accent that she suffered from a Victorian malady: unhappy love. Thirty-four documents, 125 dollars in cash, all the secret meetings. and above all Shapiro—no lawyer could win the case. The lawyer finally left her. She got a new one, whom she later married.

Judy's tender "love story" ended with the brutality of the Treason Act. In wartime both parties would have been shot. But during a cold war one is inclined to believe that Pomerantz, the Communist's lawyer, was probably right when he called them "a crazy, crazy man and a crazy woman."

GUATEMALAN INCIDENT

This happened before Fidel Castro introduced Communism to Cuba. It all began in Poland.

The world of Otto Lange had never at any time extended much beyond the frontiers of Europe and certainly not as far as Central America and the Republic of Guatemala. Yet, more than any other, this stocky, middle-aged German was responsible in 1954 for the downfall of the Government there —an almost bloodless revolution achieved, as it were, by remote control.

Otto Lange was not, of course, his real name and his hidden identity is of no consequence. Of the known facts concerning him it seems that he was born in Koenigsberg in East Prussia, which today is a Russian city. From the very start Lange was involved in the growth of Communism and he fell in step quite easily so that he was recognized as a reliable follower and called to Moscow for indoctrination and training. After the war he worked under the Red Flag in East Germany and was then sent to Poland to help the People's Republic rebuild the country's heavy industry, such as it was. He possessed a wide technical knowledge and was a skilled organizer, and infused new life into bombed and shattered plants. Under his guidance, and with the help of forced labor and corrective battalions, many factories were got to work again so that he became a key figure wherever expansion took place. One of Lange's biggest jobs was the rebuilding of the machine-tool works at Stettin, the capital of Pomerania which once had a population of 150,000. Lange found there were less than 5,000 Germans living there but many Russians and Poles watched over by political commissars.

Nobody escaped their attention, not even Lange, although he had many times been "cleared by the Secret Service. Conforming to Party discipline he never allowed himself to become involved in it, but he was respected for his loyalty and his devotion to work. Engaged in setting factories going he took no interest in factional disputes or what went on in smoke-filled rooms where Party policy was surveyed and often refashioned.

Lange had married an attractive Polish girl and was the father of two children. His home life was exemplary, after the Bolshevik model, and his only indulgence was the leisure time he gave to outdoor sports. He loved country rambles and hunting and fishing and, occasionally, he would take the family out for a day's boating in a small motor launch he owned.

But on that lovely early season day in April 1954, when Oto Lange sat on the bank of the Oder, at a place which overlooked the harbor at Stettin, he was alone with a fishing rod, a picnic basket containing sandwiches, fruit, pastries and a bottle of wine, and a pair of field glasses of a type usually carried by those with a liking for observing nature. During the few hours he remained there Lange paid little attention to his line, but quite often he would raise his field glasses to watch the birds as they rustled from one tree to another before turning them towards the harbor where many freighters were being loaded for the return journey to Soviet Russia through the wide Baltic. Certainly no one watching Lange would have regarded him as other than a somewhat indolent amateur or guessed that the Zeiss field glasses were so constructed as to contain a built-in camera which was taking a record of what was happening out there in the harbor.

Later that afternoon Lange returned to his spacious and comfortable office in Stettin and for an angler who had had a singularly unprofitable outing—not one fish lay in his basket —he appeared to be extraordinarily cheerful. He dictated a report to his superiors in Warsaw, a number of letters to trade combines in Dresden and East Germany and yet another letter to a firm in Paris interested, apparently, in the products of the factory which Lange controlled.

This letter, written in French and packing plenty of commerical jargon, was, nevertheless, carefully composed. It quoted prices for various automobile parts, the stock available and a proposed date for delivery. Certain tool-making machines and presses were offered for sale and quoted and it was suggested that, once equipped with such machinery, the French company would then be able to do its own manufacturing by paying a fee to Lange's department of the Polish Ministry of Machine Industry to cover the use of all patents invested in them.

The letter ended with assurances that the new Poland would fulfil all contracts and agreements and pointed out that the Government was anxious to encourage commercial relations between the East and the West. The prices quoted were considerably lower than could be obtained elsewhere and certainly underbid those of Britain and America.

Nevertheless, the deal never came off. Six months later the Communists in Poland learned that Otto Lange and his secretary were spies whom the Americans had placed in Stettin. The model business letter to a Paris firm had been a coded message directed to one of the secret offices of America's Central Intelligence Agency in Paris. Having reached its Parisian address, the letter was taken to a *salon de photographie* on Montmartre, where American microfilm technicians set to work on it. The job was relatively simple if you knew what to look for. What the microfilm specialists did was to scrutinize every full stop marked in the letter. They scratched each one carefully as they came to them and so examined twenty of these marks of punctuation until they found one which could be scratched off the page. The dot came loose. It was smaller than the point of a pin and was really a tiny speck of microfilm which had been glued on to serve as a period, and then dabbed with a drop of ink.

The microfilm enlarger was employed, and it produced a readable message, ready to be passed on to the proper intelligence department analyst. It was of course in code and the microfilm technician, while he could read it, was completely in the dark as to its meaning. All he saw was a cryptogram which used one of the most beautiful psalms of David: "My God, my God—why hast thou forsaken me?" It seemed a very odd thing to have been smuggled out of the Iron Curtain.

The coded message was flown to Allen Welsh Dulles, director of America's Central Intelligence Agency in Washington. It was promptly decoded and then returned to Dulles' desk in the purplish-blue lettering of the cryptographic machine. Here, I must point out that many of the details of Lange's connection with Washington, and the events which were set in motion as the result of his secret service, are still highly confidential, but what can be revealed is that the message described the new underground route by which armaments were to be shipped to Latin America. The port of origin was Stettin, on the Baltic. A Swedish freighter, the *Alfhem,* anchored there, had been loaded with 15,000 crates and boxes which had recently arrived by rail from Czechoslovakia. They contained ammunition from the Skoda works. The freighter had been chartered from the reputable firm of Angbats Aktiebolaget in Stockholm, who knew nothing of this traffic. The business arrangements had been made through a shipping agent in London who had rechartered the vessel to the Alfred Christianson Company of Stockholm. The cargo was supposed to consist of optical instruments destined for Dakar in French West Africa, but Otto Lange had revealed the true facts and made it plain that the ship and its cargo was not intended for West Africa.

It was a valuable piece of information. American counterintelligence found means of letting Lange know that his message had been received and properly understood. He had done his work well and he was advised to escape from Stettin as quickly as he could. He was told to make his way with his family to West Berlin where he would be protected. Lange got away, together with his wife and family and his trusted secretary.

To those who were awaiting him in West Berlin, Lange gave a fuller account of his discovery concerning the freighter *Alfhem.* He had guessed that it was bound for Guatemala, but he had to satisfy himself that his hunch was right. All he had to go on was certain information he had picked up in the Ministry of Commerce but every official document showed the ship's destination as Dakar. And so far there was no indication of the *Alfhem's* taking a different course. But Lange had two friends aboard the ship, supposedly good Communists, and they had taken a look at the cargo and found the crates packed with small arms and machine guns.

Two days before the Swedish vessel was due to reach Dakar, a shortwave message in code was received by the

Central Intelligence Agency. The news was that the *Alfhem* was changing course and heading for Trujillo, Honduras.

The ship and its dangerous cargo now became a matter of concern for the intelligence department of the U.S. Navy. Communist weapons were being smuggled into the Western Hemisphere and emergency sessions were held in Washington. London was notified. The U.S. fleet stationed in the Caribbean was put on the alert and submarines received special orders. Of course the *Alfhem* never landed at Trujillo, because two days out the captain of the vessel received fresh orders. He was to proceed to Puerto Barrios, the Caribbean port of Red Guatemala.

The United States had no legal power to halt the vessel and confiscate the arms. Moreover, Washington was eager to learn the strength of the Communist conspiracy in Guatemala. This was a vital factor, for if the United States was to back the opposition in Guatemala, it had first to know what resources the existing régime had at its disposal.

It was a hard decision, *not* to stop the arms shipment, but to let it pass. On the other hand, the incident could be used as a lever by which the Communists could be ousted from the Republic of Guatemala once and for all. A certain element of danger was involved, and the whole plan was liable to miscarry. Mr. Allen Welsh Dulles' greatest concern was lest some U.S. senator, and Senator McCarthy in particular, got wind of the maneuver. If the secret leaked out and the papers carried the story, McCarthy would be sure to accuse Dulles of sheltering Communists in his department.

. . . . .

The Communists in the Guatemalan Ministry of Defence were present at the docks when the *Alfhem* was unloaded at Puerto Barrios. The harbor area had been sealed off and was under guard. The crates and boxes were loaded on military trains.

A few hours later Washington had its first report from Guatemala. The 15,000 boxes and crates contained 1,900 tons of small arms and ammunition. Armed in this way the Communists in Guatemala would have been able to overrun the neighboring republics of Honduras and El Salvador, and could then march through Nicaragua and Costa Rica and on to the Panama Canal.

It was May 17th, 1954.

When the United States presented these significant facts to the Governments of Nicaragua, Costa Rica, El Salvador and Honduras, they were so alarmed that they asked America to intervene. But this was not what America desired, nor what Dulles had planned. The patient spy chief's master play unfolded slowly.

Order followed hard upon order and a huge fleet of America's latest super Globemasters ferried twenty-five tons of rifles, machine-guns, pistols and hand grenades to Honduras and Nicaragua. Whether or not small atomic bombs were among these weapons has never been officially stated. It is highly unlikely. Destruction of Communism in Central America was the goal of the master plan.

It was, too, the moment for Colonel Carlos Castillo Armas, a former officer of the Guatemalan Army, exiled in Honduras, and who had recently visited America, to go into action. Colonel Armas was now able to rally every anti-Communist refugee in Central America to his cause. He armed those who were willing to fight the Communists in Guatemala and began the armed invasion of the country.

The resignation of Jacabo Arbenz Guzman, the Red puppet President, was demanded and Colonel Armas sent two outworn aircraft over Guatemala City. Then came the biggest surprise of all.

The Communist stronghold fell overnight. The war had not lasted twenty-four hours when the army went over entirely to the side of Colonel Armas. The smuggled arms had never been intended for the army anyway, but for some of the Communist-dominated trade unions. The army accepted the support of the neighboring republics and the U.S.A. and made a clean sweep of the Communist elements in their midst. The Cominform had delivered them the weapons with which they hoped to extend their domain, but quick and resolute action by democratic forces had curbed their ambitions. For the resolving of the Guatemalan crisis, thanks are directly due to a German who went by the name of Otto Lange. Now under another name, and in some other capacity, he is working in some far-away country inside the Soviet Zone, visiting port after port to build up the harbor espionage system for the Allies, a modern flying Dutchman who will not rest until Communist imperialism has vanished from the earth.

The Russians did not take their defeat calmly. Indication of the resentment felt against Allen Dulles personally can be found in a comment by Ilya Ehrenburg, the keenest of the

Soviet propagandists. "Even if the spy Allen Welsh Dulles should arrive in heaven through somebody's absentmindedness," Ehrenburg said, "he would begin to blow up the clouds and slaughter the angels."

The wisecrack got back to Allen Welsh Dulles. He laughed and retorted dryly: "That may well be. But I hardly expect to discover any Red angels up there!"

THE MICRODOT

JIMMY BOZART, a fourteen-year-old newsboy, clattered down the stairs of a Brooklyn apartment house, where he had been collecting from some of his customers, jingling a handful of change. He slipped and grabbed for the handrail. The nickels, dimes and quarters cascaded to the landing below.

With the cheerful resignation of fourteen, Jimmy recovered the coins, his mind already on something else, until he picked up one of the five-cent pieces. It, literally, had split apart in the fall. The youngster noted that a tiny object had been wedged between the halves.

Here was real cloak-and-dagger spy stuff, and when Jimmy displayed his discovery to his father he remarked with satisfaction that, for once, the older man was just as impressed as he was.

"This," Bozart senior ruled, "had better go to the police."

Jimmy agreed, giving the nickel to Patrolman Frank R. Milley, the father of one of his classmates.

Four years later, on August 7th, 1957, a seedy, undistinguished man with faded blue eyes and wispy hair was indicted in the United States District Court in Brooklyn as one of the most important Soviet spies ever captured in the United States.

The two incidents—Jimmy Bozart's discovery of the split nickel and the arrest of Rudolf Ivanovich Abel, colonel of the K.G.B., the overseas intelligence arm of the Soviet Union—are connected.

How close the connection is, we don't know. It may be years, if ever, before that information can be safely released. We do know that Patrolman Milley, turned the nickel over to the F.B.I. We know that F.B.I. technicians found the object inside the coin was a microfilm of a card bearing six numbers. And we know that Jimmy Bozart, then preparing to enter college, was alerted to testify, if necessary, at Colonel Abel's trial.

Understandably, the F.B.I. declined to discuss the precise importance of the nickel but indicated that, while it did not lead them directly to the Russian spy, it did help them complete the jigsaw puzzle of the Abel-directed espionage network.

The investigation that led to his arrest and conviction—he was sentenced to thirty years' imprisonment although he could have been executed under the law—was probably typical. Its many ramifications included the tracking down of hundreds of tips, most of them false observation, and patient questioning of suspects and the piecing together of thousands of seemingly unrelated items.

The extent of Abel's depredations against the United States is suggested by the three co-conspirators named with him in the same indictment. None was brought to trial, since all are believed to be in Russia. They were Vitali Pavlov, linked with the Canadian spy ring whose break-up in 1946 figured in the arrest of Dr. Klaus Fuchs, Harry Gold and the Rosenbergs; Aleksandr Mikhailovich Korotkov, who was high in the Soviet secret police; and Mikhail Svirin, once a member of the United Nations Secretariat in New York.

Colonel Abel's arrest by agents of the F.B.I. and the United States Immigration and Naturalisation Service in July, 1957, caused hardly a ripple. He was charged with illegal entry into the United States and was placed in an alien detention camp in McAllen, Texas, to await deportation. The stranger-than-fiction story didn't come out until more than two weeks later, with his indictment.

He had been living as "Martin Collins" in Manhattan's little Latham Hotel off Fifth Avenue but maintained a photographic and artist's studio on the top floor of a building at 252 Fulton Street, Brooklyn. The colonel had done what no writer of spy fiction would permit a character to do—that is, had operated directly across the street from the United States Courthouse.

While agents questioned Abel expertly in Texas, others searched the "studio," turning up a treasure trove of evidence that convinced them their prisoner was no mere violator of immigration laws.

Residents in Fulton Street had known him as Emil R Goldfus, an unobtrusive but friendly enough man whose profession was photography and whose avocation was painting.

He had a genuine talent and, one artist predicted, "would have been a very good painter within another five years."

He had entered this country in 1948 from Montreal under a phony European passport that bore the name Andrew Kayotis. It was only one of several aliases. Customarily, he carried birth certificates of Martin Collins, born on July 2nd, 1897, in New York City, and also of Emil R. Goldfus, an actual Manhattan infant who had been born August 2nd, 1902 (just one month after Abel's real birthday, July 2nd, 1902), and who had lived but two months.

Well supplied with cash, he lived modestly, blending easily into the background of shabby hotels and his cluttered studio. He made friends with people, paid his rent on time, dropped into the Music Box Bar for an occasional drink, and gratified nearby storekeepers by addressing them as "mister."

F.B.I. agents were hardly surprised to discover in his studio the tools of his supposed profession—cameras, lights and other photographic equipment. They did note with interest his powerful short-wave radio receiver, and other gear that was difficult to associate with an innocent photographer.

Altogether, they dredged 126 items out of the Fulton Street studio, ranging from a blowtorch to glass cutters, batteries, hollowed-out nails, pencils, coins, cuff-links and ear-rings; documents, powerful lenses and movie films. He was equipped to record messages in "microdots," a technique that enabled him to condense documents to the size of a pinhead. The agents refused, of course, to discuss their haul in detail.

Squads of G-men fanned out, following every lead, so far as possible, to its source. One item, for example, was a thank-you note from a Fulton Street acquaintance. Curious to learn how Abel had earned this person's gratitude, agents heard an explanation that satisfied them but did not help their case. The person in question had married recently and "Emil Goldfus' considerably had sent a wedding gift. The couple was astounded to learn their well-wisher was Colonel Abel, of Russian Intelligence.

Other messages were suspiciously cryptic. One handwritten note was obviously significant.

"I bought a ticket for the next ship—*Queen Elizab.* for next Thursday, 1-31," it read. "Could not come because three men are tailing me."

Another: "In Mex—signal T pole opposite No. 191 Chihuahua st. using sides of pole toward roadway Sat. or

Sun., Tues., Thurs. Met on Wed. Thur. Fri. 3 p.m. movie Balmora."

Still another: "Aveida Oberon 3 pm. display left of entrance. Is this an interesting picture. Yes. Do you wish to see Mr. Brandt? Smokes pipe and has red book in left hand."

Abel's position in the Soviet espionage system was that of a resident chief of an apparatus that may not yet be fully exposed. He served as an executive, directing the work of others. He received his instructions from Moscow by short-wave radio and passed them along to members of his network, sending results to Soviet headquarters through an elaborate system of codes.

Some of the "drops" used by his underlings for the transfer of information were revealed in notes found in his hotel room. They ranged as far off as Mexico. Some were of obvious interest to spies: Quincy, Massachusettes, is the site of an important shipyard and naval air station; New Hyde Park, Long Island, is near a plant producing electronic instruments for missile production. Agents were mystified though, by Abel's assignment of a subordinate to Salida, Colorado, a small resort town in the heart of the Rocky Mountains.

Messages of various kinds, documentary and photographic, were passed in the numerous containers such as the hollowed-out nails, coins and jewellery. In some cases, microscopic documents were carried to Western Europe, thence to Russia, by agents. Others may have been dispatched directly to the homeland.

At the time of his arrest he was an espionage agent of some thirty years' experience. He was no deluded, pro-Communist American such as Harry Gold or the Rosenbergs, nor one of the heavy-handed minor functionaries attached to the Soviet Embassy who have occasionally exposed themselves by their clumsiness.

He probably was the most formidable foreign agent. ever caught by United States counter-espionage and there is no reason to believe Moscow does not have many more like him loose. Subjected to the stern training of a professional, he operated so smoothly that the amount of harm he did may never be established.

An expert photographer and cryptographer, he was also a trained electronics engineer, an accomplished sketcher and artist, well versed in nuclear science.

In addition to his native language he speaks fluent and colloquial English, French, German and Italian.

Equally mysterious was his subordinate, Reino Hayhanden, who reported to Abel late in 1952. Associated with the K.G.B. since 1939, Hayhanen has done most of his foreign service in Finland. It would be safer not to speculate too much about Hayhanen, who defected from Russia and served as a key witness at Abel's trial.

Characteristically, the Russian Government and its Embassy in Washington studiously ignored Abel's arrest and the colonel, as a professional, accepted his abandonment as the fate to be expected by a trapped spy.

Abel, asked whether he wanted an attorney, did request a United States marshal to "contact Abt." The only lawyer of that name in the Manhattan directory is John J. Abt, long-time counsel for United States Communists. In this case, however, Abt decided he was "too busy" to accept a new client.

Eventually, displaying his familiarity with American legal procedure, Abel appealed for a lawyer through the Brooklyn Bar Association. The organization went out of its way to find him a good one. Its selection was James. B. Donovan (he gave his 10,000-dollar fee to charity), who served as war-time counsel for the Office of Strategic Services and who participated in the prosecution of Nazi leaders at Nuremberg.

Even more than Hayhanen's testimony, what probably influenced the jury of nine men and three women was the story of an unexpected witness. M. Sgt. Roy A. Rhodes, who confessed he had betrayed secrets to Russia while working as a mechanic in the American Embassy in Moscow, and for which he had recently been sentenced to five years.

Returned to the United States in 1953, Rhodes had agreed to continue his activities for Russia in this country. Hayhanen, he said, made contact with him under Abel's orders.

Abel, stony-faced and silent, heard his sentence on November 15th, 1957. Judge Mortimer W. Byers fixed his penalty at thirty years' imprisonment, although he could have imposed a death sentence under the Espionage and Sabotage Act, a general tightening of internal security laws passed by Congress in 1954.

Just one day earlier, Russia broke the silence it had maintained since Abel's arrest. A Moscow literary newspaper that mentioned the case didn't discuss the evidence against Colonel Abel nor did it so much as admit the existence of such a man. It reported merely that the F.B.I. had arrested an "artist-photographer named Goldfus" and then produced a piece of paper of "low-brow crime fiction" to convict him. The purpose, Moscow explained, was to get the minds of the American people off "the dirty side" of the F.B.I.

THE FROGMAN

THE COLD, clammy, oily waters of Portsmouth harbor were calm that morning of April 19, 1959. A grotesque figure, clad in rubber, slipped through the sludge, never to appear again. Fate can play dirty tricks once she has buried her claws into her victim, and on this occasion her prey, resembling a Man from Mars as envisioned in a Hollywood science-fiction film, was merely a frogman serving Her Majesty's Royal British Navy.

He had left behind him the busy port with its red-bricked and white-tiled warehouses and the freighters and schooners rocking against their piers and moorings.

Swimming like an eel, the eerie dark figure, equipped with the latest underwater cameras and detection instruments, slithered toward the two Soviet destroyers which lay at anchor, the temporary floating Kremlin of the Soviet Union's chief, Nikita Krushchev and Premier Bulganin.

"This man was involved in a plot to kill our Comrades, Krushchev and Bulganin," maintain the Soviet Secret Service. Even today they claim this daring British underwater swimmer intended to bring death to the dreams and lives of the two Soviet leaders. The heroic era of Communism was a part of the past. An epoch of practical men had begun. An unknown frogman, protested the Russians, carried explosives designated to blow up the two Soviet ships, taking with them their nation's chiefs.

It is a gargantuan theory indeed. But it seems improbable that a single man could ever have carried out such an intricate plan of sabotage and assassination . . . not under water.

When Commander Lionel Crabb, equipped with his flippers and oxygen tank, left the solid soil of England to plunge into the murky waters, he descended, not only into the depths of an undersea world, but into a labyrinth of world intrigue and annihilation.

The mighty Stalin had been succeeded by Khrushchev and his temporary Premier Bulganin. Both attempted to charm the citizens of Great Britain. During this, their first "summit meeting" they scored. "Bulge" and "Khrush," as they were dubbed immediately by the Londoners, doled out candies to the English children and were never photographed without smiles. The pictorials showed the two shaking hands with Sir Anthony Eden, having tea with the important government and labor leaders, clinking glasses with Charlie Chaplin, and as a total effect, behaving like the world's most gracious and well-groomed personages.

But, while the Soviet potentates enjoyed themselves in their roles of two Greek Gods bearing the olive branch of peace, British and American Intelligence were less dignified. With audacious scheming they created a plot to disturb the pontifical aura set by the master promoters of modern Russian propaganda.

The man chosen to create the havoc was far from being an unknown secret agent. He was the world's outstanding forgman, a World War II underwater ace and hero, a knight in shining rubber armor. To his friends, colleagues, and compatriots, he was affectionately known as "Crabbie."

His targets were the new Soviet cruiser *Ordzonikidze* (pronounced Our Johnny Kids Kay) and the small Soviet flotilla anchored in the Portsmouth harbor.

A year before, the *Ordzonikidze's* sister ship *Sverdlov* had docked in Plymouth and created a rousing stir among naval authorities. She was the sleekest, most modern war vessel they had ever viewed at a distance. And, at a distance they were forced to remain, for the Soviet skipper flatly refused to allow any British pilot, or personnel, to come aboard. The British stood on the wharves and shore and watched with amazement as the cruiser breezed through the crowded port, and docked with the ease and precision of a racing car.

The Western world had never seen such a ship. Indeed, the Russians had every reason to boast her radical design which gave their craft sensitive maneuverability and record speed. The experts made their guesses and naval intelligence authorities pondered the Soviet secret. Each would have given his right arm to have been able to make a blueprint of the *Sverdlov*. She must, they thought, have an entirely new hull design, auxiliary screws and several rudders.

The Soviets, who wanted to impress the West, succeeded. Furthermore, they added to the effect by keeping their secret out of reach of the Western powers.

When the *Ordzonikidze* slid now into Portsmouth with Comrades Khrushchev and Bulganin on board with their doves of peace in one hand and their plot to break Great Britain away from the United States in the other, the secret service chiefs made up their minds. It was high time to have a close look at the new "tub."

The choice for the man with the radar eyes and radar mind was not a difficult one. Crabbie combined all virtues needed for such a daring project. He possessed the needed stoic calmness, was slow blooded and had proved his unselfish resoluteness. All his life Crabbie had been a dashing daredevil, eager to throw himself fearlessly into new and greater adventures. The spice of danger was his whole life and the Navy had long before deemed him to be one of those phenomena who crystallized into a being more fish than human. His friends jocosely declared he was born with fins on his feet and scales instead of hair. He was blind in his recklessness, but skillful in his tasks. During his outstanding career, Commander Lionel Crabb had fulfilled dozen of secret missions for the Admiralty and set a record by swimming two-hundred-fifty feet deep in simple, unprotected gear with a new German camera, following the movement of fishes, and surveying naval routes and underwater defenses.

One set of pictures showed the screw of a ship as it threatened to cut him in two, but and more important, the films showed the belly construction of an enemy vessel. Another pictorial sequence recorded a torpedo being shot from a submarine at a distance of only fifteen feet. Crabbie roamed the shifting sands of the sea with the same pioneering bravery that had sent the first explorers to the North Pole, or across the American plains and deserts.

Crabbie was not born on the sea. His life was filled with bumpy interludes, and often lonely, to prove others were mistaken. There were many ebb tides in his existence and many alibis for his failures.

He experimented with many trades, from selling paintings in Paris to filling gas tanks in New Jersey. His peregrinations were always filled with restlessness and endless search.

When Hitler invaded Poland in 1939, thus lighting the conflagration that was to sear all Europe, Crabb wondered what he could do for England. "The mere thought of the sea is poisonous to me," he told one of his friends. "I get seasick just looking at the water in my bathtub. Guess I'm just a landlubber. Hell, I don't even know how to swim!"

Swallowing his aversion, however, Lionel volunteered for

the Royal British Navy and was promptly rejected. The doctors poked and probed the skinny little five-foot-six man and pronounced him unfit for service. His tobacco-stained lungs showed a suspicion of cancer and he was almost blind in one eye.

More angered than discouraged by the rejection, Crabb joined the Navy Volunteer Reserve and, without any medical examination, was promptly sent, as a lieutenant, to Gibraltar where the former salesman was placed behind a desk doing such tedious things as making out long forms, endless reports and complicated requisition orders. He chafed under the inactivity.

On September 19, 1941, Lieutenant Crabb was growling over his assignment of requesting several hundred swagger sticks for the officers, based on the rock fortress, when a tremendous blast shattered all the windows of the office buildings.

With stunned fascination the garrison watched the scene being played in the Grand harbor below them. The Naval tanker *Denbyvale* was on fire. She quickly sank into the sea. Moments later two other tankers exploded and followed her into watery graves.

It was obvious a new underwater campaign had started. Mussolini's Italian Navy was increasing her activity and strength in the Mediterranean. Was this a submarine attack? Certainly Gibraltar had always been considered one of the world's most protected harbors. Or were the explosions the result of sabotage?

The Admiralty had to know the answer immediately. Divers descended. Within a few days they had found the information. Holes had been cut in the submarine nets— huge gaping holes made by compressed-air cutters. In addition, the frogmen found parts of a cigar-shaped, battery-powered craft, containing a sort of saddle seat for one or two people. In the front was a detachable nose-cone or warhead. This was a new type of human-propelled torpedo. Gibraltar was in danger.

If maturity ever can be traced to a single event in Commander Crabb's life, perhaps this was the time. Naval Intelligence was still locked up in a conference room to evaluate, determine and analyze the new dangers of underwater warfare, when Lionel Crabb and his friend, Bill Bailey, teamed up with three other officers and evolved a working unit of their own, called UWWP (Under Water Working Party).

Crabbie was both mad and glad. His objective was simple: "I want to stop the Italian underwater attacks. It's our personal war against Mussolini."

It seemed Crabbie was overactive and underwise. But he actually created, without knowing it, the first Allied frogmen unit in the area.

He was still unable to swim a stroke and his floating ability resembled that of a lead balloon, but what he lacked in ability, he made up for in courage, perseverance and dogged determination. His aquatic lessons lasted for hours and he was determined to lick the enemy.

The Italian underwater squads were well-trained and expertly equipped with wool-lined and silk-padded rubber suits, sturdy fins and the latest in compressed-air breathing gear, or lungs.

The British crews seemed a ludicrous lot primitively equipped. They wore their own bathing trunks, lead-weighted tennis shoes and antiquated breathing equipment. Pressures were growing. By now the Italians were developing deadlier methods; mines which clung to the hulls of British ships like lamprey eels, were detonated by timing devices. New, intricately-designed, explosives trailed in the wake of ships and in sudden spurts of power, split the sterns of the enemy vessels.

"One day," Crabbie later told one of his friends, "I found myself embracing a cylindrical monster. A strange mine had clamped itself to the side of our ship in the region of the engine room. It was greenish in color and about three feet long. I put my ear to it and could hear the hellish telltale ticking inside. I fooled around with the firing mechanism, trying to dislocate it. Time seemed to be running against me, and I suddenly realized the clock inside might detonate the explosion chamber any second. It would be the end of the ship and everyone on board.

"I panicked and rose to the surface. 'Captain,' I yelled, 'order all hands off the ship. The engine room first.' I gulped down a slug of rum to warm me, for it was December and the Mediterranean was bitterly cold, and went back down again.

"On a second look, the mine was the most unusual type I had ever seen. I feared there could be a booby-trap which would explode if I tampered any more with the fuse section. The only solution, as I saw it, was to remove the entire mechanism from the ship's hull by cutting off the three clamps that adhered to the metal.

"The first clamp, to my joyous surprise, came off easily and the second followed in a matter of minutes. It was that bloody third one that gave the trouble. I felt the tension of knowing at any time we all might be hurled into eternity.

"Not only time, but my oxygen was running out. I surfaced for another tank. When I went down again, the over-exposure in the icy water had swollen my hands, which were scraped, cut and bruised from the work. Scratching against the iron, with the movement of the water, had sanded them raw.

"After what seemed centuries, the last clamp gave way and the mine was separated from our ship. Later, we found it was one of the most dangerous types, an ingenious affair which operated with neutral buoyance, floating under the water at random until it was magnetically attracted to its prey."

Most of the Italian mines belonged to the pressure models. To elevate them to the surface of the sea usually meant their explosion. Knowing this, Crabbie anchored the sinister cylinder between two buoys at the same depth as he had found it and towed it away from the ship. At a safe distance, he carefully removed the detonator, thus rendering it harmless. Later, when the mine was thoroughly inspected, the clock-device inside showed the explosion would have come in a matter of seconds—twenty-three, to be exact.

Early and imperfect radar was unable to measure the speed of unidentified objects in the water and often showed large schools of fish to be submarines and vice versa. But there was a danger from strange and dangerous fish which Crabbie's outfit had to combat—human fish.

Crabb related one of these experiences to his friends after the war was over. "I remember," he said, "when I came upon a tremendous shadow in the half-darkness of forty-feet depth. It wavered closer and closer toward me, a hooded creature from the court of King Neptune.

"As it approached, I could see its goggled eyes and glaring white long hands. You guessed it. It was a well-equipped enemy Italian frogman.

"He attacked with the sharpest, most wicked looking knife I have ever seen. I drew my own to parry, and the underwater duel began. We both knew one or both of us would die. Fighting under water is a battle staged in slow motion. I am sure we were a weird spectacle, but neither of us had the mood or the time to be amused by our languorous movements and misaimed slashes through the murky ocean.

"My attacker's complete and scientific underwater suit was his defeat. My old bathing shorts and tennis shoes gave me more freedom and speed of motion than his heavy rubber suit and long rubber fins. I made a final plunge at him. My knife slit his suit, and big fat bubbles of air soared upward as his uniform collapsed and filled with water. He tried to reach the surface. Four days later, we fished his body out of the bay."

Thus, Lieutenant Crabb was probably the first living creature to fight a hand-to-hand commando-trained underwater duel.

He was also the first Allied naval officer to pilot a two-man enemy submarine. This product of World War II was called a "pig." Lionel and some of his men salvaged and reconstructed one from the three enemy craft which had been sunk by depth charges. The twenty-two-foot monster was put into working order and formally christened *Emily*.

"I never liked her," Crabbie told his friends, "any more than the woman for whom she was named. Each time I took her out, I went through some of the worst moments of my life. The first time, an unexpected underwater current smashed her into the steel meshes of an anti-torpedo net. It nearly tore my head from my shoulders."

On his next trial run on the *Emily*, he very nearly drowned. The battery chamber was faulty and began to leak at a depth of fifty feet. "It was jolly hard to pull up from the dive," he recalled, "and I was nearly suffocated when he oxygen valve refused to open."

The third trip was the last for the *Emily*. An outside pipe broke, the tanks flooded and she nosed down to a final resting place on the shifting sea bottom. Crabb, however, wormed free from his temperamental craft and reached the safety of land.

During this time the tides of war were also shifting. Italy deserted Hitler and Mussolini in favor of the Allies.

Crabb's mission was to locate all surviving Italian-trained frogmen and work with them to detonate the mines lying in wait in the heavily populated Italian seaports. He, with the assistance of an American naval hero, Anthony S. Marsloe, a former legal advisor to Governor Tom Dewey, was commissioned to set up the Allied Navies Experimental Station in Venice.

"He was not unlike a knight out of the past," Marsloe says of Lionel. "His body belonged first to his King and then to Queen Elizabeth. This blind loyalty inspired him to overcome all obstacles. I am sure he wanted to die doing something daring."

Mussolini had been defeated. The new Italian Government sided with the Allies; loyalties and inter-dependencies switched rapidly. All Italy was suffering from the wounds of war when Crabbie discovered that his fame had spread into the camp of his former enemies. His task to recruit Italian frogmen was not difficult at all. They came to him voluntarily, eagerly and admiringly. One day the frail little Britisher confided in Marsloe, "To have a friend like you is one thing, but when your enemies respect you, that is a real honor."

A deep friendship grew between the American and the British frogman.

The Crabb-Marsloe team, assisted by their Italian frogmen officers, organized history's first and largest team of "human mine sweepers." They worked twenty-four hours around the clock to make Italy's ports free of the treacherous, death-dealing cylinders and iron-clad mines that lay in the blue waters.

Crabbie, who had wrestled in the underwater wilderness for almost five years, found himself at the end of the war hearing the applause of a British crowd who deliriously approved his war record. The man with the bad lung and the blind eye emerged from the war a hero, the world's most celebrated frogman. He was awarded the rank of commander and decorated with the seven highest combat medals, including the Order of the British Empire and the King George Medal.

The postwar world treated the war hero less kindly. The man who had established such high marks for his courage, tenacity and valiancy, no longer received such profuse accolades.

British Naval Intelligence rehired him, but only after he had experienced many ups and downs in the commercial field, including establishing a partnership in a furniture company in London.

The apparent impotence of the great Allied powers against the domination and growing strength of the USSR reactivated Crabbie's adventuresome life. As a "hobby" he took up underwater photography and produced for the Western governments some of the rarest aquatic pictures ever taken, many of which are still classified as "top secret" in the files of the various security departments.

Crabbie successfully convinced some of his naval superiors that, in his opinion, the contest between the East and the West was not only in the race for outer space, but also in the race for "underseas."

His activities were not always as a straight salaried employee of Naval Intelligence. Crabbie built his own organization and his own private unit, composed of former Navy frogmen and experienced underwater warriors, began their work for the government.

The British Navy endorsed the setup, knowing if some projects would fail and backfire, the Government officially would face embarrassment and blame.

There was a long period in 1950 when Crabbie vanished. No one saw him for months in his luxuriously decorated flat in the Knightsbridge district of London, nor did the waiters or bartenders remember serving him in his favorite hangouts.

The last time Commander Crabb visited Portsmouth harbor for his "shave and haircut" was April 17, 1956, shortly before the *Ordzonikidze* docked with comrades Khrushchev and Bulganin on board. With the Britisher was a tall, bespectacled blond man, who seemed to be his friend. Together they registered at the old Sally Port Hotel in rooms apart from each other.

Neither of the two men spent much time in his hotel room. No one knows where they were during the following hours, but Crabbie was seen the same night in some of his old favorite hangout places as the Nut Bar and the Keppel's Head Hotel. He made several phone calls to his old partner in the furniture company, Mr. Maitland Pendock.

The following night, on the 18th of April, Crabbie was again seen by the waiters and bartenders of his favorite bars and restaurants.

The events which followed are unknown to the public. The Soviet Secret Service may know the details. The British and American secret services have their speculative theories, but the real and true story can only be guessed from the puzzling, frightening, contradictory, provacative bits of unsure evidence and information that, like flotsam, continue to turn up on the beaches of fact.

What is known through intelligence and counterespionage is abysmal, leading only into darkness:

April 17, 1956
Crabb and friend checked in at the Sally Port Hotel.
Friend wore glasses.
Crabb around the docks.
Crabb visited bars and restaurants.
Crabb made a phone call to his partner.

April 18, 1956
The man wearing glasses who registered under the name of "Smith" checked out of the Sally Port Hotel at 3:30 p.m., paying both his and Crabb's bill.

April 19, 1956
At 10:30 a.m. Crabb phoned his business partner about a check. All further activities unknown.

April 20, 1956
Pat Rose, an attractive young lady who was very fond of Crabb, spent an impatient night waiting for Crabb, who did not arrive, nor did he phone.

On April 21, Mr. Pendock, Crabbie's business partner, began to wonder what had happened to his partner who had not been in the office since the 16th of April. Something must have gone wrong, Pendock thought, and he decided to report the matter to Scotland Yard where he was met by stony faces and, in terse words, told, "Stay out of this. You should know better than to ask questions."

The newspapers caught wind of the story and uncovered confusing facts. A certain Bernard S. Smith had bought a Danish armchair from the Pendock-Crabb Company. He paid with a personal check but had misdated it. "That's all right," Crabb had told his partner by phone at 10:30 on April 19th. "Smith will write another check. I expect to see him in Portsmouth soon."

Naval Intelligence remained silent. M.I. 5 remained silent. Scotland Yard remained silent. Not even Crabb's mother could receive cooperation from official sources. Her son had not returned from Portsmouth.

Others of Crabb's close friends and associates took up the search. One commander went straight to the Admiralty. "Don't worry," he was told. "Crabbie will show up right enough. You must realize we are in no position to divulge any information due to the Official Secrets Act."

Marshall Pugh, a writer and close friend of Crabb's, reached the Deputy Chief of the Naval Staff. He was informed, "Commander Crabb is missing after testing some classified new equipment. There will be an official announcement very soon."

Pugh was not satisfied with such a vague, cryptic answer. "Humph," he grunted sarcastically, "and I suppose the announcement will say Crabb fell overboard during a thunderstorm."

"Oh, no," answered the Deputy Chief seriously, "this is no laughing matter. We have far too much respect for Commander Crabb to say anything so ridiculous as that."

Nine days after Crabb's disappearance, an agent of M.I. 5 Intelligence Department visited the Sally Port Hotel in Portsmouth and tore four pages from the guest registry. But it was too late to keep "Smith's" name out of the case. The papers had all reported and duly constructed their own suppositions about the man who had misdated the check for the chair.

On Sunday, April 28th, forced by the public clamor, the Admiralty issued their terse communique:

"COMMANDER CRABB DID NOT RETURN FROM A TEST DIVE. HE IS MISSING AND PRESUMABLY DROWNED."

The report went on to say the tests took place in Stokes Bay (three miles from the position of the anchored Soviet ships) and the hour was given as 10:20 in the morning.

The press still was not satisfied. How, they asked, could Crabb have been lost in a test dive at 10:20 in the morning and call his business partner at 10:30 the same day to discuss the matter of a misdated check? They voiced scepticism that Crabb made his test three miles away from the Soviet ships, and later turned up evidence that the Commander had indeed visited the *HMS Vernon*, the frogmen's training ship and a cover-up center for Naval Intelligence in Portsmouth. The *HMS Vernon* lay in the harbor only five hundred feet from the *Ordzonikidze*.

It took the Soviet Government a week to compose their angry two-page note to London. However, when it arrived, it was a masterpiece of stinging accusations which claimed British Naval Intelligence had ordered Commander Crabb to spy shamelessly on the new Russian ship and the activities aboard the Soviet vessel. It went on to state they had no knowledge of the whereabouts or the fate of the British frogman.

In the files of British Intelligence, there is a different set of facts which contradict the Soviet statements. During a farewell party, before the *Ordzonikidze* sped from the Portsmouth harbor, one of the Russian sailors, caught in the spirit of too much vodka mixed with Guinnes stout, confided to his feminine companion, "A couple of days ago we caught one of your men." But he refused to say more, having realized he had already said too much.

Still the theories raged. What had happened to the frogman hero? Had he been electrocuted? Or speargunned? Had he been killed by Communist frogmen who discovered him while attempting to blow up the ship in order to kill Khrushchev and Bulganin? Was he planting mines on the ship? Or perhaps the dive was made to discover the secret of the maneuverability of the new vessel. Did he place sound instruments? Microphones?

Whatever the unknown truth was, it seems apparent Commander Crabb was caught by the demons of destruction.

The Soviet press dived on the case like a tern after a fish. The propaganda machine went into full speed and screamed to the Communist world that Commander Crabb either spied on the Russians while they were on a friendly peace mission or still worse, had attempted an assassination plot.

Still other comrades in Moscow and Peking wove the threads of evidence into a fabric that accused the American Intelligence Service of having hired Crabb to install on the ship's hull a *sonar* system which would give the West information about the new cruiser's navigational range, through underwater sound waves. These electric spy instruments with small anchors could release themselves after a time. Had Crabb tried to attach them?

In the age of science anything is possible. Crabb could have been installing a microphone system to pick up the conversations of the crew or beamed to hear the conversation of the Soviet leaders.

In a fast answer to the Soviet note, and the unfavorable reaction of the Russian press, the British Government stated: "The charges that the *Ordzonikidze* was spied upon are untrue. We assume no responsibility for Commander Crabb. If he did anything wrong, he did it on his own."

Marshall Pugh was incensed by what he felt was Governmental side-stepping. "Crabb died doing his duty," he said bitterly. "Now they are trying to make him look like a bad boy. They are dragging his good name into the mud."

But if Crabb had been drowned in the harbor, where was his body?

Sydney Kowles, an exfrogman and wartime buddy of Crabbie, came to Portsmouth to search for the Commander's remains. He was stopped at the docks by an Admiralty official.

"Don't dive. Crabb isn't down there, so just don't bother."

"Then his body has been recovered?"

"I didn't say that," was the answer. "But don't risk any more questions. I am sworn to secrecy. But don't dive because I would hate to see a friend of the Commander stick his neck out when there is nothing to be gained. I know he isn't there. Don't ask me how I know; I just do. Now go home, please."

This conversation could mean anything. Perhaps the Navy recovered the body and kept it secret. Or Crabb was alive and a Soviet prisoner.

On May 10th, an Admiralty officer returned some of Crabb's belongings to his mother. They had been collected from the Sally Port Hotel by the mysterious "Mr. Smith."

Mrs. Crabb's hopes soared. "There is one thing missing here," she said, "that makes me know my son is still alive. His cane is not among these things! It is really of little value to anyone else, but Crabbie would have taken it with him— just for good luck."

Yes, some agreed, if the Commander had been captured, the Russians, out of respect for the British hero, might have permitted him to have his cane.

With the passage of time, public interest in the case died down.

Four weeks later a headless torso was fished from the harbor, but the body was too deteriorated for identification. Those who clung to the idea that Commander Crabb was killed by the Russians called the case closed.

But those who felt Crabb was still alive found new hope in a strange event that occurred some weeks after.

One morning a strange, stout woman, who spoke with a foreign accent, appeared at the Pendock furniture store. She handed a check to one of the clerks and said in a shrill voice, "Give this to Mr. Pendock and tell him to tear up the one dated 1955." By the time the astonished clerk delivered the check to Pendock, the woman had vanished. The check was signed "Bernard S. Smith."

The visit of the mysterious woman opens two more vistas of thought. It could be conceivable that British Intelligence, in an effort to close the case forever, issued a new check so that Mr. Pendock would not be tempted to pry further into the affairs of Mr. Smith.

As an alternate, the check might have been sent by Commander Crabb, who was, and perhaps still is, alive. To support this possibility there is the incident of the two missing British diplomats who vanished behind the Iron Curtain and managed to send checks to their families in Switzerland as a sign of their being alive.

The British Parliament went through numerous stormy sessions on the Crabb case. At last Prime Minister Anthony Eden put his foot down on the debates by saying, "It would not be in the public interest to disclose how Commander Crabb is presumed to have met his death."

Soviet diplomats remained close-mouthed on the Crabb incident, but they frankly admit that the *Ordzonikidze* was a ship well worth an investigation. She is, they stated proudly, not only as fast, light and maneuverable as a flying fish, but also equipped with a new type of anti-magnetic armor which repels conventional mines and torpedoes. She is also equipped with new sound and radar systems and all modern sound and counter-sound detection systems. Equally radical are her built-in anti-frogman devices which include magnetic traps.

These boasts, coming from the Russians, were verified by Finnish Intelligence after watching the maneuvers of the *Ordzonikidze* in the Gulf of Finland. The magnetic pull, according to the reports, can draw the frogmen's oxygen tanks into the magnetic field and suck them onto the hull of the warship where they are held until their life's breath is exhausted and they suffocate.

"If that was Crabbie's fate," his old friend Marsloe declared, "he was prepared for such a death. One night, many years ago, over a bottle of Italian Chianti, he said to me, 'I don't want to die with my slippers on . . . give me my flippers instead.'"

But there are still those who believe Commander Crabb is being held by the Soviets, who rescued him while he was fighting for his life p101ioned on the hull of the cruiser *Ordzonikidze*.

From a very practical standpoint, it would be folly to kill

a man who knows so much about British-American underwater intelligence, radar, sonar, and the specialized scientific naval advancements.

This is an opinion shared by a high-ranking French diplomat who recently returned from Moscow. He states that, during a Kremlin reception, a high government official admitted, "We have the British fish-spy."

"Do you mean Commander Crabb is still alive?"

"Sort of," the Commissar smirked. "He is Number 147 in the Lefortovo Prison. Dangerous character . . . that Crabb! He almost escaped, but he was recaptured after a struggle. Now we keep him in solitary confinement. Perhaps we will put him on trial . . . perhaps not. It all depends on the British attitude. In any event, he won't be seeing London for a long, long time."

But, whatever the truth may be, Commander Crabb will not be forgotten for a long, long time either. If there is a human chance for him to return to England, he will do so.

FRANCIS G. POWERS: MODERN SPACE SPY

It happened on the first of May, 1960.

Under clear, blue, sunny skies the soldiers in Major Mihail Voronov's Ural Command relaxed. They had every reason to claim a vacation after the weeks of arduous drills and difficult maneuvers.

In addition, it seemed the entire world was looking for peace. Comrade Nikita Khrushchev was to celebrate the First of May parade in Moscow in accordance with the respect due the Soviet revolution and was preparing to fly with his entourage of commissars, secretaries, interpreters, spies and secret service personnel to Paris for the summit meeting.

Russia's reigning dictator was scheduled to sit down with General de Gaulle of France, President Eisenhower of the United States and Prime Minister Macmillan of the United Kingdom.

Tensions could be reduced and co-existence between the Soviet dictatorship and the free world would be discussed. It was agreed in the hearts and minds of serious thinking men that this historic meeting in the spring of 1960 could wipe out the fears of atomic war.

Then it happened: A spy incident which shook the world,

broke up the summit meeting in Paris and changed history in our day.

Major Voronov's men had captured the first American space spy.

Far away, the Soviet radar screens saw their first blip, an unidentified object. A cloud . . . a Russian plane . . . a mistake in their own instruments . . .

Dials spun; buttons were pushed. Air alerts sped along the Soviet air defense network. "This is not a flying saucer," said Major Voronov. "This is a foreign plane. The pilot knows he has been discovered. Watch . . . watch . . . he is zigagging. He is trying to change his course. Yes, see, he is trying a long circle around our rocket launching base. Get him into your range. Fire!"

One American pilot tried to outwit the Soviet air defense system.

Francis G. Powers stood a slim chance.

From Pakistan to Norway, traveling at 65,000 feet in his bullet-like jet, Captain Powers' plane was no more than a dust mark on the tracking scope.—

The Soviets were ready to shoot down the first U-2 plane that came into their range. For six months they had eagerly hoped to capture one of these high-altitude aircrafts, manned by only one pilot and filled with an amazing array of the latest electronic and photographic equipment. The spectacular capabilities of the American U-2 had puzzled and challenged the Russians since they first discovered that such a plane existed.

Soviet authorities were well aware that the miracle plane of 1960 had given Washington new confidence. The U-2 was equipped to detect atomic tests inside Russia itself; and for many months the planes had been skirting the USSR, scanning the defense perimeter of the Western World and taking air samples at high altitudes. This ability of the U-2 to detect atomic tests, coupled with its sensitive photographic equipment which permitted it to record miles of terrain in a single flight, made the U-2 a prize well worth dropping from the sky.

Pilot Francis Powers breathed pure oxyegn for two hours in order to rid his system of all nitrogen before he climbed into the cockpit of the sleek aircraft. His pressure suit was as complicated and fantastic as those worn by Buck

Rogers and, despite his vantage point high above the earth, he kept an alert eye on the dial-filled instrument panel which guided his flight.

But the lone man, flying at an incredible speed in the thin air of the stratosphere, was discovered.

It took only seconds.

A rocket blasted out, gathering momentum and speed as it broke away from earth.

Voronov peered into the screen. Two specks headed toward each other.

Then the screen was filled with confusion.

"We hit the target."

Major Voronov ran into the sunlight and focused his binoculars on the sky. The sunlight glinted on bits of the metal. Then there was a small figure mushrooming down in a parachute.

Francis Gary Powers was captured by Voronov's men of the Soviet aurhotities. His U-2 aircraft had penetrated the USSR and flew 1200 miles over the heart of the Russian missile-launching area. Reputable sources say that his was the forty-eighth plane sent by the United States on reconnaissance missions in a period of four years.

Powers was thirty-one years old when he was shot down. He was a normal, clean-cut American from Georgia, a frank-faced young man with closely cropped hair and a perpetual smile, a Southerner with a deep pride of Southern traditions and heavy languid drawl. Francis Powers never dreamed he was to make history.

In the last analysis, Powers himself was not a spy but only the pilot of a plane which contained spy equipment, all electronically controlled. The cameras spun on by themselves; the instruments which tested the air for atomic radiation operated automatically. Powers was the human element encased in a modern espionage machine; nevertheless, the handsome flier has come to be thought of as a spy for Democracy, a modern Nathan Hale who risked his life for his country as all modern astronauts are prepared to do if necessary.

Powers carried with him an injection needle, a tiny instrument filled with such a strong poison that death is almost instant. This was to have been used to take his own life if faced with capture . . . if there were time. But for the U-2 pilot, there was no time. His plane careened to earth in Russian territory and into the hands of Soviet soldiers.

There remains only the mystery of those crucial seconds at the moment and after Powers' plane was hit.

The U.S. U-2 was exhibited in Gorki Park, a strange, warped, mangled bit of wreckage, macabre evidence, according to Khrushchev, of the evil plans of the United States against the Soviet Union.

Powers was indicted and held incommunicado with no access to the U.S. Embassy, American lawyers or any member of the Red Cross. The three-judge collegium, the highest military court in Russia, tried Powers under Article 2 of the Criminal Code which provided a minimum penalty on conviction of seven years imprisonment. Maximum penalty is death before the firing squad.

The court was the same Soviet legal body which conducted the infamous purge trials of the 1930's. The majority opinion rules on the court, and there is no appeal after the court's decision.

With Powers in prison, Russia's Khrushchev glowered on his arrival in Paris. The clown-like little man raised his fist and demanded Power's life as a spy. The United States, he added, was entirely to blame for an aggressive and unfriendly act of espionage. The world shuddered. What was to have been a peaceful summit meeting dissolved into a vat of nitroglycerin!

President Eisenhower laid the cards on the table. Yes, he said, the United States has organized space espionage because it is the only way to protect the fifty states and the free world against surprise attacks from behind the Iron Curtain. Since Soviet dictators decline the idea of aerial inspections for all nations by the United Nations, sky-spying is the only form of self-protection the United States possessed.

The President of the United States defended Francis G. Powers' actions.

The Soviet Union has woven a network of spies through the free world. Through the activities of the Rosenbergs, the first atom bomb secrets were sent into Russia.

But space espionage is new.

A new breed of spies has invaded outer space. These are not only pilots, astronauts, analysts, technicians . . . the human animal . . . but mechanical espionage agents which see, listen, remember and talk to only those who understand their strange language.

World-wide, globe-girdling spy networks of electronic equipment have been installed . . . the missiles, the anti-missiles, and the anti-anti-missiles, to name but a few. All major powers pride themselves on a fence of giant radar screens to combat counterespionage in the air. There are "sniffer" aircraft which take photographs and air samples, picket submarines, balloons bearing radios and cameras, radio ears which make tape recordings anywhere in space—and hear everything.

In the electronic world, the masters over the spy-organizers are the "brains" and the "computers" which digest and analyze all space reports. The "eye in the sky" can photograph any area on earth and transmit it through television to us earthlings.

The first hint of the use of aerial espionage came in 1917 when French, German and United States planes buzzed back and forth over the front lines gathering information about numbers and movements of troops.

A later, and unique case, developed when Hitler was in power. The Nazi Secret Service was baffled by a sky-writer who spread his trail of smoke across the sky, advertising soft drinks. When this story was unravelled, it was discovered the pilot was giving coded trip-offs concerned with German troop movements. A French spy in Berlin then informed his intelligence chief in Paris of planned troop military movements.

The Nazis themselves used air spies over Iceland and Greenland. Using the excuse that the planes were gathering weather data, a fleet of aricraft operated for over two years until they were destroyed by an American naval expedition, aided by the courageous Danish and Norwegian sky patrols.

Göring's Luftwaffe officers photographed large sections of the British Isles in order to "blitz" them with greater accuracy. The United States air-raid attacks on Berlin brought back aerial photographs of the secret V-2 rocket launching sites of Peenemunde which were later wiped out.

The United States Consul in Gothenburg, Sweden, William C. Corcoran, learned of the secret Peenemunde base and suggested the photographic attack, thus helping to save London.

To combat the growing strength of aerial espionage, the Nazis developed counterespionage methods, camouflage, to confuse the pilots and bombadiers. As one example, the Germans built a make-believe river through Hamburg. Thinking it to be the Altser, American airmen misdirected their bombs for a considerable time. Aircraft factories, train stations and strategic areas were also painted and disguised in the United States.

A forerunner, radio spying is closely akin to space espionage. The OGPU operated some fifty secret radio stations in France, Nazi Germany and Belgium during World War II. Important information was relayed directly to Moscow.

Just as modern radios have been developed, specialized cameras are now so advanced that two jet planes can photograph a strip of the globe five hundred miles wide and more than twenty-five miles long in a single shot. Francis G. Powers was in the process of photographing only a small section of the vast USSR when he was shot down and exposed as a space spy by two bits of evidence: pictures and a poison needle meant for his own suicide.

The range of feats a modern spy camera can perform is impressive. Jet planes can fly day or night through good weather or bad, using infrared devices from heights as high as fourteen miles. The aerial photographers can take pictures of anything they wish . . . the Kremlin, airfields, airstrips, factories, harbor facilities, highway systems, missile launching pads. For the men who dart through the atmosphere at supersonic speeds, the Iron Curtain behind which dictators like to hide is nonexistent.

The Soviet sputniks and U.S. space satellites are now piercing and probing the universe. Each can be thought of as a potential spy vehicle, exploring a realm where no human being has ever been.

It is not the purpose of this book to give a political or legal analysis of the U-2 incident, but its author would like to interject one editorial view:

The U-2 incident that cascaded the Soviet Union and the United States down to a nadir in political, public and human relations has also, for the first time in many years, placed the Soviet Union on the defensive.

Since 1945, one country after another has been conquered and ground into submission by the Soviet—from Estonia to Red China, from Indo-China to Tibet. The march toward World Communism may not have been slowed down by the capture of Francis Powers and his jet aircraft, but the Soviets are less likely to rush into a Third World War now that they know the United States has in her possession accurate photographs of Russian secret rocket and missile bases.

The United States is proud of the country's industry, ingenuity and scientific prowess that gave birth to such a miracle plane. America's citizens feel an awed humility when they hear the name Francis G. Powers, pilot and patriot, who was willing to risk his life to perpetuate the freedom of the country of his birth as well as for the entire free world. The one great and shocking difference lies in the fact that Hitler's troops never held in their tentacles one-third of the world, as do the Soviet soldiers, nor were they ever orbiting the globe in outer space.

Francis G. Powers will long be remembered and discussed. But, in reality, he is only a symbol of our age which has reached new frontiers. This young man from Georgia has suffered for his country. His name will be listed among the American heroes, but even he, the first American space spy of flesh and blood to be made an example of by the Russians, has been replaced by technological developments: the USD 5, a pilotless jet plane, and two new space vehicles, the SAMOS and the MIDAS satellites.

Both of these space travelers carry cameras and infrared equipment as they orbit the earth. The pictures fall back to earth in space capsules. Their television-like equipment transmits pictures directly to earth stations.

The MIDAS is capable of giving an immediate warning of any missile launched any place on earth and of sending up a counter missile which directs and corrects itself to make a direct hit. All this in a matter of minutes.

Half a dozen such MIDAS satellites, orbiting the earth over the poles, will cover and photograph every mile of the globe on a twenty-four-hour-a-day schedule.

Pioneer Midas II, the robot spy in outer space which guards world democracy, talks to many listening posts in the free world: Kaena Point in the Hawaiian Islands, Chiniak and Kodiak in the Alaskan chain, Point Mugu and Vandenberg, California, New Boston, and Grenier, New Hampshire and Cape Canaveral, Florida.

It seems likely that this tremendous, unbelievable spy system will, in a few years, be outdated and improved, but the electronic spies of today's universe admirably demonstrate that the spies for Democracy are guardians in outer space, whirling monotonously onward to insure that no dictator on earth can ever destroy the free world from within or through surprise attacks.

Espionage seems to be eternal. Man says he does not believe in war . . . but he always speaks of war and threatens war. The Soviet Union alone controls seventeen countries since 1945. These countries were subdued through war, revolution and captured by aggression and are held by force, never through the free elective voices of the people. While men mouth statements of peace, they expend their brilliance in making bigger, better and more fantastic weapons of destruction.

The lesson these new space spies teach us today is that there is a shocking lag between our ability to build machines and our ability to solve our human problems and to iron out political difficulties. Until this gap between Twentieth Century technology and our primitive urge to fight is eliminated, we cannot hope for an everlasting peace.

Until the beginning of this century, it was considered a sort of madman's dream, like the legend of Icarus, that man could fly. He now can travel at speeds faster than sound, and scientists ponder what will happen when he reaches the speed of light. All this in less than sixty years. But the real dream of all men that we will live as nations together without conflict still remains unaccomplished.

But the day should come when our great-grandchildren will battle no more seriously than on the football fields of the moon, the Olympic tracks on Mars, the lawns of Eton and the sandlots of America . . . instead of on the bloodstained banks of the Rhine, through the bullet-riddled forests of the Argonnes, over the cold mountains of Italy or Korea.

Let us pray that the space age will prevent another war!

THE HUNTER AND THE HUNTED

THE YEAR: 1960
THE SCENE: A modern school in Nebraska.
THE OCCASION: A new school assembly for the entire student body. The author of this book delivered a talk about spies and traitors which was followed by a question-and-answer period. As the time was rapidly drawing to a close, a twelve-year-old boy raised his hand and asked a question, the same question the speaker had heard several times before:

"Mr. Singer, just who was this man, Adolf Hitler?"

The lack of knowledge about the madman of our century is not shocking, for there is emerging in our midst a new, young, generation who know very little about past history of whom Hitler is a part, and even less about his inhuman concentration camps, the Nazi hatreds, and mass murderer Adolf Eichmann who gassed six million Jews to their death at the staggeringly efficient rate of two-hundred human beings every fifteen minutes.

But there are those who *do* know and *do* remember with bitterness. In the eternal city of Jerusalem, next to the tomb of David, exhibits and mementos of Eichmann's horrors and atrocities are stored away as reminders to the coming generations that there are no limits of man's cruelty to man once the passions for evil and pain are unleashed. There in the unholy shrine of barbaric inhumanity are the replicas of Eichmann's misdeeds: the blood-stained holy scrolls, soap bars made from human tallow, parchment of human skin, bones whittled and sculptured, gas ovens and pits which served as mass cemeteries into which the wizened and tortured bodies were dumped with less care than cordwood.

The author, who had lost sixty-six members of his own family in the macabre game of the "hunter and the hunted," had hoped he would never have to write about the man who gassed his mother and his seventy-year-old grandparents—but fate is not that kind.

And so it falls to his duty to give an impartial, dispassionate report on the greatest spy hunt of the century, for Tuvia Friedmann and the Israeli Secret Service spent sixteen long and discouraging years before they successfully tracked down Adolf Eichmann, war criminal, torturer and mass executioner of six million people of the same race that gave Jesus Christ to the world.

Tuvia Friedmann is a mild-mannered man, a thorough, systematic agent who indeed has the patience of Job. In some respects he looks like Israel's Prime Minister Ben-Gurion although he cannot boast the Prime Minister's heavy head of hair. Friedmann lost his while interned in a Nazi concentration camp in Poland.

This is the story of a chase that bridged two continents.

In 1945, Israel had not yet been born, but the idea was a persistent dream. The British ruled their Palestinian mandates with a firm hand and weapons. The Zionists were busily organizing their own government, educational system, and a courageous underground army, the Haganah. The day of their uprising and subsequent independence was near.

The Haganah, which smuggled ten thousand Nazi victims

into Palestine, developed a well-organized and well-trained spy network. The Palestinian Jews knew the techniques of war. They had fought with the British to defeat Hitler; they were now ready to use their knowledge to fight for a country of their own.

The secret service of the Haganah organized branches in many places. The intelligence chief in Europe was Asher Ben-Nathan, a young man with military training, clear vision and astuteness. After V-E day, he summoned one of his lieutenants, Tuvia Friedmann, and delivered the simple directive:

"From this day on, your job is to find Adolf Eichmann. He is not dead; he has merely escaped. He is wanted as a war criminal, and he has murdered our people. We want Eichmann!"

Friedmann was no Sherlock Holmes, nor did he have a pocket-sized crystal ball. There was no picture available of Eichmann and only a few sketchy descriptions of his appearance. Where was he to start his search?

Working on a thin logical path, Friedmann visited one refugee camp after another, talked with hundreds of displaced persons, any survivor who might possibly have seen the wanted man. He reaped only a meager harvest. Eichmann appeared to be an average Teutonic type with no outstanding physical characteristics. In accordance with Nazi prejudices, Eichmann had not fraternized with Jews. He was a hated name, a malevolent shadow with no face nor form.

Friedmann turned to the police official in many countries, the British, French and American intelligence agents as well as the former members of the anti-Nazi underground in Germany.

The sparse facts, dates, descriptions only lead into a maze of dead ends.

At one point Friedmann's hopes soared. The Austrians reported that Frau Eichmann often visited an isolated shack in upper Austria. Underground members watched, waited and finally arrested the man who was her host. With impetuousness born of war-torn nerves, they seized the man and shot him without a trial. But he was not Eichmann. Their victim was just one of many Nazis who had hid from the finger of guilt.

The United States Central Intelligence Agency was of little more help, although they were able to piece together a clear verbal description of Eichmann. Eichmann had been a prisoner of war in a camp. During his internment, U.S. Counterintelligence conducted three hearings with him. The sessions, however, had been routine, and since the war was over, Eichmann plead the same old familiar case: he was an innocent victim of misplaced patriotism, was shocked but knew nothing of gas chambers and concentration camps, and had been forced into a Nazi uniform by the combined forces of fear and circumstance.

On his written forms and in his interviews with the American captors, Eichmann lied about his name, his past, his military history. The CIC in Ansbach deemed him to be just another Nazi. He was placed in prison and forgotten.

In 1946, Eichmann and four other Nazi prisoners escaped from the loosely guarded prison camp and, equipped with forged indentification papers listing him as Herr Otto Henninger, he made his way to Northern Germany.

One of the inmates in the prison had a brother in Eversen who helped the escapee. Finding a job in war-torn Germany was not difficult. The Mayor of Eversen accepted Herr Henninger's registration card, and Eichmann relaxed in a period of peace and safety in the Kohlenbach Lumber Camp deep in the wilderness of the forests.

Tuvia Friedmann continued to build his net. He alerted every cooperative spy service to help in tracking down the arch-enemy of the Jews.

Tuvia, the hunter, was spurred on by his own memories. He had watched his own parents pulled from their homes and executed on the orders of Eichmann in Poland. Granted that the world is finite, time is infinite and patience was Friedmann's greatest virtue. "If I cannot find Eichmann," he reasoned, "perhaps I can find his family."

Among the millions of confiscated Nazi papers, Friedmann finally found a new lead. One paper, signed by Eichmann dated October 30, 1934, was an application for permission to marry Veronica Liebel, a woman of "purest Aryan blood and descent, an asset to any storm troop leader."

On January 23, 1935, the SS and Nazi Security Office had granted permission for the marriage with a decree that the racical check was satisfactory.

On May 17th of the same year, Eichmann married Veronica Liebel.

Again the search continued, the fruitless follow-up of every lead. Veronica Liebel-Eichmann was as hard to pin down as her husband. Rumors hinted she was in Egypt.

Rumors whispered she was in South America. The entire globe seemed to be Friedmann's oyster bed.

The hunter went to Prague. The Czechs had captured one of Eichmann's closest assistants, Dieter von Wisliczeny. Von Wisliczeny was verbose and cooperative. He hated Eichmann, he declared, because he had never felt safe during their association. Fear was Eichmann's whip. Von Wisliczeny suggested one idea worthy of investigation—Eichmann's mistress. No, he did not know her name, but he was certain she once owned a factory in Doppl.

Friedmann continued his work in Austria but sent a trusted Haganah co-worker to Doppl in search of Eichmann's one-time mistress.

Friedmann's choice of an agent was excellent. Manos was a handsome man with excellent manners, a fluent linguist with a natural flare for dramatics which made it possible for him to pose as a former Nazi officer. In Doppl he was told the *"gnadige Frau"* was vacationing at the spa of *Bad Aussee*.

At the resort, Manos checked into the best hotel, registered as a citizen of the Netherlands but, over coffee, and at breakfast, lunch and dinner, and with everyone with whom he talked made it quite clear that he was really a German with special sympathy for all the poor, sorrowing wives of Nazi leaders who seemed to have taken refuge at *Bad Aussee*.

A woman took his bait. But it was not Eichmann's mistress. To his surprise, he found himself in the circle of Frau Eichmann herself.

Manos played his prize catch carefully. He was a *bon vivant*, charming attentive, and sophisticated. He turned his ebullience, not toward Frau Eichmann, but to her best friend, a widow. For several days he saw her for afternoon coffee, for supper, for a late glass of wine. At last he reached his goal, an introduction to Frau Liebel.

"It is a pleasure to meet you" she murmured, as he bent over her hand. "You remind me so much of my brother. He was killed in the war."

The next step was as easy as inevitable. Manos saw Frau Eichmann often. There were afternoon teas in her home, evenings of bridge, walks in the park, occasional swims, all accompanied by a reserved and respectful flirtation. The house needed a man since Frau Liebel's husband had been killed in the war.

And Manos needed access to the house. During each visit

he tried to find pictures of Eichmann but his prowling uncovered not even so much as a picture of the children, Klaus, Horst and Dieter, who were becoming increasingly fond of Manos, the new family friend. Nor were the children of help in giving information. On boat trips, when Manos took them out alone, they gave only the official version that their father had been killed during the closing days of the war.

During Manos' visits, Nazi names were mentioned and discussed: Hitler, Bormann, Göering, Goebbels . . . Eichmann. Nothing out of the ordinary was said. Manos sensed Frau Liebel was nervous and fearful when the name Eichmann came into the conversation, but suspicion was not fact. Nevertheless, he stated his feelings in his daily reports to Tuvia Friedmann.

Manos became more deeply ingrained in the family life of Frau Liebel and her children. When she mentioned a desire for a maid, he promised to speak to the hotel housekeeper for a good woman to help with the household.

The "maid" he produced was an agent for the Haganah. She worked in the Liebel home for months, listening to every bit of conversation, reading letters whenever possible and trying to see, hear and sense everything that happened and their possible implications.

From the reports that came out of Frau Liebel's home, it seemed Veronica did not know where Eichmann was hiding and that there was no contact between the two.

At this point of diminishing returns, Manos returned to Doppl, determined to find Adolf's mistress. After some search, he met Frau Mistelbach, a gay, happy, handsome woman with a substantial amount of wealth. Manos presented himself as the brother of Eichmann's closest friend. His brother, Manos said, was holding money and valuables for Eichmann who must certainly be in need of cash.

Frau Mistelbach shook her head. She knew nothing about Adolf. Their affair was an event set in the distant past, 1938. It was over and remained a vague, romantic memory.

The contact, however, brought one bit of new information: the address of Eichmann's father living in Linz, Austria, where he ran a small business. When Manos visited Herr Eichmann and asked for his son's address, the old man answered with a brief but loud tirade: "Get out of here! I have nothing to do with my son!"

With this contact severed before it began, Manos returned

to Frau Mistlebach in the hope of finding a new, unearthed lead.

While sitting under a leafy arbor, sipping a glass of wine, Frau Mistlebach brought out her picture album. She thumbed through the pages, explaining each picture, mentioning family ties until she suddenly paused. "And here," she said, "is one picture of my old friend, the close friend of your brother . . . this is Adolf."

Manos stared at the one and only picture of Eichmann which the careful, clever Nazi leader had failed to destroy. The one picture which would identify Eichmann legally and identify him as the Nazi executioner.

Not wishing to incite an incident by taking the picture by force, Manos went to the local police. Together they plotted and executed a search of the Mistelbach household on the pretense of seizing hoarded ration stamps. The picture was removed from the album, and the police corps excused themselves and departed.

During all this time, Eichmann hid in the shadows of his forest, slashing at trees, working as an ordinary lumberman. But Destiny writes its own laws. The lumber company went into bankruptcy, and Eichmann was forced to move again.

He told his fellow-workers in the camp that he would go to Scandinavia. Later, these men told stories about the character of the mass-murderer which can be summed up as: "He was a nice man. We liked his honesty. Eichmann always saw that our rations were divided equally. He was a hard worker. A woman visited him from time to time, but he was a lonely man who told us his family had been killed in the war . . . and he wished he were dead, too."

Instead of making the trip northward to Scandinavia, Eichmann and two camp members, fellow Nazis, crossed Italy. There they made an illegal entrance over the Austro-Italian border.

Eichmann followed the coast went to Genoa where he visited a Franciscan monastery and asked for rest and help. The monks asked no questions and gave him food and lodging. Eichmann worked with the Franciscan Fathers for many months. He ate, slept and prayed with the religious men, but restlessness bored in with wormlike precision. Finally he applied for a Vatican state passport, giving his name as Ricardo Clement.

With these papers, he reached Syria where he found employment in the import business with a former Nazi aid, Alois

Brunner. Eichmann was in his element of friends again, ex-Nazis in the Middle East who had found favor in the eyes of the Grand Mufti, the Pan Arab League and Moslem Brotherhood. The vocabulary, ideology and methods were familiar: "Jews are not wanted in the Arab world. Jews must go. Jews must be killed." The group were active in procuring arms for the Middle East and organizing military training and espionage service for the extremist groups.

This reopening of the past continued until 1949. From time to time papers reported Martin Bormann and Adolf Eichmann were still alive, but the majority of people were forgetting such names. The passage of time lessened the impact of the true meaning of such personalities.

Eichmann's whereabouts were kept a secret. He did not contact his wife, but he read daily the German and Jewish newspapers to find out what was being written about him.

During this period, the State of Israel was created. The Middle East underwent its own grave political upheavals. Eichmann was again out of a job. In a vain search for old friends, Adolf journeyed to Spain, back to Genoa and there, on June 14, 1950, he received his visa to immigrate to Argentina. He sailed a month later aboard the SS *Giovanna C.*

Although Eichmann had never written his wife directly, it later became clear there was some communication through a third person because Veronica tried once more to help her husband. She filed a falsely-sworn statement saying her sister and two other witnesses had seen Eichmann killed by Czech partisans at the end of the war.

The affadavit was given credence in many quarters. So many reliable people believed Veronica's statement that Friedmann, Manos and their agents were called fools who were fighting windmills, described as insanely motivated by hate and vengeance. Even the Israeli Secret Service was willing to call the chapter closed and to admit they were shadowboxing.

Tuvia Friedmann was not convinced. With the acuteness of a bloodhound, he continued his search. The finances came from his wife, his doctor, friends, acquaintances who believed a smoke screen was protecting Eichmann. "Eichmann is alive," Friedmann said. "I know it . . . I feel it . . . I know it!"

Adolf Eichmann arrived in Buenos Aires, the splendid capital of Argentina, and registered himself under the alias Ricardo Clement . . . unmarried . . . born in Bozen on the Austro-Italian border.

At last Eichmann felt free. Not free from his conscience, but free from statelessness. Soon he would be a citizen of Argentina and could work for a new life. At forty-four he was ready for a worthwhile, better future.

But somehow, somewhere, it seems that most criminals make one fatal mistake that leads to their apprehension. The man who killed six million Jews and spent the rest of his life running, now sensed peace and respite, and with the security came the longing to see his wife and children. This human, natural desire was the downfall of the inhuman, sadistic beast.

Shortly before Christmas, an airmail letter reached Frau Veronica Liebel. It said very little but was signed Uncle Ricardo, Tucaman Province, Argentina.

Frau Eichmann told her sons their kind Uncle Ricardo had asked them to join him in South America. Uncle Ricardo, she explained, was an engineer with the Capri Company which built dams for the Government.

Veronica took out passports for herself and the boys under the name of Liebel and left Europe without the knowledge of the Israeli Secret Service or the agents who had almost given up the search. In July, 1952, the Liebel family docked in Buenos Aires.

After a few days of rest, they boarded a train north to Tucuman. At a small station in a rural area, the engine growled to a stop. A man in working clothes stood waiting for his family. After seven long years, there was little to recognize except common memories. Frau Eichmann pulled herself together. "Children," she said, "This is your Uncle Ricardo."

The household of five carried three different names—the second mistake the Nazi executioner made. He lived as Señor Clement, introduced Frau Eichmann as his "sister," Veronica Liebel and the three children as Klaus, Horst and Dieter Eichmann.

The reunited family seemed happy. The children especially enjoyed the open life with its hunting, fishing and the warm friendliness of the South American people. Adolf's salary was comfortable and life fell into a normal pattern.

Thousands of miles away Tuvia Friedmann fermented in his frustration. His friends called him mad to continue his chase. Leads became few, and each was more irrational and discouraging than the last. Eichmann was reported in New York, Vienna, Tel Aviv, Syria on the same day. And then no report for weeks.

Again destiny made a move. The Capri dam was completed, leaving Adolf out of a job. For a short time he worked in a fruit juice plant, then tried to open a laundry which immediately failed. His shrinking bank account brought new worries and incited old restlessness.

Eichmann worked for a year on a ranch in Brazil, showed up in Paraguay in 1954, in Bolivia in 1955. He was also in Chile, Peru and Uruguay. A man without a country, a migrant, an itinerant worker.

Each time Friedmann's agents caught wind of Eichmann's latest job but arrived too late for the capture.

By 1956, Eichmann returned to Argentina. Jobs were scarce, and Adolf drifted spasmodically from one to another . . . mechanic, clerk, farm foreman.

The next year found him back in Syria where he offered his services to the United Arab Republic. When Prime Minister Nasser did not even reply to his application, Adolf Eichmann, alias Señor Clement, returned to Argentina.

Friedmann was beginning to believe that Eichmann had escaped into a corner of oblivion. A new spark soared out of the darkness when Dr. Edwin Schiela, Attorney-General in the German state of Württenberg-Baden, wrote him on October 1959, "I have received secret information that Eichmann is in Kuwait, working in the Persian Gulf area."

Friedmann asked for four men and funds to follow the scent. The disillusioned Israeli Secret Service refused the request.

With characteristic determination Friedmann gave the letter to a leading Israeli newspaper for publication on the eve of Yom Kippur, the Day of Atonement. Public opinion became so strong that Prime Minister Ben-Gurion ordered the Central Institute for Intelligence and Security to intensify their search for Eichmann. New agents were flown into each place where Eichmann had been reported seen recently.

In April, 1960, the Eichmanns made their third error. Frau Eichmann returned to Austria and renewed her passport. The clerk recognized the name Liebel and notified the Israeli agents.

From there on Frau Eichmann led agents to Ricardo Clement. There remained only the major question of legal proof. During the past fifteen years of the manhunt, twenty men had been arrested in the belief they were Eichmann, but each was cleared after handwriting tests.

Frau Eichmann herself was a key to her husband's identity. Since the moment she left the passport office, she was under constant surveillance. An Israeli agent disguised as a travel bureau official took her to the airport. Agents were on her plane to Buenos Aires. The cab driver from the airport to the apartment at Chacabuco 4261 was a member of the Israeli intelligence department.

In a room directly opposite the Eichmann apartment more Israeli agents watched every move the family made. Eichmann, who now worked in an automobile factory, was unknowingly surrounded by spies, on his way to and from work, at the restaurant where he ate his luncheon, at the bench beside him as he accomplished his daily tasks.

Little did the hunted man know that many of the men with whom he rubbed elbows daily bore serial numbers which had been burned into their bodies during their days in the Nazi concentration camps.

Although Eichmann was surrounded, treed, virtually within their hands after all these years, Tuvia Friedmann was faced with still one gigantic problem. How could Eichmann be removed from Argentina? During the lengthy extradition procedure, Adolf, escape artist extraordinaire, could easily evade their grasp. He could not be taken on a plane through customs and visa inspections. The one answer was kidnapping— and this answer was against law. International law. An international law which, if broken, would lead to grave complications between Argentina and Israel.

Inspired by the event of the celebration of Argentina's 150th anniversary of independence, during which time a new airline route was to be inagurated by the Israeli government between Buenos Aires and Tel Aviv, an enlarged Israeli delegation arrived in the capital city. This would be the way Eichmann would be ferreted out of Argentina and flown to Israel to stand trial for his massacres.

The kidnapping was easy. Four men waited in a rented car for Eichmann to return from work. A fifth watched his apartment. There was no violence, no confusion. Eichmann was hidden in a room for nine days until the Israeli plane left to take him to face an Israeli trial.

Frau Eichmann, fearing the worst and unable to speak outright, checked the morgues and the hospitals cautiously. After three days she went to the police.

The hunter and the hunted finally faced each other. The thin-faced man with a troubled conscience and the weariness that comes from running wrote these words before he faced his accusers and final justice:

"I am tired of traveling over continents and lands as an anonymous wanderer. I wish I could have made peace with my former enemies.

"I was not a murderer. I was nothing but a loyal, orderly, correct, efficient soldier, and did what I did only out of idealistic devotion to my Fatherland and to the SS. I was never a traitor.

"After a careful self-analysis, I am now convinced that I have never been a murderer or a mass-murderer, nor were my subordinates. But to be entirely honest, I see myself as one of those who helped in the killings, for after all I did receive and relate the orders for deportation, and a part of the deportees were killed—though by other units.

"My belief in the Nazi leadership and the necessity of total war made me fulfill my duties with clean conscience and willing heart.

"I was a good German, I am a good German, and a good German I shall always be."

The flight that kidnapped Eichmann from Buenos Aires and took him to Tel Aviv was a violation of international law. The case was brought before the United Nations, before which Mrs. Golda Meir, the Foreign Minister of Israel, stated she wished to apologize to the Republic of Argentina for the incident but added that, in this case, moral law was on the side of Israel.

Eichmann, who has tried to change the course of history by his desire to liquidate all Jews, is ending his chase in their own hands.

A modern David has conquered Goliath.